Is It a Sermon?

Is It a Sermon?

*Art, Activism, and Genre Fluidity
in African American Preaching*

Donyelle C. McCray

WESTMINSTER
JOHN KNOX PRESS
LOUISVILLE · KENTUCKY

First edition
Published by Westminster John Knox Press
Louisville, Kentucky

24 25 26 27 28 29 30 31 32 33—10 9 8 7 6 5 4 3 2 1

The Scripture quotations are from the New Revised Standard Version Bible: Anglicised Catholic Edition, copyright © 1989, 1993, 1995 the Division of Christian Education of the National Council of Churches of Christ in the United States of America. Used by permission. All rights reserved.

Chapter 2 expands on material in "Quilting the Sermon: Homiletical Insights from Harriet Powers," Religions (2018) and is used by permission of the author. Excerpts from unpublished Toni Morrison Papers at Princeton University, copyright © 2023 by the Estate of Chloe A. Morrison. Reprinted by permission of H. Ford Morrison, Literary Executor for the Estate of Chloe A. Morrison.

Photo of Harriet Powers's *Bible Quilt* reprinted by permission of Division of Home and Community Life, National Museum of American History, Smithsonian Institution. Photo of Harriet Powers's *Pictorial Quilt* © 2024, Museum of Fine Arts, Boston. Reprinted by permission. All rights reserved.

Book design by Sharon Adams
Cover design by Marc Witaker / MTWdesign.net

Library of Congress Cataloging-in-Publication Data

Names: McCray, Donyelle C., author.
Title: Is it a sermon? : art, activism, and genre fluidity in African
    American preaching / Donyelle C. McCray.
Description: First edition. | Louisville, Kentucky : Westminster John Knox
    Press, [2024] | Includes bibliographical references and index. |
    Summary: "An informative and daring call to blur the boundaries of the
    sermon genre, exploring the "shoreline" of homiletics, or the place
    where preaching laps up against other modes of discourse"-- Provided by
    publisher.
Identifiers: LCCN 2024023484 (print) | LCCN 2024023485 (ebook) | ISBN
    9780664266875 (paperback) | ISBN 9781646983940 (ebook)
Subjects: LCSH: African American preaching. | Preaching--United States. |
    Sermons--United States.
Classification: LCC BV4208.U6 M33 2024 (print) | LCC BV4208.U6 (ebook) |
    DDC 251.0089/96073--dc23/eng/20240610
LC record available at https://lccn.loc.gov/2024023484
LC ebook record available at https://lccn.loc.gov/2024023485

Most Westminster John Knox Press books are available at special quantity discounts when purchased in bulk by corporations, organizations, and special-interest groups. For more information, please e-mail SpecialSales@wjkbooks.com.

Contents

List of Illustrations

Acknowledgments

I have a deep well of gratitude for the tenderness, wisdom, and ebullience of my friends. New friends bring bursts of energy to my life, and I am grateful whenever these bonds blossom. But my old friends are like the finest of wines—layered, complex, full-bodied, and still evolving after decades. To know them is to be in awe. Angelisa Gillyard, Geralyn Richard, Kimberly Roberts, LaTonyia Vaughn, Lori Anne Brown, Nikki Stewart, and Stephanie Burch, your names are poems to me. Music. If it were up to me, I'd rename all the planets in the Milky Way after you. You are my Mercury, my Venus, my Neptune, Saturn encircled with braids and kinky twists. Love is too weak a word.

And ten years ago, I joined a conversation on race, church, and theological practices with four lovable human beings: J. Kameron Carter, Mark Ramsey, Jemonde Taylor, and Denise Thorpe. Our conversation has yet to end, and the friendship we've forged is one of the most surprising gifts of my life. I am also blessed to have colleagues in theological education who witness to God's love inside and outside of the classroom. I owe a special thanks to my homiletics colleagues at Virginia Theological Seminary and Yale Divinity School: Ruthanna Hooke, Carolyn Sharp, and Nora Tubbs Tisdale. A gem of a dissertation advisor, Charles L. Campbell remains a trusted conversation partner about all things homiletical, and his encouragement to color outside the lines is an inspiration. My extraordinary colleagues in the Academy of Homiletics and Societas Homiletica delight and inspire me. I am also grateful for the lasting influence of Judy Fentress-Williams and John T. W. Harmon.

I've had the joy of learning alongside students whose brilliance was equaled by their compassion, humility, and bravery. My students at Virginia Theological Seminary and Yale Divinity School continually renew my hope in the church and in God's action in the world. I've taught a course at Yale called "Is It a Sermon?" since the spring of 2017, and I'm grateful for the genre-bending sermons preached by students and the many discussions that challenged my thinking.

This project has been inspired by the clergy and especially the faithful lay witnesses at Alfred Street Baptist Church, Alexandria, Virginia; Shiloh Baptist Church, Alexandria, Virginia; Trinity Episcopal Church, Washington, DC; Saint Ambrose Episcopal Church, Raleigh, North Carolina; Saint Titus Episcopal Church, Durham, North Carolina; The Episcopal Church of Saint Paul and Saint James, New Haven, Connecticut; Saint Paul African Methodist Episcopal Church, Madison, Georgia; Saint Philip African Methodist Episcopal Church, Atlanta, Georgia; and Griggs Chapel African Methodist Episcopal Church, Monticello, Georgia.

Finally, I have lived long enough to know a loving family cannot be taken for granted. Thank you, Mom, Dad, Korey, Lauren, Nichelle, Olivia, Kassius, and Rocket. Our life together feels like one long Christmas, and you each offer daily reminders of God's grace.

Introduction

Albert Ayler was known for screeching and groaning through his horn in songs like "Our Prayer" and "Ghosts." Audiences found the music blood-curdling, a wrenching experience of anguish and bliss. Many of those who were mesmerized by the music struggled to describe his atonal wailing. For Ayler, it was simple. He was preaching. Yawping through his saxophone was a means of bearing a holy message. He'd discerned his call while listening to John Coltrane and was now a "missionary" and sounder of "truth for those who can listen."[1]

In 1959, Mack Charles Parker, a young African American man, was abducted in the middle of the night and lynched near Poplarville, Mississippi. Pauli Murray, an attorney in New York, read about the case and penned two poems, "Collect for Poplarville," a nighttime prayer for all those hunted by the dogs, firearms, and viciousness of the lynch mob, and "For Mack C. Parker," pondering the implications of lynching on the afterlives of perpetrators and victims.[2] Some twenty years later, after being ordained as an Episcopal priest, Murray recognized poems like "Collect for Poplarville" and "For Mack C. Parker" as early sermons and was convinced poetry and sermons were overlapping genres.[3]

This book is about the shoreline of homiletics, the place where preaching laps up against other forms of expression. The examples just mentioned are not flukes. They form part of an aspect of preaching with a long history. There were, for instance, sermonic performances: Isaiah walked naked and barefoot for three years, Jeremiah fashioned a yoke and put it on his neck, Symeon the Stylite lived on a pillar fifty feet in the air, Julian of Norwich made a pulpit out of her anchorhold.[4] We also see preaching that merges with prayer, singing, or everyday discourse. Consider the Baptist deaconess whose morning prayer rhythmically flows into a sermon, or a singer like Mother Willie Mae Ford Smith, whose gospel solos included sermonettes. From time to time, even a simple committee report sheds its banality and gives everyone a taste of the good news. The gospel dances in and out of the forms we create for it. What modes of preaching get overlooked due to genre classifications? What types of proclamation go unrecognized because they don't meet our expectations for what a sermon is supposed to look like?

The concept of the sermon genre was not always construed so narrowly. In medieval England, for instance, Christian commentary, treatises, letters, poetry, and drama came under the umbrella of sermon along with some spiritual writings that were never even brought to speech.[5] An item could begin as a sermon and grow into a treatise, start as a letter and turn into a sermon, or flit back and forth between these categories.[6] This fluidity required openness on the part of the audience and reflected a culture that prized spiritual counsel. The English intuited that, as evidenced by the different genres of Scripture, divinely inspired messages might take a range of forms.

From its inception, Christian preaching has been a parabolic venture, indebted to patterns of Greco-Roman rhetoric but not beholden to them. "Sermon" and "homily" are slippery, "notoriously ambiguous" terms among biblical form critics.[7] As C. Clifton Black stresses, "God has made nonsensical (ἐμώρανεν ὁ θεός) [emōranen ho theos], 1 Cor. 1:20) everything in this world we ever thought wise—about power, prestige, wealth, church growth, biblical scholarship, homiletics, *everything*. No word could be more witheringly and healthily parabolic than Christ the crucified."[8] Doesn't this suggest that Christian preaching has an inherent elusiveness? That we lose something vital by pinning it down?

The lines of demarcation around sermons are blurry in Black sacred discourse as well. Martin Luther King Jr.'s "Letter from Birmingham Jail" is a case in point. It begins in the margins of a newspaper, runs on to bits of paper, and eventually flows on to full pages of a tablet once King receives one. By straddling epistle and sermon, his message has visceral impact. Surely, King's carceral setting and preacher-activist vocation shape the message in his case. Yet the fluidity I am describing also arises in church sanctuaries with preachers who are much less engaged in bodily witness in the public square. Many a pastor has preached a forty-minute oration of a sermon that climaxed in ten minutes of song, parts of which consisted of solo and parts of which were sung by the entire congregation. The very runniness of the venture is what's provocative here; the message's underlying instability provides a helpful vantage point for thinking about the nature of preaching. Like a river, the sermon's movement is a sign of life and an indication that an invisible current is at work beneath the surface.

Scrambling and even violating the boundaries of genre is a reappearing feature of Black radicalism. The search for fullness of life in the face of social death leads to a passionate disregard for structures that muzzle truth. As Fred Moten explains, "Blackness—the extended movement of a specific upheaval, an ongoing irruption that anarranges every line—is a strain that pressures the assumption of the equivalence of personhood and subjectivity."[9] When this conception is applied to preaching, the pastiche nature of the venture becomes prominent. Dynamism at the boundaries of the genre is part of Black preaching's genius. The fluidity mirrors the Holy Spirit's tendency to spill past human confines set around a message as all things are made new.

Holding to rigid boundaries around the conception of the sermon presents serious problems. First, if sermons are considered solely as messages preached from a pulpit during a worship service by an ordained person, the very definition of preaching mutes too many of the church's preachers, particularly women, queer people, laypersons, and people who preach outside of liturgical settings. Yet such people play an essential proclamatory role in African American faith communities, both within liturgies and beyond them. And since homiletical approaches that work for charismatic straight clergymen sometimes hinder those who move through the world differently, research that considers a range of identities is vital. The sources we choose for examining Black preaching are critical in determining which voices are foregrounded and in shaping the norms of the discourse.[10] Privileging a few voices at the expense of others has propelled a warped vision of power and contributed to the delegitimation of the preacher.

A thorough exploration of Black preaching requires attending not only to the clergyperson but to the singer in the choir stand, the painter before an easel, a quilter and her needle, and protesters who understand themselves to be engaged in work that is fundamentally proclamatory. On a practical level, this means taking a painter like Aaron Douglas seriously when he describes a painting as the visual equivalent of a sermon and compares his use of light and shadow to "call-and-response."[11] What does it mean to assume a visual artist has homiletical insight to offer? How do such proclaimers participate in the sermon genre and expand it?[12] And how might they even challenge assumptions? These preachers might, for example, challenge the assumption that a thirty-minute oration by an ordained person on a Sunday morning still "counts" as a sermon if the oration is deflating or scolding rather than encouraging. Can a hate-filled tirade ever be a sermon? Should a message still count as a sermon if it bores the listeners or wilts the listeners' imagination of God? There are, of course, simply bad sermons. The question is whether certain criteria indicate that another classification is in order altogether. And is categorization within the sermon genre determined primarily by ecclesiastical authority and liturgical space, or more by the Spirit's efficacy in spreading a divine message regardless of the medium? I lean toward the latter and suggest that these blurry modes of proclamation are areas where preaching flourishes.

This book is about preaching, but it is also about genre. Genre is never pure, and this must be exponentially true of preaching if the gospel envisioned is a living word and if the church is a living community that continues to evolve in the power of the Holy Spirit. I realize genre fluidity can be disconcerting to some degree because so many of us have been taught to understand reality by naming and categorizing it. One question that tends to come up when we suspend the traditional walls around a sermon and consider visual art, music, letters, and the like is "Well, is everything a sermon?" While I'm not eager to guard the borders of the sermon genre, the short answer here is no.

Yet rather than reestablish new and roomier boundaries, I want to urge a turn from this boundary-setting reflex. Instead, receive the different preachers illumined in this book on their own terms and examine the approaches, intentions, and fruits of their work. Consider the arguments and how they are made. What modes of listening to Scripture and to life do they encourage? What troubling patterns of sermon composition do they interrupt? The proclaimers in this volume produce meaning in a variety of ways that are helpful in strengthening the practice of preaching whether in traditional or innovative forms. And in a world trembling under the weight of violence, pollution, consumerism, and alienation, gleaning these insights is critical.

Increasingly the church's gaze is being turned outward to the broader world. The emptying of many Protestant churches puts new pressures on the remnant. The call is not to prop up the church of the past but to follow the Spirit's leading in this new moment. While there is much about the thirty-minute oration that must be preserved, it is also necessary to remember that the Holy Spirit is the source of the church's preaching. This book is about becoming attuned to the realm of the Spirit's proclamation inside and outside church walls.

Because this book is about genre, it's also about power. How we refer to a given message matters a great deal. In many cases, honoring a message as a sermon values its substantive and pedagogical heft, but there are surely cases when the designation could add a layer of "preachiness" to something that is not intended to be dogmatic. Genre classifications generate questions about authority and shade the kind of disposition one has when receiving discourse. Christian power dynamics are crystallized and amplified in the pulpit. And since we live in a moment when some of the received assumptions of clerical power have withered, egalitarian modes of preaching and power sharing are essential.

Amid the polarization and verbal jousting that has become normative in contemporary American discourse, preachers face a bit of a conundrum. On the one hand, the amped-up, hyperbolic speech often associated with the pro-phetic tradition is vital. By speaking in extremis, prophets summon our atten-tion and communicate divine pathos. Yet at the same time, extreme speech abounds in the current rhetorical landscape. As a result, discerning prophetic authority has become more difficult.

The urgency surrounding the power issues is heightened by the attention-starved culture of the United States and the tendency to idolize immedi-ate results. So in exploring genre fluidity in preaching I am not suggesting genre-bending for its own sake or as a means of wowing a congregation. That approach would reify brittle assumptions about the purpose of preaching. I believe you will find that the witnesses in this book walk the shoreline of preaching for reasons other than self-aggrandizement. They play at boundar-ies as a means of following the Spirit's revealed trajectory for a given message and teach others to do the same. In doing so, they reveal the sermon as a husk for divine encounter. Sermons are vehicles that question and, in some cases, deepen faith. They sharpen people's recognition of divine action in the world, expanding affective and perceptive capacities in the process. Rather than being defined solely by form, sermons are characterized by the kind of energy they yield and their capacity to build up people of faith who actively and at times joyfully disrupt the manifestations of evil in the world.

As I hope will be clear, I am also curious about the nature of divine revela-tion—specifically, how it is molded by the memory of past generations who discipled us in the faith. Like the apostle Paul, through preaching we pass on what was entrusted to us. That which is relayed is discerned and sifted, of course; nevertheless, it is inherited and rooted in the hope of communal sur-vival. African American preaching is often laced with memory of the ances-tors, those whose bones populate the underwater cities of the Atlantic—owing to the Maafa—and their succeeding generations. These ancestors include famous exemplars, lesser-known figures who are known by their posterity, and many whose names are known only to God. No longer captive to empire, they have been made whole, and though unseen, they are understood to have an ongoing presence. These benevolent spiritual guides find ways to assure us, lead us, and warn us. According to Kurt Buhring, "In some African societ-ies, the ancestral realm is similar to the human, visible world; in others, the ancestral realm is a utopian paradise. Either way, there is a certain reciproc-ity to the relationship between the ancestors and humans."[13] And since the beloved dead are believed to encircle and uphold the living, illuminating their continuing influence is an ethical obligation and an important though often overlooked dimension of the preaching vocation.

The proclaimers highlighted in this volume demonstrate accountability to the ancestors. Their genre-bending sermons do not arise out of a vacuum.

They reflect a certain kind of anamnesis that remembers the action of God and the ways God has spoken to and through the ancestors. This means foregrounding some of the modes of wisdom-sharing cherished by the ancestors—such as dance, song, and storytelling—and reckoning with the ways these discourses were censored and maligned under the conditions of slavery and colonialism.[14] So as novel as some of these approaches are, they reflect the proclaimer's familial history, skills, life circumstances, and spirituality. This book is not about preachers who went hunting for innovative sermons, but, as Malan Nel suggests, more about sermons that sought out preachers who would provide the appropriate brooding space in their hearts for God's dynamic truth.[15] Further, by focusing on preaching as wisdom-sharing and as a means of corresponding with the ancestors, I also hope to address a problem Kenyatta Gilbert identifies: the "present-future" preoccupation in Black religious practice.[16]

The chapters in this book are arranged as a series of cases. Each case presents a proclaimer who engages in genre-bending preaching and illumines unique insights about the nature and potential of the preaching craft. Since the inner lives and spirituality of preachers profoundly shape strategy, I begin with biographical sketches before turning to their approaches. Chapter 1 begins with a focus on Mahalia Jackson, who described her vocation in apostolic terms and used the choir loft as a functional pulpit. "I can't sing a song that doesn't have a message," she explained, and melody proved as vital to her work as lyric.[17] Drawing on vocal stylings modeled by her elders, Jackson sought to drape her listeners in an experience of grace and transcend the division between sacred and secular space. I explore her techniques and tease out practical implications for contemporary preachers.

Musicality is a crucial frame for Black preaching but not the only one. So visual art drives chapter 2. I introduce Harriet Powers, a nineteenth-century African American woman who described her *Bible Quilt* as a sermon. I explore her aesthetics, hermeneutics, and sense of voice. African American women have used quilts to claim voice, preserve memory, and express themselves artistically since antebellum times, so I present Powers as a preacher intent on stewarding Black tradition. I pair Powers with a more contemporary quilter, Rosie Lee Tomkins (also known as Effie Mae Martin Howard). Tomkins's quilts function as eulogies, diaries, testimonies, and scriptural meditation—sometimes all at once. Her quilts are inspirations for people who are overwhelmed by the fragmented nature of life and need to see it pieced together again. Both quilters offer insights on quilting as a mode of discourse.

In chapter 3, I turn to the invaluable gifts dancers bring to preaching. The focus is Sister Thea Bowman, a Roman Catholic who joined the Franciscan Sisters of Perpetual Adoration and used dance as catechesis. For Bowman, dance expressed the gospel in ways that drew on the model of the ancestors. Bowman also felt dance strengthened the link between the church's preaching and its public witness in street activism and the public square.

The challenge of energizing faith-driven activism arises again in chapter 4, which profiles Howard Thurman. I focus on his meditations because he intended for them to provide a contemplative refuge for activists and an experience of divine intimacy for all who were wearied by the fast pace of life. Thurman's meditations have a hybrid quality in that they shuttle between sermon and prayer and between the visible and invisible worlds.

Then in chapter 5, I reflect on the relationship between preaching and literature with a turn to Toni Morrison. After discussing some preacherly aspects of her novels, I home in on her Nobel Prize acceptance speech—a parable about storytelling and ancestral wisdom. I detail some of the ways her strategies mirror those used by Jesus to deepen moral imagination.

All the cases above involve improvising on the sermon, and this entails straining certain conventions and extending them like taffy. While the proclaimers in this book have different approaches, they share similar approaches to authority, ephemerality, and memory of the ancestors. They either directly stir political action or do so indirectly, providing the necessary spiritual foundation. And in different ways, each preacher profiled in this volume shows us how to say something that matters, how to reach a deeper substrate of truth. Together these preachers urge a new, multivocal vision of preaching that reaches a broader population and engages the human person more holistically.

Of course, many other modes of discourse could have been included in this book. I considered Pieter Bruegel's group dialogues, Mamie Till Mobley's justice-driven addresses, as well as testimony, retreat-meditations, lectures, letter writing, picketing, and sculpture, just to name a few.[18] Yet rather than attempt an exhaustive catalog of preaching mediums, I selected a few exemplary approaches that foreground the significance of ancestral memory while offering transferable practical strategies. In choosing the cases, I drew heavily on the preaching of African American women and laypeople. I am convinced that a thorough examination of African American women's preaching must consider the significance of genre-bending when claiming voice, navigating masculinist spaces, and nurturing strength for resistance. These dynamics seem doubly relevant for Black feminist or for womanist preaching.

Finally, let me say that I love a good sermon—I mean the traditional oration offered in the pulpit as part of a Christian liturgy. The reflections about preaching beyond these bounds are not offered to undercut this aspect of the church's preaching but rather to appreciate the Holy Spirit's work on broader terrain.

1

The Singer

A musician is a kind of preacher.
—Rashied Ali

When Mahalia Jackson comes backstage after a two-hour performance, she is parched and collapses in a chair with exhaustion. Ready hands reach out with a glass of cool water, which she gulps as another is poured. Other eager hands reach around the water glass to blot her sweaty face and neck with towels. She drinks in this care for her body, as she did the water, and on an internal cue springs up, helpful hands still blotting, and marches back to the stage for an encore. She croons out another hymn, and the sound rises out of her and through the wave of listeners who rock, weep, or close their eyes in reverence. For a few more minutes they are churched by the deep softness she and her longtime accompanist, Mildred Falls, offer up in the dark theater. Then Jackson comes back to the dressing room for good this time, dripping with sweat and exhausted.

Her sweat is not just the natural result of the stage lights. It arises from the exertion of vocalizing her convictions. And in this respect, she sweats like many of the Black Baptist preachers she saw growing up who, whether they chanted on a given Sunday or not, ended their sermons by falling into a cushioned chair drenched and exhausted. Her sweat also clues us into the nature of her work. "I can't sing a song that doesn't have a message," Jackson explained in an effort to distinguish spiritual edification from entertainment.[1] Singing was a missional endeavor to soothe and energize people of faith. Jackson thought of herself primarily as an evangelist, and she is as essential to the roster of twentieth-century African American preachers as she is to the history of gospel music, though the tendency to minimize laywomen's preaching clouds her contribution. Jackson drew directly from Black preaching traditions in her music and activism. Through her music she made an offering, embodied an argument, interpreted the church's texts, and ushered listeners into an experience of the Holy Spirit that often matched or exceeded what might have been experienced in a liturgical setting. What Jackson did so beautifully is illumine the overlay between the sermon and the song.

In her songs, Jackson sought to capture the "cry" that she heard in the Baptist church of her youth. "I would always find myself drawn to the church. And it's because I liked the songs and I liked the way that the preacher, the old preacher, would preach in his method. He weren't educated like some of our ministers today, but there was a way that he would preach, would have a singing tone in his voice that was sad. And it done something to me."[2] The affective impact of the preacher's cry was so visceral that it shaped Jackson's vocation. The preacher's cry became a template, a sound she sought to explore and improvise on in her ministry: "Really, it was the basic way—it is the basic way—that I sing today, from hearing the way the preacher would sort of preach in a cry, in a moan, would shout sort of like in a chant way, a groaning sound, which would penetrate to my heart."[3]

MAHALIA JACKSON: A BIOGRAPHICAL SKETCH

To understand Jackson's preaching, it is necessary to first have a sense of the life experiences and spirituality that animated her proclamation. She was born on October 26, 1911, in New Orleans.[4] Her mother, Charity Clark, had recently arrived from Pointe Coupée, a remote community about 150 miles to the northwest, where her parents, Paul and Celia Clark, chiseled out a life as farmers.[5] Charity's move to New Orleans allowed her to start a new life in the city and join her siblings—Porterfield, Hannah, Bessie, and Mahala, called "Duke," for whom Jackson was named.[6]

Jackson's father, John Jackson Jr., had come to New Orleans from nearby Kenner, Louisiana, and labored as a stevedore and carpenter.[7] He also seems to have been a substitute preacher that local Black Baptist preachers could count on when needed.[8] Much of the effort to sustain the father-daughter relationship was borne by Mahalia. John was already married to someone else when Charity gave birth, and he eventually had children with a number of different partners.[9]

Little "Halie," as she was then known, was enfolded in the Clark family's circle of love and immersed in the Black community that lived near the levee and the Mississippi River. As a youth, she sang in the Mount Moriah Baptist Church Junior Choir and had a spiritual home in four sister congregations in

New Orleans: Plymouth Rock Baptist Church, Zion Travelers First Baptist Church, Broadway Mission Baptist Church, and Mount Moriah Baptist Church.[10] This spiritual nurture proved vital. Charity died while Halie was quite young—less than eight years old. Her Aunt Duke became her guardian and was known to be a harsh disciplinarian. Within that household Halie's labor was instrumental, because she provided childcare for her young cousins, cooked, and cleaned. Duke worked outside her home as a domestic and took Halie along to assist with the laundry, childcare, cooking, and cleaning of white households. The result was a truncated childhood. And though she would later look back and describe New Orleans as a jolly city full of people who knew how to enjoy life through music and food, her memories would be tinged with sorrow.[11]

In these early years, she spent hours listening to Bessie Smith sing the blues and taught herself to sing by following Smith's example. What she gained from Smith was more than style; she also gained an epistemology and a vision of how music could shape the psyche.[12] Other formative influences included a certain vegetable salesman who announced his goods with a somber tone in his voice and laborers who sang work songs as they laid railroad tracks. These different notes of melancholia had a direct impact. "I sang what I, myself, had heard. I put in the sadness I heard in the men's voices as they worked on the railroad tracks nearby, and the trains themselves."[13] That somber quality contributed to her distinctive sound.

By the time she reached young adulthood, Halie was longing for change and moved to the South Side of Chicago in 1930 or 1931 to join her Aunts Hannah and Alice. Around this time "Halie" became "Mahalia." She took jobs at a date factory, at the Edgewater Beach Hotel, and as a domestic worker for a white family in Hyde Park, but she directed her creative energy to singing—her true source of joy and mission.[14] She loved singing with others in the choir at Greater Salem Baptist Church and later as one of the Johnson Singers. This group functioned as a gospel quartet even though there were five members: Mahalia Jackson, Louise Lemon, and brothers Prince, Robert, and Wilbur Johnson.[15]

Yet it was clear early on that Jackson had gifts as a soloist. Her legendary voice was first recorded by Decca Records in 1937, which released "God's Gonna Separate the Wheat from the Tares" (with "Keep Me Every Day" as the B-side) and "God Shall Wipe All Tears Away" (backed by "Oh My Lord").[16] While these were not commercial successes, they introduced a soloist who was on the rise. Her talents were quickly recognized by Thomas Andrew Dorsey, the composer and musical pioneer who would be celebrated as the "Father of African American Gospel Music." He asked Jackson to sing his compositions at various churches and concerts and eventually began calling her the "Empress" of gospel music.[17] The two collaborated closely during the early 1940s, and during the same period, Jackson became a regular soloist with the National Baptist Convention. This role exponentially increased her visibility and led to more invitations to sing.

Jackson's blossoming influence did not indicate the absence of detractors. Some listeners in Baptist circles preferred a more reserved worship experience and were alarmed by her gesticulations. Her natural expressiveness was sometimes read through an overly sexualized lens or met with contempt by those who sought to distance themselves from the boisterousness they associated with slave worship. Jackson defended her approach from such critics. "I want my hands . . . my feet . . . my whole body to say all that is in me."[18] Regular visits to Sanctified churches convinced her that bearing witness required physical as well as oral expression.[19]

Despite resistance, Jackson's popularity steadily increased and then catapulted in 1948 with the release of her hit song, "Move On Up a Little Higher." Listeners were treated to a bouncy melody over which Jackson describes the beauties of heaven. As the song unfolds, she imagines moving up higher and higher, first meeting biblical figures like Daniel, Paul, Silas, and Jesus and then reuniting with deceased loved ones. In other words, she testifies to the unseen world where relationships are not bounded by time or space. Her voice envelops anguish in joy but conveys both to yield a hard-won hope. She also narrates a vision of mobility and freedom for a Black female body that far exceeds what is afforded in everyday life. Swirling around heaven, she becomes a singing and dancing prophet who invites others into her experience of delight.

"Move On Up a Little Higher" was an artistic achievement due to Jackson's vivid storytelling and singular voice. Invitations abounded. Before long, Jackson had a packed recording and concert schedule, a contract with CBS, and her own radio and television shows. Her voice was sometimes at odds with television's mandatory levity during the 1950s and early 1960s, but her ability to churn sorrow into hope intrigued audiences. As she brought gospel music to secular audiences, she also crossed racial barriers, eventually singing in Carnegie Hall, on *The Ed Sullivan Show*, and at the Newport Jazz Festival. International audiences beckoned too. She held concerts in the Netherlands, Sweden, and Israel, and she sang for the king of Denmark and for Queen Elizabeth in England. In short, "Move On Up a Little Higher" made her an international celebrity. A savvy businesswoman, during the late 1930s and early 1940s she had funneled her resources into personal ventures such as Mahalia's Beauty Salon, Mahalia's House of Flowers, and real estate holdings that included an apartment building. By the early 1950s, she had accumulated considerable wealth.

Financial success also compounded some of Jackson's struggles. Early experiences had taught her to insist on being paid in full and in cash before the end of her performances.[20] This meant she had a practice of carrying large amounts of cash—nearly $15,000 in one case.[21] She would hide money in a secret compartment in her purse as well as in her shoes, bra, and money belt. Carrying these large sums made her vulnerable to muggers and rogue police officers. Jules Schwerin remembers a meeting with Jackson shortly after a frightening encounter with Louisiana State Police near the Mississippi border in the Vicksburg vicinity.[22] After a full day's drive from Chicago en route to New Orleans, she was searching the dark countryside for a gas station and a motel that would accommodate African Americans when she heard sirens. Apparently the sight of a Black woman driving a lavender Cadillac triggered suspicion.

Once pulled over, Jackson presented her license and registration with an extra dose of courtesy to de-escalate the tension. Her efforts were not reciprocated. Two officers circled her car and then one got in her face. "Bitch, tell us why you're drivin' this here car! Ain't yours, for sure." She tried to bring a quick end to the encounter by acquiescing: "This here's my madam's car. She don' drive, she even makes me have the registration in my own name. Miz Dorsey flew herself down to New Orleans couple days ago, Sir, she had me drivin' it from Chicago to New Orleans, to meet her." But her response did not quell the hostility: "Take off your shoes, bitch. You better be tellin' the truth, or you'll find yourself in the lock-up." Sweating with terror, Jackson removed her shoes and then emptied her purse when commanded as the officers searched for cash. They took her wallet and then escorted her to the home of a local judge. Still in his pajamas and slippers, the judge listened to the officers' claims and promptly charged her a $250 fine for speeding. One of the troopers opened her wallet and counted the fine out aloud before returning it to her. Jackson could immediately see that $200 had been stolen, but she rushed to her car and on to New Orleans.[23]

Schwerin could see that Jackson was still shaken hours later as she recounted the story to him and to her brother, Johnny. But her rage was mixed with relief because she knew the encounter could have been worse. "They would have just as soon put me in the pokey, if they had found all that money I was carrying in my bra and other places. They would have figured, no black woman could make that kind of money honestly . . . would have held me for a week, maybe, ripped me off besides, by the time I could find myself a decent lawyer."[24]

This police encounter arose around the same time as another experience of racism and sexism in her life. In 1956, she sought to purchase a red brick ranch house in the Chatham section of Chicago. Until then, the neighborhood had been almost entirely white. Threatening phone calls awoke her in the middle of the night. "You move into that house and we'll blow it up with dynamite. You're going to need more than your gospel songs and prayers to save you. Wait and see what we do to you!"[25] The threats prompted a critical period of prayerful discernment. When she decided to proceed with the purchase, rifle bullets were shot through the windows.[26] She had to hire police protection for close to a year.

As a neighborly gesture, Jackson invited local children to her home for cake and ice cream during a filming of Edward R. Murrow's television show *Person to Person*. Several children came. "But those white folks wouldn't stay there with me as a neighbor," she later recounted. "One by one they sold their houses and moved away." Though she was disappointed, white flight did not lessen her peace: "Today the neighborhood is almost entirely colored. . . . The grass is still green. The lawns are as neat as ever. . . . The same birds are still in the trees. I guess it didn't occur to them to leave just because we moved in."[27] This incident, like the encounter with the Louisiana State Police, underscored the fact that Jackson's fame and wealth did not protect her from experiences of racism and sexism. Conscious of the need for systemic change, she became a formidable voice in the civil rights movement—a movement Richard Lischer rightly describes as a preaching movement.[28]

She met Dr. Martin Luther King Jr. and Rev. Ralph David Abernathy in Denver at a Baptist convention during the height of the Montgomery Bus Boycott.[29] Feeling a call to embolden the activists, she agreed to sing in Montgomery to raise money for the boycott.[30] Multiple collaborations would follow as her friendship with King and Abernathy deepened and as song proved to be an instrumental resource for nonviolent activism.

Through hymns and gospel songs, Jackson expressed the pain and faith shared by many of the activists. Her performances at rallies might better be described as instances of testimony. She testified to the need to persist in the struggle for freedom despite fatigue or threats. Perhaps only second to King's "I Have a Dream" speech, her rendition of the Negro spiritual "I Been 'Buked and I Been Scorned" is one of the most memorable moments of the 1963 March on Washington. The song voiced the anguish of centuries of enslavement and hatred and the pain of experiences like her own with the Louisiana State Police and her Chicago neighbors. Song was a means of protest, lament, and a way to summon divine courage to move forward.

While Jackson was celebrated for her visible role in the civil rights movement, her actions behind the scenes added credibility to her public witness. When Emmett Till was murdered in Money, Mississippi, in 1955, Jackson contacted his mother and purchased his headstone.[31] Jackson was also known for giving money to those in need when asked on the street and for inviting destitute men to her home for dinner. A skilled cook, she fed them hearty meals and later developed a chicken franchise, Mahalia Jackson Chicken Systems, designed to provide job opportunities and foster entrepreneurship.[32] Seeing people without food or housing tapped a well of sorrow for her, as did contempt directed at people in need. Perhaps this sensitivity resulted from her own early experiences of poverty and the pressure to assume adult responsibilities as a child. In any case, she responded to hunger and homelessness with the same missional impetus that propelled her singing.

Jackson's sense of responsibility to minister to others enriched her life by expanding her web of friends, enabling her to travel extensively, and giving her fulfillment. But ministry also exhausted her and strained her intimate relationships. Her schedule of performances from 1956 to 1966 hovered around two hundred shows a year.[33] She was twice divorced, and her spouses, Isaac "Ike" Hockenhull and Sigmund "Minters" Galloway, added to her stress. Hockenhull had a vexing gambling problem and pressured Jackson to sing secular music. Galloway sought to control her career and ran up expenses with abandon. Neither Hockenhull nor Galloway provided the consistent emotional support or deep respite she craved.

On January 27, 1972, after a series of cardiac events, Mahalia Jackson died at Little Company of Mary Hospital near Chicago. She was sixty. Thousands who had received her lessons of love in song came to pay their respects at services in Chicago and New Orleans.[34] They mourned a messenger of hope who had not only stood in front of pulpits to sing truth but raised her voice outside church walls to reach people in concert halls, rallies, and their own homes.

SINGING AS PARADIGM FOR PREACHING

The long marriage between sermon and song has received considerable scholarly attention.[35] In African American preaching, the two do not merely feed one another but become entwined in the Negro spirituals, chanted sermons, and sermon celebrations that bubble over into hymnody. This interweaving underscores the sermon's consanguinity with other highly potent ancient speech forms such as incantation, oracle, and spell.[36] But apart from the more explicit instances where sermon and song overlap, preaching is at its plainest a kind of song in that it is a heartfelt utterance that aims to glorify God. In this respect, even the preacher's unsyncopated speech holds cosmic power, blending with the chorus of the morning stars and the woodland trees that sing out with joy (Job 38:7; Ps. 96:12). Singing provides a fitting paradigm for preaching because it indicates a homiletical posture for truth telling. The preacher shares not just the church's official truth but a personal truth. And similarly, singing indicates a posture of listening. Members of the congregation are invited to internalize, ruminate on, and apply the message by setting it to the tune of their own lives.

Many iconic African American preachers who were Jackson's contemporaries bore truth through musicality. For example, Caesar Arthur Walter Clark Sr., celebrated pastor of Good Street Baptist Church in Dallas, had a pattern of beginning with a crawling delivery that steadily increased in tempo and energy. As the sermon reached its climax he would sometimes chant familiar hymn lyrics that were in turn taken up by the congregation in a collective utterance of the Christian hope. In cases such as these, the hymn is not simply an appendage to the sermon but its heart. The hymn functions more like a parallel text that is illumined through the preceding scriptural exegesis. So song is both the seed and fruit of the sermon—the seed because the preacher latches on to a song that is already nourishing spiritual vitality within the listener's heart, and fruit because scriptural exegesis enfleshes and interprets the song.

Gardner Taylor stressed this fluidity in his remarks at the funeral of Sandy F. Ray, another of Jackson's contemporaries who expertly wove speech and song in his sermons: "It was hard to tell whether one heard music half-spoken or speech half-sung. When the glad thunders of that voice reached its climactic theme, the heavens seemed to open, and we could see the Lord God on His Throne."[37] One could say that in such sermons music is the capsule for truth or, perhaps better, that the music itself is the truth born through the sermon. Part of the sermon's function is to put a song in the heart.

With this well-established history in mind, it will suffice to simply note a few salient areas of rhetorical correspondence between Black sacred music and African American preaching. First, despite the preparation and imagination involved, both find their genesis in the realm of the Spirit rather than human intellect. And at the most organic level, preaching and singing are holistic face-to-face endeavors. Both involve the full self—the whole mind, heart, voice, body, and life story. Similarly, both are climate-sensitive ventures. Enthusiastic listeners can often coax new depths of truth out of a preacher or singer, molding the message and strengthening its grasp; resistant listeners can sometimes deflate or constrain the process even if the proclaimed word has an ultimate sufficiency due to its divine mandate. Either way, the atmosphere in the room (or on Zoom) makes a discernible difference.

Likewise, singers and preachers tend to select from the same menu of rhetorical devices. Chief among these is repetition-driven progression.[38] Through this artful approach, new variations of color and energy emerge with each round. This strategy has much in common with classical rhetoric, which extolled the orator who, by amplifying and refining, found multiple ways of communicating a single concept.[39] Repetition offered a path to depth as well as retention. And more, repetition facilitated divine encounter. In much the same way that icons elicit an increasingly rapt gaze and draw viewers past the image to the living God, in the best cases repetition leads the listener past the orator to the Truth, the Holy One.

Other rhetorical methods include rhythm, melody, and time-honored devices like exempla (brief illustrative stories), injunction, metaphor (such as the haunting comparison to people and lambs in Roland Hayes's "Hear de Lambs a-Cryin'"), and apostrophe (speaking to someone who is absent or to an inanimate object, as in Greg O'Quin's "I Told the Storm"). Immediacy is achieved through in-the-moment supplications, bestowals of blessing, apotropaic prayers, exclamations, and rhetorical questions. Dialogue also plays a defining role, whether involving singers, musicians, and listeners, or preacher, musicians, and listeners. Whatever the combination, these methods reflect an intention to speak to the deepest part of the human person. Neither the singer nor the preacher is content with merely saying something about God; each seeks to facilitate a moment of union.

Further, when the visions of Christianity that inspired and sustained past generations are recalled through word and song, something beautiful happens. The viewpoints, values, and survival strategies of the ancestors become compasses for the present moment, and the unity between the living and the dead surfaces. And more, the winding terrain of spiritual life is represented through the singer's melisma and ornamentation, suggesting the human capacity to persevere. Mahalia Jackson's approach provides a window into these rhetorical dynamics.

A SONOROUS SAGE

If one takes the images of Mahalia Jackson on the concert stage in secular venues like the Newport Jazz Festival as seriously as the images of Jackson on church fans or in the choir loft in the 1959 film *Imitation of Life*, it becomes clear that Jackson did not aspire to fit the archetype of the whooping or chanting preacher or of the pastor-singer. She brought a bluesy sensibility to liturgical settings and made the depths of church music accessible to her secular audiences in swingy renditions of spirituals such as "Didn't It Rain" and "Walk All Over God's Heaven."[40] She never pastored a congregation, nor did she seek ordination. Though she considered telling Bible stories to local children part of her ministry, she did not have a practice of exegeting Scripture through traditional sermons from the pulpit. Instead, she had a lay ministry that flowed in church settings as well as secular spaces, and in both cases she gave melodic addresses that captured the heart of what sermons are and what they should do. Her preaching voice emerges best when one sets aside the prophetic model and thinks of her as a sage, a preacher who "functions as a wise observer of life" and encourages fellow lay listeners along "their God-guided search for wisdom in daily life."[41]

As Kenyatta Gilbert notes in his study of African American preaching, the sage has a "wisdom-focused, dialectical, communal voice" and interprets the "signs, symbols, and texts" in the community's cultural archive.[42] In Jackson's case, this proved to be a sonic archive, and gospel music was a form of wisdom with its own sounds, arrangements, emotional palettes, and ancestral linkages. In other words, Jackson treated gospel music as a body of knowledge that schooled the human spirit, offering interpretations for the full range of human experience and taking moments of anguish and perplexity as seriously as the authors of Job and Ecclesiastes.

Alyce McKenzie's insights about the preacher as sage are especially pertinent to Jackson's case. McKenzie observes that in Proverbs 1:5, wisdom (תַּחְבֻּלוֹת) [tahbulot] is understood as a form of aural "steering" that feeds the "formation of an interior disposition."[43] Jackson's music functioned in a similar way by fostering suppleness in the hearts of listeners. Sometimes she charted an affective path from sorrow or ennui to hope, and other times her music became a container or conduit for pain. "That's the way with the songs," she explained. "There is sadness, but always there is the hope and the faith in the Lord, and the forgetting of sadness and trouble in praising him." She hoped her songs "would soothe the minds of the listeners, give them faith, and make them believe more in God."[44] In other words, her music offered a salve as well as a certain clarity about human experience. In some instances, the music could prompt an immediate 180-degree turn in a listener's outlook, but cumulatively, it equipped people with the melodies and lyrics they needed to interpret their lives. She revealed gospel music's capacity to shape memory, facilitate self-awareness and self-transcendence, and increase tolerance of ambiguity so that people could face the unknown.

To be clear, gospel music does not become an end in itself; Jackson believed God's presence gave the music its power and meaning. Similarly, biblical Wisdom literature cannot be reduced to a set of propositions or principles and proves brittle apart from God.[45] The mediation of God's guidance is itself a divine encounter of sorts and one that directs and edifies the faith community.[46] Jackson's music had this dual function of guiding and enlivening. The contours of her wisdom-bearing emerge when attending to her approaches to dialogue, authority, and embodiment.

DIALOGICAL EXPERIENCE OF TRUTH

The sage is involved in an ever-deepening search for truth, and dialogue partners are instrumental to this process. Together their mutual curiosity leads to new discoveries even in the most familiar sources. For example, Ralph Eubanks remembers the continuing conversation his father had with Jackson every Sunday morning when he played her song "In the Upper Room":

> Even today, I can see him standing over the record and watching its incantatory spin as he listened to the music flowing from the scratchy speakers. . . . "In the Upper Room" is a traditional spiritual, one whose power comes from its slow, meditative call to prayer followed by a call-and-response affirmation of belief. The lyrics ask the listener to believe, but the singer must express belief for the song to get its message through. What captured my father each Sunday was that Mahalia Jackson sang "In the Upper Room" as if she was making a personal profession of faith and asking him to do the same.[47]

Eubanks puts his finger on a crucial element of Jackson's sagely voice through this attention to dialogue. For Jackson, singing was a way to be in dialogue with God and invite others into the conversation.[48] Dialogue anchors a line of homiletical theory called conversational preaching that could be applied here, but Eubanks cuts directly to the chase when he explains, "Mahalia Jackson always preached through her music, using the powerful delivery of the lyrics she sang to get her message across to an audience. . . . Through her testimonial style of singing, Jackson was preaching to my father."[49] Jackson's favorite hymns included "Jesus Lover of My Soul," "My Faith Looks Up to Thee," and "Just as I Am." Personal memories shaped her performance of these hymns, and audiences could see her emotions rise as she reflected on her journey. On these and similar occasions, hymn singing is revealed as a practice of testimony. *Marturein*, the New Testament term for physically bearing witness and a cognate for "martyr," is applicable here because of the personal investment in the testimony and the effort to connect with listeners.

Along this line, Willie Jennings uses the religious icon as an analogy for understanding the dynamics of Jackson's singing: "The iconic expression, and therefore the iconic movement, begins when the singer sacrificially offers up her own pain and suffering in the act of singing. Here the singer displays the depths of Jesus' own empathetic embrace in the midst of her struggles, while simultaneously embracing the hurt of the congregation by cradling them in song."[50] Jackson weaves three cords in her testimony: her own story of suffering, the listeners' pain, and Jesus' tender response.

Eubanks and Jennings are not alone in their interpretations. Johari Jabir similarly describes Jackson's music as "her testimony," observing a dialogical dimension that Mildred Falls, Jackson's accompanist, stirred by responding to Jackson's vocals.[51] With her left hand, Falls "provided a walking bass line that gave the music its 'bounce' reputation," and with her right hand, she "compensated for the lack of horn players common to a jazz band," staying in continuous conversation with Jackson's voice.[52] Together, in songs such as "Didn't It Rain," the "dynamic duo" revealed how "swing has a spiritual and philosophical purpose" and drives the search for truth.[53]

A shift in consciousness accompanied this dialogue for Jackson. "I truly have a divine feeling . . . within me when I'm singing these gospel songs. I don't seem to be myself. It seems like I'm transformed from Mahalia Jackson into something divine. And I just feel good all over."[54] The exchange with the audience was not entirely within her control; it was something that unfolded. Her role was to be open, present, and let herself be carried by the music, willing to improvise. And improvisation does not suggest a failure to prepare. Rather, it indicates a true understanding of the ephemeral nature of performance. The full integration of person, message, and moment enables the improviser to spontaneously draw from an internal well of knowledge. Within this understanding of improvisation, "performance and composition occur simultaneously—on the spot—through a practice that values surprise, innovation, and the vicissitudes of process rather than the fixed glory of a finished product."[55]

Improvisation entails genuine expression and authentic openness to the other. This exchange hinges on a fresh and lively vision of truth in which new dimensions continually surface. The sage mines ever deeper substrates of truth with her listeners. These new depths do not break down easily into takeaways or into a portable set of "how-tos," but elements of the exchange can echo in the hearts of the listeners. These remainders can include melodies, certain phrases, onomatopoeia, or vocal flourishes, but in every case they suggest an ongoing process of mulling over the music and a desire to continue the conversation.

PURPOSEFUL AUTHORITY

Jackson had a unique form of religious authority with multiple tendrils. The moral ground of her authority stemmed from being a seeker and bearer of divine wisdom. These dual dimensions indicate an "egalitarian" understanding of authority.[56] The sage respects the varieties of human experience too much to exert power over others and instead uses both differences and areas of agreement as springboards for further exploration. At the same time, Jackson's moral authority worked in tandem with other aspects. For example, expert power emerged whenever she drew on her incredible skill of reading the energy of an audience and when she controlled sound as it moved through her body. By partnering with her audiences, performances became joint ventures of seeking the sublime together. Artistic skill and stardom in turn contributed to Jackson's charismatic authority.

Yet one aspect of Jackson's authority that stands out and has significant transferability for those without musical genius is the "authority of purpose."[57] Letty Russell uses this term as a contrast to empty clerical authority. She understands that without divine purpose and a commitment to the equality and well-being of all, clerical authority can have ruinous effects. Authority of purpose describes the credibility that inures from clarity, conviction, and earnestness when reaching out to others. Unlike charismatic power or expertise, which tend to elevate one above others, authority of purpose is nonhierarchical and seems especially suited for bearing witness.

Authority of purpose helped Jackson claim her space whether on a dais in a church or on a stage in Carnegie Hall. And the authority of purpose helped her trust her own body, devise her own way to tell stories, and interpret songs that resonate with the depths of human experience. Free from the trap of exerting herself over others or proving herself worthy, she could devote her energies to the larger purpose of connecting deeply with her listeners.

Jackson's audacious aim was to touch the souls of her listeners, and this took time. Henry Mitchell explains that the use of slow delivery in Black preaching facilitated an "impact on the whole person: on cognitive, intuitive, and emotive consciousness," and he describes the spiritual as the "homiletical twin" to the sermon because of the use of slow delivery in each.[58] Jackson sang spirituals often, and even when singing other songs or hymns she extended notes or slowed the meter for effect. She used deliberate pacing to feel the haptics in the room and facilitate shifts in consciousness. This refusal to rush gave each song gravity, underscoring her sense of purpose.

Jackson's sense of purpose was also bound up with exploring the power of sound. After all, it was not theological propositions that drew her to church but the magnetism of the sounds she heard: "I would always find myself drawn to the church. And it's because I liked the songs and I liked the way that the preacher, the old preacher, would preach in his method. He . . . would have a singing tone in his voice that was sad. And it done something to me."[59] It had a visceral impact, and her call was to summon that sound and search for its antecedents, which I would ground in the ache of the spirituals sung by her ancestors. Jackson reached for consolation of the same Jobian depth. This effort required the authority of purpose.

EMBODIED WISDOM

Jackson's performance preparation process was also telling. Her weeks included multiple rehearsals that equipped her to internalize songs so that she could improvise on stage when desired. But in the hours just before getting on stage, she began her process by reading and meditating on Scripture. "Before I go on stage, I read my Bible. . . . It's my strength, and it is the strength and spirit of my songs."[60] This meditative reading surely centered Jackson but also indicated missional focus. She knew she was telling a Christian story through song, and readiness to tell that story was crucial. She had to get beneath the lyrics and incarnate her beliefs. When this happened, the impact on the audience could be electric. One reviewer, stunned after seeing her at Carnegie Hall, explained that "some inner spiritual force has given her the power to tell a story in song with as much passion and rapture as any prima donna who ever graced the stage. And you have the innermost conviction that in her heart she feels and lives the text of each song."[61] For Jackson, song was a means of publicly interpreting Christian doctrine, and this required an embodied hermeneutic.

The emphasis on embodied wisdom turns on the assumption that a sermon is less like a speech and more like a performance of a biblical text or a performance of Christian truth. This notion of performance accords with the Anglo-French etymology of the word *perform*—*per-* (thoroughly) + *furnir* (to complete or furnish).[62] The rhetor carries the truth to completion so that propositions come alive.[63] Similarly, Jackson brought Christian teachings to life by involving her whole body. When singing, her eyes communicated as much when open as when closed. Closed eyes revealed an intensity of concentration rather than retreat. Hands were often clasped in prayer or waved for emphasis. Her facial expression conveyed emotion, and the muscles of her neck tightened and loosened visibly. Her jaws moved to shape the sound. Viewers could not see her diaphragm, but it, too, was active in sustaining her breath. All this bodily engagement indicates an enfleshed understanding of wisdom.

The fact that Jackson was a larger, round-bodied woman raises critical issues concerning performance. Sometimes she was haunted by the mammy stereotype. For instance, during the production of *The Mahalia Jackson Show*, she received an anonymous note comparing her to Beulah, a radio and television character who was an African American maid (played for a time by Hattie McDaniel) and in many ways analogous to mammy.[64] The note was a discouraging reminder of how narrow the conceptions of Black womanhood were. Indebted to Bessie Smith's blues influence, Jackson embodied a Black vernacular aesthetic that scrambled the sacred-secular divide as well as the binary between cultivated and vernacular music.[65] As a consequence, she was not estranged from her body or her sexuality, as many in Chicago's Black Baptists circles knew, and her brightly colored gowns accentuated her curves. Even on the occasions when she performed in choir robes, the robe was not designed to hide her girth but to serve the music.[66]

In a 1952 interview for the *Chicago Tribune*, Jackson spoke of dieting, saying she was easing off her celebrated cooking: "I'm reducing, and it's quite a struggle. I weigh 240 pounds now, but by the time the Chicagoland Music Festival comes around, I expect to be down to 200. . . . You need strength to sing the songs I sing. . . . You could say that 200 pounds is my singing weight."[67]

But in addition to misreading the ways Jackson used her body, mammy associations also misread her joy. She had a buoyant personality behind the scenes and under the stage lights, not a cheap joviality put on to please white audiences. Her commitment to Black political empowerment would not allow that. For example, she enjoyed giving offertory appeals. In one playful episode, she openly competed with a pastor to see who could contribute the most to the offering plate and pulled money from her bra to outdo him.[68] It is true that television muted some of this freedom, but not enough to render her as a mammy figure.

Despite the hostile climate of show business, Jackson believed her body was a gift, and she relished in her sonic capacity to bridge the visible and invisible worlds. One of the clearest examples of this took place at the March on Washington. At the request of Martin Luther King Jr., she sang the spiritual "I Been 'Buked and I Been Scorned."[69] The song had special resonance that day on the steps of the Lincoln Memorial because it articulated the pain and hope of the enslaved in their own language and cadence. Among the many lyrics she could have selected for the second verse, she chose "Ain't but the one thing I've done wrong / Ain't but the one thing I've done wrong / Ain't but one thing I've done wrong / You know I've been in the valley for too long." The striking thing about the last line is that it suggests those who were enslaved have an ongoing presence that is being mediated through song. They are summoned by the voicing of their testimonies. Of course, this idea challenges the Western notion of the body's materiality and the rigid wall between presence and absence, but it reflects an important dimension of African American spirituality and reveals the metaphysical landscape of African American preaching. Being attuned to the presence of the living and the dead is part of what it means to be fully embodied.

The third verse builds on this idea: "You know I'm gonna tell my Lord when I get home / You know I'm gonna tell my Lord when I get home / Yes, I'm gonna tell my Lord when I get home / How you've been mistreating me for so long." "Me" is broad enough to encompass all African Americans, living and dead, and indeed all who suffer. Jackson's stress on "tell"—extending the note, closing her eyes and bending her knees for emphasis—was especially poignant because in that moment she functioned as emissary for her enslaved ancestors. Their strength was bequeathed to the vast crowd. Their warning of the cosmic consequences for evil was announced before the marchers, human adversaries, and the powers and principalities.

   Surely this role as intermediary also prompted her interjection during King's speech when she famously encouraged him to tell the listeners about the dream. After having first heard "I have a dream" as a refrain in a prayer led by Prathia Hall, King had drawn on the theme before, but Jackson sensed that the dream was ripe for the moment. What I want to stress here is that Jackson's homiletical counsel, which helped inspire one of the most celebrated speeches of the twentieth century, was preceded and undergirded by her embodiment of ancestral wisdom.

   Through her song and prompting to King, Jackson braced the demonstrators for the violence that would come in the immediate future as a backlash to that march. In less than two weeks, these horrors would include the bombing of the Sixteenth Street Baptist Church in Birmingham that would kill Addie Mae Collins, Carol Denise McNair, Carole Robertson, and Cynthia Wesley, and the shooting deaths of Virgil Lamar Ware and Johnny Robinson. Jackson could not have known exactly what lay ahead, but the wisdom she embodied as an intermediary for the ancestors makes it clear she knew much was at stake. Preachers are called to relate concrete contextual realities to the transcendent world, and Jackson did both.[70]

LEGACY AND PRACTICAL INSIGHTS

Overall, Jackson's music reveals the porosity of the African American sermon genre. Here it helps to note that genres are not fixed categories but fluid ones. They are expanded, modified, and performed in fresh ways as new voices inhabit them and as new situations arise. Belonging within a genre is not always a simple "type/token" or "general form/particular instance" question.[71] Genres are stretched by experimentation and on occasions when the guidelines that typically govern them are only partially adhered. This means one can partake in a genre without seeming to belong.[72]

   Mahalia Jackson did more than sing gospel music; she was one of its architects. Her sound influenced a host of contemporaries, including Willie Mae Ford Smith, who also played with sermon hybridity and is credited with originating the song and sermonette. This practice of inserting a short story or mini sermon in a song was also taken up by other artists such as Edna Gallmon

Cooke and Shirley Caesar who underscored the intersection between sermon and song. "The Lord called me to the melody of song and the ministry of the Word," Caesar explained. "He called me to use music to preach. . . . I sing a sermon and I preach a song."[73] In these cases, the turns from song to discourse or vice versa are more distinct. It was not uncommon for Jackson to offer short exhortations between songs when in concert, but her preaching was not limited to these orations. Rather, her approach challenged listeners to discern a sermon *in* song. Within this frame, preaching involves putting a song in the listener's heart and performing a sacred text in a way that provides a link to the faith of the ancestors. Through the sung word, the living and dead are shown to be in a continuing communion.

Jackson also provides an example of preaching that is not overdetermined by a colonialist framework. Her model is not haunted by the specter of a domineering man telling others what to do, or using fear, coercion, or manipulation to achieve its ends, or objectifying the listeners so that they become pawns—only finding power as they cede to the preacher's vision. Yet her sagely approach is still grounded in conviction and lived experience. Were she to counsel preachers, I suspect she would stress the importance of communicating the substance of a message sonically. This would mean proceeding as if the contours of the message had to be sculpted through rhythm, pitch, tempo, and other elements of music rather than by the lyrics alone. Composing the sermon to music or treating the manuscript like a musical score that charts the arc of the message for emphasis could serve as starting points.

Gardner Taylor was once asked why he did not have a practice of whooping or singing in sermons, and he replied, "Your words should sing!"[74] Even as a nonsinger, he appreciated the vital links between sermon and song. This vibrant pairing is helpful for thinking about the sermon in relation to other forms of discourse. What if the fluidity between visual art and sermon were as legible as that between song and sermon? What other ways of knowing might emerge and what new levels of wholeness might result? In the next chapter, I consider what it might mean to preach a soundless message and *see* a sermon.

2

The Quilter

Narrative quiltmaking has become my voice on cloth.
—Peggie L. Hartwell

Rosie Lee Tompkins takes a piece of bright blue fabric adorned with yellow, white, and orange flowers. With bright tangerine thread, she moves in and around the crevices of the flowers to stitch a phrase with painstaking care: "Let not your heart be troubled: ye believe in God; believe also in me" (John 14:1 KJV).[1] This little blue quilt square is surrounded by other patterned patches. Tompkins combines more than two dozen different fabrics with vibrant floral designs that run horizontally, vertically, diagonally, and in curling vines. Together they form a lush and living garden encircling a central square that features an image of Jesus. Several small black velveteen squares signal mourning in the garden, but they are buoyed by the surrounding jubilance and other uplifting verses of Scripture. This quilt is also an exhortation.

Some may find the notion of a proclamatory quilt puzzling—especially if one has limited familiarity with quilting and tends to lump it with flower arranging or scrapbooking. Quilting is a craft in this vein, but for some it is also a highly expressive medium for testifying and consolation. Since the late nineteenth century, African American women's quilting has been an embodied practice that has often transferred cultural knowledge. As Gladys-Marie Fry, a quilt historian, explains, "Denied the opportunity to read or write, slave women quilted their diaries, creating permanent but unwritten records of events large and small, of pain and loss, of triumph and tragedy in their lives. And each piece of cloth became the focal point of a remembered past."[2] And more, quilting was a means of drawing on ancestral traditions of spiritual expression.

For many African American women, quilting became a form of discourse. Some quilts tell stories; others memorialize the dead and recount divine action. Aesthetically, quilters communicate through symbolism, color, and texture and by harmonizing that which seems discordant. Inspired by the divine power to reorder and restore, they sew fragments into kaleidoscopic wholes, finding beauty in chaos. And much like traditional preachers who exegete patterns in Scripture and in life, quilters study patterns as well.[3] They arrange cloth to first build and then usurp patterns, to render gradations and create visual energy.

In addition to this artistic dimension of healing, quilters address practical needs like warmth and comfort. For newborns, newlyweds, the sick, and bereaved, quilts function as material signs of intercession. These tactile messages of consolation and affection grow out of prolonged periods of concentrated meditation. Because of the deep spirituality that tends to manifest in quilting, it is not an exaggeration to describe a quilt as a "visual chant," "requiem," or "voice on cloth."[4] Quilting is a form of memory speech and is especially adept at communicating truth.

I have offered a general framework about quilting for context, but the proclamatory potential in quilting emerges best through examining the witness of individual quilters such as Rosie Lee Tompkins (1936–2006) and Harriet Powers (1837–1910). An examination of their compositions leads us to ask how God's truth manifests through the visual and tactile medium of quilting. What if gazing at or touching quilts is expected to sharpen the viewer's spiritual perception, mimicking the posture of deep listening that is experienced in aural sermons? How might such quilts function as sermons?

ROSIE LEE TOMPKINS: A BIOGRAPHICAL SKETCH

Rosie Lee Tompkins, née Effie Mae Martin, was born on September 6, 1936, in Gould, Arkansas, a rural community located about thirty miles southeast of Pine Bluff and eighty miles southeast of Little Rock. Details on her early life are scant, but she was the daughter of Sadie Bell and MacCurey Martin and one of fifteen half-siblings.[5] She had a deep affection for her mother, who taught her how to quilt and who had learned from her mother, Lovely Bell.[6] Young Effie Mae left Arkansas to live for brief stints in Milwaukee and Chicago and then settled in California in 1958.[7]

Upon arriving in the East Bay area, she tried to construct a life for herself that would not have been possible in Arkansas. She married Ellis Howard in 1963, raised five children and stepchildren, and found fulfilling work serving in convalescent facilities as a practical nurse.[8] She also found a spiritual home in the Beacon Light Seventh-day Adventist Church. Given that the Seventh-day Adventist Church has emphasized a link between health and spirituality since its founding in 1863, it is also likely that she found continuity between her faith and her chosen vocation as a practical nurse.

Yet Beacon Light offered more than spiritual support; it offered a sense of belonging. The congregation was founded in the 1950s by a small group of African Americans who had, much like Howard, journeyed from Mississippi, Louisiana, Arkansas, and Texas to California as part of the Great Migration.[9] Having witnessed brutality in the South and new iterations of racism in the West, they banded together and formed an extended family. After worship they invited one another into their homes for Sabbath lunch and organized activities for their children.[10] And despite the challenges stemming from the mostly white administrative structure of the Seventh-day Adventist Church, they made an impact on the city of Richmond, California, sometimes teaming up with nearby congregations for joint missionary projects.[11] At Beacon Light, Howard found an anchor and a sense of home.

But life in California brought struggle along with joy. She would eventually divorce twice and feel the loneliness of being far from home. Quiltmaking provided a restorative outlet. By 1970 she was making quilts and selling them at local flea markets. She even had business cards made that read, "Effie Howard/Crazy Quilts and Pillows All Sizes."[12]

While there are few specifics, at some point during the late 1970s Howard's mental health suffered, and she experienced a nervous breakdown. Medication proved ineffective, and its side effects were intolerable.[13] While she continued to hear voices and have mental health challenges long afterward, in quilting she found a salve and a sense of closeness to God. "The reason it makes me feel so good," she once said of her work, "is that I put Christ in the center of it."[14]

For Howard, piecework was a sacred task. Each quilt began with prayer. And though she liked to sew to disco music, she believed God guided her hands as she worked.[15] Given that disco grew out of gospel, she may have had a similar affective experience of the music. When quilting, she understood herself to be "God's instrument" and was convinced that God gave her the designs for her quilts as well as the color schemes.[16] Quilting became a way to self-soothe, remember, pray, and express her faith. Ultimately, she hoped her quilts would "spread a lot of love."[17]

Many African American women of Howard's generation treasured their privacy, but apparently this was doubly true in her case. While warm and vivacious privately, she avoided the limelight and interviews, and rarely allowed others to photograph her. She even responded to one request for a portrait by positioning one of her favorite outfits in an empty chair "as if an invisible woman were sitting in them."[18] Her hesitance may have stemmed from the stigma associated with mental illness at the time or for other reasons. Either way, she was resolute about protecting her privacy. Around 1987, Eli Leon, a quilt scholar and collector eager to get more of Howard's work into the public sphere, suggested she use a pseudonym, and the name "Rosie Lee Tompkins" was created. The pseudonym mirrored the syllables and prosody of her actual name while shielding her privacy.[19]

Although she was ambivalent about the art world, Rosie Lee Tompkins's quilts were regularly exhibited in art museums and publications, earning her considerable acclaim during the 1990s. In 1997, the Berkeley Art Museum of California held a solo exhibition for her, *Rosie Lee Tompkins/MATRIX 173*. In 2002, her quilt *Three Sixes* (1986) appeared in the Whitney Biennial prior to its historic exhibition of *The Quilts at Gee's Bend*, which brought renewed attention to African American women's quilting.

While Tompkins was not formally trained, her mother's tutelage and the insights she gained from her independent study of art proved sufficient. She created compositions that excited quilt lovers, museum goers, and art critics, and they fulfilled the spiritual and proclamatory aims that were of utmost importance to her. Rosie Lee Tompkins died on December 1, 2006, at age seventy. Shortly after her death, the Shelburne Museum in Vermont held her second solo exhibition, *Something Pertaining to God*. The "category-defying" and "boundary-blurring" breadth of her oeuvre came into fuller view in 2018 after Eli Leon bequeathed around 200 of her works to the Berkeley Art Museum and Pacific Film Archive.[20]

VISUAL AND TACTILE EXHORTATIONS

Tompkins's quilts carry a good deal of affective energy and surprise. Her eclectic approach to asymmetry often resembles collage, and a fondness for experimentation and breaking conventions becomes immediatcly obvious. Tompkins liked to skew borders and make incomplete or imperfect squares. She integrated crosses regularly, and these, too, are imbalanced—often lopsided. Beading, ornamentation, and trim are also recurrent on her quilts and on her many other patchwork creations—such as clothing, purses, and pillows—as well as on sculpture-like assemblages that she created out of small bottles.

In fact, it may be a stretch to call her fabric compositions "quilts." Technically, quilts involve a top layer, often with a design that is pieced or appliquéd, a middle layer of filling, and a "back" or lining on the bottom. The three layers are sewn together. Tompkins focused on the top design and showed less interest in assembling her tops into completed quilts. She also took liberties with the size of her compositions. Some are much smaller than traditional bed quilts, and others are considerably larger. Unlike with most bed quilts, her orientations are often uncertain.

Despite these departures from typical quilting practices, she made vibrant, arresting compositions. Her larger quilts have the immensity of murals and layers of depth. Tompkins had a pattern of incorporating miniature quilts within her quilt designs. These miniatures draw the viewer's eye in and emphasize the significance of small things. Preferring to be guided by intuition instead of by a ruler or template, her instincts yield generosity and freedom. Constellations of unmeasured shapes undulate and give her quilts a sense of animation. They also stir emotions. Eli Leon spoke of a woman whose tears streamed down her face as she stood before Tompkins's *String* (1985), a quilt another viewer described as "an outpouring of spirit, an avalanche of love."[21]

Color plays a central role in her spirituality and in her creative process. "I think it's because I love them so much that God let me see all these different colors," she once said.[22] She sometimes linked a color with a specific loved one—red and black for two of her brothers, for example.[23] And Tompkins was not only drawn to color but to certain trios of color. A repeated yellow, purple, and orange combination honors three family members with sixes in their birthdays. Sometimes a quilt was a prayer for the relationship of loved ones, whom she portrayed through select color combinations. Tompkins even created memorial quilts that function as eulogies for deceased loved ones. These mournful quilts use color to extol the dead and point to inner truths that the person radiated. Color, then, was a means of meditating on the Christian witness of ancestors.

Texture is as important as color. Velvet and velour were among her favorite fabrics.[24] In addition to reflecting light, these plush fabrics reveal her fascination with tactility. For example, an eight-by-twelve-foot untitled quilt from 2002 incorporates buttons, velour, cotton, canvas, polyester, fleece, and wool—a feast of textures.[25] To these, Tompkins stitched scriptural references along two sides of the quilt. These references—to Luke, Acts, James, and Psalms—are hard to make out visually against the bright colors and busy patterns but appear to be easier to make out tactilely. Touch, then, whether experienced directly or approximated through eyesight, functions as a primary medium for meaning making. And in contemporary digital cultures that are essentially bereft of touch and prone to consuming images quickly and broadly disseminating them, Tompkins's call to slow contemplation has increased potency.

TOMPKINS AS TRUTH TELLER

While Tompkins regularly incorporated Bible verses, crosses, and images of
Jesus, her quilts maintain a certain dreaminess. Symbolic numbers sometimes
float alongside cascading yo-yos. Clusters of Bible verses on related themes
dance together and allude to shared meanings as they might in a sermon.
She does not demand a decision from the viewer in accord with traditional
kerygmatic preaching. Instead, as visible and invisible worlds swirl together in
her work, viewers are "given permission to wonder."[26] Such pondering is itself
a form of edification.

Sometimes Tompkins's penchant for the whimsical also emerges. In an
untitled pistachio-green composition that she finished in 2002, amid crosses,
biblical references, and allusions to her geographical moves, she tucked in the
phrase "Love is like an ice cream cone; it gets better with each lick."[27] Given
her playfulness and eclecticism, it is no surprise that she sought to envelop the
viewer in an experience of grace rather than rely on verbal statements about
grace. Tompkins once told Eli Leon, "If people like my works, that means the
love of Jesus Christ is still shining through what I'm doing."[28] This goal of
touching the soul is evident even though some of her thinking is deliberately
opaque. I think of her quilts as visual testimonies. Through them she shares
her inner experience of truth and invites viewers into it.

Tompkins's attention to the mysterious and the sublime does not, however,
suggest she had no interest in addressing the realities of evil. Sometimes
her didactic aims were more explicit, such as when she reflected on the
complexities of patriotism, anti-black racism, and oppressive social structures.
In an untitled 1996 quilt, Tompkins arranged images of eight famous African
American men—Michael Jordan, Magic Johnson, O. J. Simpson, Nelson
Mandela, Martin Luther King Jr., Malcolm X, Elijah Muhammad, and Louis
Farrakhan—and juxtaposed eight crosses constructed out of men's neckties.[29]
The piece is a meditation on Black male suffering and the cross.

In another 2005 quilt, she fashioned over a dozen crosses out of smooth,
brown fabric and affixed them to a white background.[30] The crosses are of
different shapes and sizes and are positioned next to rectangular blocks. This
quilt similarly invites reflection on present-day Christ figures. The fleshy
crosses draw on "haptic visuality," which, as Laura Marks explains, requires
that we gaze for an extended period before making conclusions about what
we are beholding.[31] Tompkins's combinations of color and texture hinder a
quick or distant view. Instead, the eyes must function as "organs of touch."[32]
Through this sensory skewing, Tompkins cultivates an enchanted form of
vision—the vision of a seer. It is in this respect that Tompkins's participation
in the sermon genre becomes most evident.[33] She seeks to edify viewers,

nurturing their powers of perception and discernment through a visual and tactile experience. And isn't the nurturing of perception and discernment consistent with what most preachers aim to do? More than exegete a specific text or communicate an idea, preachers try to sharpen listeners' perceptive capacities so that they can better discern divine action in the world.

Examined homiletically, Tompkins's work offers a nonargumentative approach to Black preaching. That is to say, rather than trying to be persuasive, she relies heavily on divine revelation to achieve its own ends.[34] In the current rhetorical landscape, such a position may seem naive, but there is strong homiletical foundation for it. As Amos Wilder explains in *Early Christian Rhetoric*, the gospel is governed by divine revelation rather than by the established rules of rhetoric.[35]

Instead of explaining biblical texts, Tompkins invited viewers to look at them obliquely—to experience them through color, texture, and symbol. She also seemed to revel in making viewers search for biblical texts. For instance, she liked to inscribe biblical references in a manner that made the letters blend or recede into the pattern and colors that foregrounded the quilt.[36] The viewer must look beyond the busyness of the quilt's design to make out the words she has hidden like little treasures in the background. These hidden words are often sewn in writing that seems to come from a cryptic hand. Tompkins's vision of faith combines hidden truth and revealed truth.

Though Tompkins's quilts often include overt Christian references and affirmations, her didactic elements are presented with a certain reserve. Using fewer words may reflect an apophatic sensibility—a consciousness of divine transcendence that leads to a retreat from language. The apophatic tradition within Christianity offers a helpful corrective to the word-heavy traditions typically found in Western Christianity. As Peter Kline argues concerning apophatic discourse, "To speak of what cannot be said, even to speak of it as 'unsayable,' is a betrayal of what cannot be said."[37] Tompkins's use of abstraction seems to lean in this direction by shifting our attention to the ineffable. But beyond her attention to the "unsayable," she demonstrates a more fundamental aspect of apophatic discourse by maintaining a position of elusiveness, refusing to "master" her theological subject matter.[38]

Alternatively, Tompkins may be providing a respite for her viewers. Her approach brings to mind what Judith Butler calls the "vulnerability of address," which stems from the psychic violence to which language has been put and the automatic power listeners yield to speakers through the act of listening.[39] Even if one is relying on ego defense mechanisms, listening makes one at least initially receptive to the speaker and vulnerable to the consequences that may result from a toxic message. A paradox ensues, as there is both a need to be addressed *through* language and a need to be protected *from* language.

This vulnerability may be especially acute among African Americans and others for whom language has been a tool of racialized oppression. From antebellum times, Christian preaching has been coopted as a means of undermining Black personhood, sanctioning racialized violence, encouraging assimilation to white norms, discouraging self-determination, and denying the freedom God intends for all human beings. In such instances, listeners have had to brace themselves against the preached word as they might against a slur, thus hindering the absorption of the more wholesome content in the sermon (if any). And sadly, these forms of psychic aggression have been perpetrated by preachers from multiple racial and ethnic backgrounds. Consequently, the sermon has a long history as a site of violence and as a time of scolding, shaming, coercion, and manipulation. Tompkins, in contrast, deals gently with the viewers' gaze. Using abstraction, she finds a way to "speak tenderly to Jerusalem" (Isa. 40:2). Her quilts invite consideration but do not compel or jolt the viewer into attention. Her images find their fullest life in the imagination of the viewer.

Overall, Rosie Lee Tompkins provides a helpful case for thinking about the sermon genre. She adheres to certain requisites of preaching, such as engaging in public Christian edification, but refuses others, such as orality. This partial adherence reveals the shoreline of the sermon genre. As John Frow argues, drawing on Derrida, "The law of genre is 'a sort of participation without belonging—a taking part in without being a part of, without having membership in a set.'"[40] A quilt can also be a sermon. Such multiplicity is indicative of the energy of individual texts and the fluidity of the genres intended to classify them. Primacy rests, according to Frow, on the effects of a given form of discourse. "Genres are to be defined not in terms of the intrinsic structure of their discourse but by the *actions* they are used to accomplish."[41]

To be clear, Rosie Lee Tompkins does not explicitly call her quilts "sermons." Yet she is intentional about using quilting to testify, "spread" Christ's love, and reflect on contemporary social problems in light of the gospel. It helps to put Tompkins's work in conversation with that of another quilter, Harriet Powers, who voices an intention to "preach the gospel in patchwork, to show my Lord my humility," and to "show where sin originated, out of the beginning of things."[42]

HARRIET POWERS: A BIOGRAPHICAL SKETCH

Harriet (or "Harriett") Powers was born to an enslaved mother in Clarke County, Georgia, on October 29, 1837.[43] It is unclear exactly where she was born or what the details of her early life were. In 1855 she married Armstead Powers, and after emancipation they eventually moved to a farm near Athens,

Georgia. She and Armstead had nine children, though six of them died at a young age. Eventually the couple purchased a four-acre farm and supported themselves and their children there. When Powers was not absorbed with farmwork, housework, or child-rearing, she quilted. Inspired by religious themes, Powers understood her work as a form of sacred rhetoric and treated her quilting as a vocation. Her reflections conveyed confidence that she was a "channel through which a greater power was speaking."[44]

Harriet Powers made at least five quilts. Three have not been found, including one with "4 thousand and 50 diamonds" made in 1872; a "star quilt," which won a prize in Athens's 1887 Colored Fair; and an undated quilt depicting "the Lord's Supper from the New Testament."[45] A finely detailed quilt, *The Lord's Supper*, included a design with 2,500 diamonds.[46] Powers completed it after she joined Mount Zion Baptist Church and began fervently studying Scripture.[47] Two quilts remain. Powers called one "Adam and Eve in the Garden of Eden," though it is now commonly referred to as the *Bible Quilt.* [48] It is dated around 1886 and part of the permanent collection of the National Museum of American History in Washington, DC. The other remaining quilt is Powers's *Pictorial Quilt*, which is dated 1895–1898 and part of the collection at the Boston Museum of Fine Arts. Some of the panels may have been inspired by sermons Powers heard at church, but her original arrangement proves her to be a skilled interpreter and proclaimer in her own right.[49]

Powers's *Bible Quilt* was displayed at the 1886 Athens Cotton Fair and drew considerable attention. The quilt caught the eye of Oneita Virginia Smith, a local white artist and teacher, who offered to buy the quilt. But Powers said she was not willing to sell it "at any price."[50] A few years later circumstances changed. The Powers family was struggling financially, and Powers offered to sell her quilt to Smith for ten dollars. Smith counteroffered five dollars, and with pressure from Armstead, Powers agreed to sell.[51] Smith remembered the reluctance in Powers's voice when she explained that Armstead had urged her to accept the five dollars and noted, "Not being a new woman she obeyed."[52] Yet before parting with the quilt, Powers insisted on explaining the interpretation of each quilt panel while Smith took notes.[53] Still heartbroken, Powers made several return trips to visit her quilt, prompting Smith to call it the "darling offspring of her brain."[54]

The fact that the quilt was so valuable to Harriet Powers is important. Beyond pride in craftsmanship or the family members who may have been memorialized in the fabric, Powers's attachment to the quilt also hints of the necessity for Black women to preach to themselves as a means of seeking intimacy with God—a need Ntozake Shange alludes to when she speaks of finding and loving God within oneself.[55] The personal spiritual meaning the quilt carried should not be discounted and likely contributed to her initial refusal to sell.

But Powers's quilt would have a broader public life. After the pained sale, the quilt was displayed in an exhibition on Negro progress at the Cotton States and International Exposition held in Atlanta in 1895.[56] This event proved historic. Booker T. Washington opened it on September 18, 1895, with his "Atlanta Compromise" speech, famously encouraging his listeners to "cast down your buckets where you are."[57] He went on to commend the Negro exhibit, noting that the progress it demonstrated through the various examples of machinery, inventions, and artistry had begun only "thirty years ago with ownership here and there in a few quilts and pumpkins and chickens."[58]

Despite Washington's somewhat dismissive comment about quilts, the *Bible Quilt* (see figure 1) again made an impact. Lorene Curtis Divers, a writer from Keokuk, Iowa, was so struck by the power of the quilt that she had it professionally photographed.[59] Later, another artist, Lucine Finch, published a copy of Divers's photograph in "A Sermon in Patchwork," an essay in *Outlook Magazine* that conveyed Powers's intention to preach through quilting.[60] Disparaging views of Blackness hindered Smith, Divers, and Finch from promoting Powers

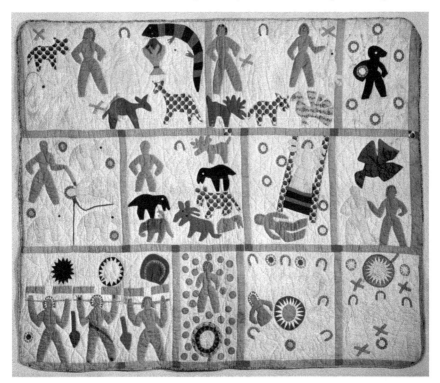

Figure 1. Harriet Powers, *Bible Quilt*, 1885–1886. Hand-stitched cotton and machine-stitched cotton, 75 in. × 89 in. Washington, DC, Division of Home and Community Life, National Museum of American History, Smithsonian Institution. Used by permission.

Figure 2. Harriet Powers, *Pictorial Quilt*, American (Athens, Georgia), 1895–1898. Object Place: Athens, Georgia, United States. By Harriet Powers, American 1837–1910. Cotton plain weave, pieced, appliqued, embroidered, and quilted, 175 x 266.7 cm (68⅞ in. × 105 in.). Museum of Fine Arts, Boston. Bequest of Maxim Karolik. 64.619. Photograph © 2024, Museum of Fine Arts, Boston. Used by permission.

or recognizing the breadth of her talent, but they nonetheless brought more attention to her work, and the Cotton States and International Exposition of 1895 played a crucial role in this process.

Yet by 1895 Powers's family life was changing. She and Armstead had separated. Nearing sixty by this time, she took care of the farm and mortgaged a portion of the land to buy a buggy for herself for $16.89.[61] Despite these changed responsibilities, Powers continued her quilting. By 1898 she had completed the *Pictorial Quilt* (see figure 2), which was exhibited at the Nashville Exposition. The quilt was either purchased or commissioned by the faculty ladies of Atlanta University as a parting gift for Rev. Charles Cuthbert Hall, a trustee of Atlanta University who had accepted a position as dean of Union Theological Seminary.

Harriet Powers died of pneumonia on January 1, 1910. Three days later, an Athens newspaper published a death notice: "Harriet Powers, an aged Negro woman who held the esteem of many Athens people, died from pneumonia Jan. 1st. Her remains were carried to her old home near the city for internment Sunday."[62] Powers was buried at the Gospel Pilgrim Cemetery in Athens.

POWERS AS BIBLICAL STORYTELLER

Powers's most celebrated work is the *Bible Quilt*. While African American quilting styles are vast and no single set of aesthetic features should be considered determinative, Powers's *Bible Quilt* includes design features that have been associated with African American handiwork.[63] First, it includes vibrant shades of green, orange, and pink. In addition to bright color, Powers uses large-scale design elements, juxtaposes multiple patterns, uses contrasting sash trim, places squares at most (though not all) of the corners, and deliberately uses asymmetry. Her aesthetic elements also carry an improvisational quality.

Comparisons have been made between Powers's design and appliqué patterns in Dahomean textiles because there are obvious similarities, but it is important to stress that there are as many differences as there are similarities. Establishing definitive familial or artistic links between Powers and Dahomean textiles proves elusive.[64] But for some scholars, Powers's use of layered symbolism to relay biblical stories suggests an ancestral influence and gives her work a certain charge—the kind associated with "the power-to-make-things-happen."[65]

Powers's usage of silhouettes gives her figures a universal dimension. Another African American visual artist, Aaron Douglas (1899–1979), used silhouettes in a similar way to signify the universality of certain biblical themes arising in James Weldon Johnson's *God's Trombones*. His renderings of *The Creation, Noah's Ark, The Prodigal Son,* and other sermonic poems are visual allegories that depict homiletical interpretations of specific biblical scenes.[66] By dramatizing pivotal moments, he expressed the struggle and triumph of faith. He also surrounded his silhouettes with emanating circles of light or shaded angles and compared this usage of light and dark to "call-and-response."[67] The silhouettes reveal a unity between the visual and the aural, showing how listening feeds seeing and vice versa.

Another part of the efficacy of silhouettes stems from their ability to depict a subject while pointing to unseen dimensions of reality that are nonetheless active. Similarly, Powers's silhouettes draw viewers beyond the surface of the images themselves and into the central themes and archetypes of the biblical story. By looking through the veil of these silhouettes, viewers get practice for the daily responsibility of reading and interpreting signs of divine action in the world.[68]

Yet carefully deployed silhouettes are not the only distinctive features of Powers's quilt. Vertical orientation was common during the time, but hers reads horizontally. And at seventy-five inches by eighty-nine inches, the quilt is not intended for sleeping.[69] Perhaps most striking, Powers composed an interpretation for each panel of the quilt, underscoring its didactic purpose.[70]

Bible Quilt consists of eleven panels arranged in three rows that unfold like David Buttrick's sermonic moves.[71] "Good preaching involves the imaging of ideas, the shaping of every conceptual notion by metaphor and image and syntax," Buttrick explains.[72] Powers's sermonic moves unfold cinematically to form an overarching argument. She begins with the story of Adam and Eve in the garden of Eden. Beautiful animals abound. With its vivid stripes and delicate orange feet, an alluring serpent dominates the upper right corner of the panel. The second panel shows Adam, Eve, and Cain—each with a pet. Cain's peacock may symbolize pride because next, Satan triumphs among the seven stars. On the second row, Powers begins with a macabre scene. A line of red depicts Cain murdering Abel. Abel's blood cries out from the ground. Exile follows, leaving Cain in the land of Nod. This panel symbolizes impending judgment and marks a turning point in the quilt and in her understanding of salvation history.

But things get more hopeful in the sixth panel, where an angel descends Jacob's ladder and comes to earth. And in the seventh, the first New Testament scene, the Holy Spirit descends on Christ like a dove. The magnitude of Christ's redemptive work is represented next in the crucifixion. While gazing at this panel, Powers is quoted as having said, "Wipe it [sin] out in the world."[73] Her next panel portrays the Last Supper. Though the sequencing is somewhat opaque, she ends with a panel that renders the Holy Family—a new beginning. In sum, she argues that the sin of Adam and Eve is redeemed through the birth of Christ.

So the *Bible Quilt* is a sermon about sin and redemption. Eight of the eleven panels warn viewers to guard against sin. The remaining three, all positioned on the right side of the quilt, include a figure that descends from the upper right corner (the angel descending on Jacob's ladder, the dove descending to represent Jesus' baptism, and the large Bethlehem star descending over the Holy Family in the final panel). In each case, these descending figures draw the viewer's eye up and to the right just as the striped serpent did in her first panel. Marie Jeanne Adams, an art historian, interprets this firm direction of the viewer's gaze as a declaration of faith, one Powers does not want the viewer to miss.[74] She makes an explicit visual argument about sin being eclipsed by the redemptive power of God.

THE DIVINE HAND OF JUDGMENT AND PROTECTION

Overt preacherly aims also surface in Powers's *Pictorial Quilt*. At 68⅞ by 105 inches, this quilt is larger than its predecessor. Fifteen panels are arranged in three horizontal rows. Didactic intent is evidenced in the fact that each panel has a corresponding description. And as Laurel Thatcher Ulrich observes, "The Boston quilt makes no pretense to being a bedcovering. It has a lining, but no filling, and therefore no quilting. The pictures march across the fabric like leaves in a book."[75] Bright orange, pink, red, green, and shades of blue help tell the stories. Like the *Bible Quilt*, the *Pictorial Quilt* includes contrasting sash trim, placement of squares at most of the corners, and deliberate asymmetry. This time, however, Powers's appliquéd silhouettes recount Bible stories as well as others outside the biblical canon that inspire her.

One central motif of this quilt is the divine hand that appears three times, once in each row. This divine hand creates, guides, judges, and protects, caring for humans and animals. Her central theme appears to be judgment, which she explores by laying biblical narratives alongside celestial phenomena and local legends.[76] The first row of panels includes (1) "Job praying for his enemies. Job's crosses. Job's coffin." (2) "The dark day of May 19, 1780. The seven stars were seen 12N. in the day. The cattle all went to bed, chickens to roost and the trumpet was blown. The sun went off to a small spot and then to darkness." (3) "The serpent lifted up by Mosses [*sic*] and women bringing their children to be healed." (4) "Adam and Eve in the Garden. Eve tempted by the serpent. Adam's rib with which Eve was made. The sun and moon. God's all-seeing eye and God's merciful hand." (5) "John baptizing Christ, and the spirit of God descending and rested upon his shoulder like a dove."

The second row includes (6) "Jonah cast overboard of the ship and swallowed by a whale. Turtles." (7) "God created two of every kind. Male and female." (8) "The falling of the stars on November 13, 1833. The people were frighten [*sic*] and thought that the end of time had come. God's hand staid the stars. The varmints rushed out of their beds." (9) "Two of every kind of animals continued. Camels, elephants, gheraffs' [*sic*] lions, etc." (10) "The angels of wrath and the seven vials. The blood of fornications. Seven headed beast and 10 horns which arose out of the water."

Her eleventh panel is described as "Cold Thursday, 10 of Feb. 1895. A woman frozen while at prayer. A woman frozen at a gateway. A man with a sack of meal frozen. Icicles formed from the breath of a mule. All blue birds killed. A man frozen at his jug of liquor." The panels continue: (12) "The red light night of 1846. A man tolling the bell to notify the people of the wonder. Women, children, and fowls frightened but Gods [*sic*] merciful hand caused no harm to them." (13) "Rich people who were taught nothing of God. Bob Johnson and Kate Bell of Virginia. They told their parents to stop the clock at one and tomorrow it would strike one and so it did. This was the signal that they had entered everlasting punishment. The independent hog that ran 500 miles from GA to VA, her name was Betts." (14) "The creation of animals continues." (15) "The crucifixion of Christ between the two thieves. The sun went into darkness. Mary and Martha weeping at his feet. The blood and water run from his right side."[77]

The chosen biblical stories are those in which God sends a sign that is either misinterpreted or disregarded—like Moses lifting a serpent in the air (thought to foreshadow the crucifixion) or Jonah spending three days in the whale prefiguring the three days Jesus spends in the tomb. She also alludes to Noah gathering two animals of every kind to go into the ark, another great sign that was not heeded. In panel five, Powers depicts John the Baptist baptizing Christ and the Spirit of God descending on Christ's shoulder like a dove. This, too, refers to a heavenly sign that is misunderstood or discounted—much like the crucifixion, which is rendered in the quilt's final panel.

The theme of impending judgment carries over when she depicts local legends and atmospheric events. For example, her second panel illustrates "The dark day of May 19, 1780," a day when mysteriously darkened skies covered much of New England and part of Canada.[78] Many thought the dark sky was an omen. Since this event took place well before Powers was born, she probably learned about it through oral history. Her eighth panel refers to November 13, 1833, a day when falling stars led many to believe the world had come to an end. In the eleventh panel, she recalls an unusual cold spell that killed bluebirds and caused humans to suffer in the freezing weather. The twelfth panel depicts a meteor shower that terrified humans and animals on the "red light night of 1846."[79] In each case, the events were understood as signs of divine judgment. Read alongside her depictions of biblical scenes, these panels portray a God who communicates in uncanny ways and whose judgment is imminent.

What I hope is clear is that neither of Powers's quilts is a sentimental assembly of biblical stories. Heroic acts of faith are recounted—a longstanding form of thematic preaching.[80] Biblical stories and oral histories are relayed. Both quilts stress God's mysterious action in human history and carry warning of divine judgment. And whether Powers knew it or not, she was not alone in treating visual art as sermonic. Centuries earlier medieval apologists described wall paintings, sculptures, stained glass, and other religious artwork as *muta prædicatio*, or "silent preaching," because of its facility for communicating theological content.[81] Visual art proved effective in familiarizing parishioners with biblical figures and scenes without boring or distracting the listeners, as was the case in much preaching in that context.[82] At the same time, silent preaching reflected an appreciation for the different ways humans recognize and absorb spiritual truth, and it was an effective way to inspire contemplation on biblical stories.

HARRIET POWERS'S HOMILETICAL STRATEGIES

Powers's role as a biblical storyteller is unmistakable. She speaks through a medium that was historically treasured by Black women to steward cultural history. A storyteller reaches into the "marrow" of a culture, touching its history, legends, "taboos, images, ancestral desires, and terrors."[83] In a similar way, "telling the story" is a fundamental aspect of African American preaching. Imagistically, Powers draws on elements of this tradition when she gives Cain a pet peacock—an example of imaginative elaboration. When she adds a dressmaker's form to her garden of Eden scene, she is immersing herself into the biblical story and treats it as if it were her own. This strategy gives the biblical text immediacy and encourages viewers to claim the text as their own.[84] She also relays certain biblical scenes as if she were an eyewitness. The turtles swimming beside Jonah and the whale contribute to her "eyewitness account." Henry Mitchell describes these narrative techniques as characteristic of African American preaching.[85]

And more, Harriet Powers does a rendering of "Rich people who were taught nothing of God. Bob Johnson and Kate Bell of Virginia."[86] The two are positioned above a famed hog, Betts, who, according to local legend, ran from Georgia to Virginia and may have been a sign of freedom.[87] If this interpretation is correct, it may also suggest that Harriet Powers saw God as one who liberates and empowers the oppressed. According to Cleophus LaRue, this approach gave her a hermeneutical foothold in Black preaching, which despite myriad differences in performance and style, tends to proclaim a message about an omnipotent God who supports those who suffer.[88]

PREACHING NATURE'S WISDOM

While one gazes at Powers's two quilts, the prominent role of animals becomes apparent. Humans and animals are paired in five of the eleven *Bible Quilt* panels, and animals are featured in thirteen of the fifteen *Pictorial Quilt* panels. Their tails, horns, feathers, trunks, udders, feet, and eyes required intricate sewing. This detailed work coupled with Powers's selected themes suggests a respect for animals as well as a sense of wonder for creation. As one studies her quilts, it becomes clear that for Powers, divine revelation involves more than Scripture. Nature, climatology, and celestial occurrences also bear divine messages. Powers's quilts carry reminders of human finitude and urge people to heed the warnings that emerge from the natural world. In Powers, one finds a nineteenth-century African American preacher who tries to cultivate a deep regard for nature as she instills respect for God.

One of the more intriguing aspects of Powers's spirituality concerns her fascination with stars. Stars appear in almost all of her *Pictorial Quilt* panels and most of the *Bible Quilt* panels, and apparently she also quilted a star (or possibly the sun) on the apron she is wearing in her carte de visite—the only known photograph taken of her. A close look at the *Pictorial Quilt* reveals that she has arranged the sun, moon, and stars in matching patterns. For example, the arrangement of celestial bodies in panels five and fifteen are inversions of one another. The arrangement of celestial bodies in panels two and twelve match and so do those of four and thirteen, six and ten, and nine and fourteen. Overall, her arrangement might refer to a hidden code, a constellation or asterism, or have some other unifying purpose. Whatever the case, the arrangement of celestial bodies demonstrates great intentionality on her part. Given Powers's repeated inclusion of celestial bodies in the biblical stories and legends she tells, one could regard them as a rhetorical refrain. The stars frame and contextualize the human and animal figures in her panels by suggesting their precarity and impermanence. Through her usage of celestial bodies, the ephemeral and the eternal are juxtaposed.

The stars also raise the issue of time. The nighttime setting for so many of the quilt panels is striking and appears to emphasize the limits of human knowledge and perception. By offering light and guidance, Powers's many stars indicate that there is help for human perception. The stars seem to serve as witnesses to the temporal events. Perhaps they even embolden holy action—much like ancestors who guide their descendants from afar.

Though tiny in scale, Powers's stars reflect considerable intentionality. She used an intricate technique when sewing the stars. Each one was sewn by hand from tiny bits of cloth that had been cut into sharp triangles and set on a contrasting background.[89] Laurel Thatcher Ulrich notes that Harriet Powers's strategy for making stars mirrors that of another Georgia quilter, Mary Bryan, of (nearby) Elbert County, Georgia, though Bryan incorporated her stars using piecework while Powers used appliqué.[90] In any case, this extraordinary meticulousness is evident to viewers but would be even more obvious to one touching the quilt.

According to one quilt historian, Gladys-Marie Fry, the tiny triangles in the stars are believed to be symbols of prayer, and anyone touching the triangles would experience a tactile reminder to pray.[91] Powers may also have been drawing on dimensions of slave spirituality in which stars served as literal guides and metaphorical signs of hope. Overall, Powers's fondness for stars contributes to an eclectic spirituality in which nature, biblical stories, and local legends all mediate divine wisdom and arrest the viewer's attention.

AUTHORITY

Powers's vision of divine revelation also has implications for homiletical authority. Her quilts emerged at a time when there were few Black women preachers, and conceptions of preacherly authority contributed to this small number. Ordinarily, the authority to preach inures from a composite of factors—ecclesiastical, charismatic, cultural, and personal—that together undergird the preacher's power to speak and influence the receptiveness of the listeners.[92] Sexism, racism, ableism, heterosexism, and other experiences of or expectations of bias complicate and layer questions of authority, but the underlying issue is power—how it is held and how it is imagined. Preaching involves navigating a faith community's grid of power assumptions as one proclaims the gospel. This process may involve adhering to convention, flouting it, negotiating it, or finding ways to compensate for perceived inadequacies.

Harriet Powers's quilts present an unusual case of a Black woman's voice that is mediated through textiles rather than through written text or performance. There is to date no record of Powers serving as an ordained or lay preacher in the Black Baptist congregations where she worshiped. As church mothers, Black churchwomen sometimes edified congregations with exhortations and claimed to be led by the Holy Spirit when doing so.[93] These women had little formal authority but considerable credibility, which they earned by offering encouraging messages, interpreting dreams, providing intercessory prayer, and giving advice. Known for being open to the myriad ways God speaks, these women incubated communal hope and epitomized the life of faith. Harriet Powers could have been such a woman, revered for her wisdom and held in affectionate regard. She may have also had a ministry of wisdom-sharing and intercession that took place informally and outside of church settings.[94] Unfortunately, we do not have records that clarify her role in the church, if she had one.

Whatever her role, calling a quilt a sermon confers an unusual degree of gravitas to its message. This framing is a form of self-authorization. At the same time, her chosen medium grounds its authority in the biblical text and gives authority to the viewers to discern whether the messages she proclaims edify the church. Consequently, Harriet Powers presents some fresh angles for thinking about authority in less hierarchical ways.

Powers claims the authority inherent in engaging in a creative act: the authority of invention. This approach to authority stresses that God is up to something new, that the gospel is enlivened by the past, not bound by it. Homiletically, inventiveness correlates with the nature of preaching itself, which as Lisa L. Thompson observes, "requires pulling together pieces for something that does not yet exist—that is, the sermon."[95] Theologically, inventiveness provides a link to imagination and the *imago Dei* and "permits us to have a vision: of the life to come after death, of life in our human existence for decades to come, of the possibility of transforming ambiguities, contradictions, anger, hostility, human limitations, into positive and creative acts touched by the Holy Spirit."[96]

An appreciation for the authorizing power of invention energizes Black sacred rhetoric on both an aesthetic and pragmatic level. Aesthetically, it carries a dynamism that is not available when authority stems from status or hierarchy; pragmatically, invention functions as fuel, yielding the energy needed to adapt, reframe, and strategize for survival. At the same time, invention involves clarity. Unanticipated connections and implications between Scripture and life come to the forefront. In this respect, inventiveness is "not cosmetical or decorative" but an "evocation"—an indication of keen perspective rather than panache.[97]

Powers's message comes through a talking needle, an instrument assumed to be confined to domestic labor. Through the needle she warns of divine judgment when she might be expected to be silent or have something merely decorative to say. She claims creative power by finding a proclamatory purpose for torn fabric—things otherwise considered trash—and uses these fragments to speak of divine acts. Gazing at her quilts involves contemplating the possible and thinking about God's power to upend human expectation.

In "African American Art and Biblical Interpretation," James Noel argues that African American art often provides critical hermeneutical insight. As a starting point, he explains that it is not sufficient to interpret African American art without considering the religious significance inherent in creative acts. "Because of the extreme deprivation to which Africans were subjected during and subsequent to their arrival in the Americas, their artistic products required a tremendous feat on their part to muster and assert a humanity that was on the brink of annihilation." He insists that "when studying African American art we must always bear in mind not only the work under interpretation but the creative act itself."[98] Harriet Powers quilted during a historical period when African Americans faced disenfranchisement, vigilante violence, and lynching. Given the assaults on African Americans at this time, her emphases on pride and divine judgment should come as no surprise. Signs of human fallenness abounded. The quilts render a longing for divine intervention, for cosmic consequences for evil.

Despite the heavy themes concerning judgment, there is a buoyancy in the quilts, a sense of delight that gestures toward the sublime. This buoyancy of hers is also authorizing because joy is a source of power and energy that kindles a spirit of play and improvisation. Joy emphasizes the Spirit's unifying work among people of faith and curbs the "flavor of separateness" that is often associated with holding power.[99]

EMBODIMENT

Harriet Powers's sermons similarly raise questions about the relationship between preaching and embodiment.[100] Usually, physicality is mediated in voice and gesture, but even traditional preaching situations involve a level of elusiveness in this regard. As David Appelbaum argues in his book *Voice*, language conceals and obscures the voice.[101] Revealing one's authentic voice requires coughing, laughing, or groaning. Gesture, similarly, reveals most when it appears natural rather than choreographed. So on one level a preacher's embodiment of a sermon involves both disclosure and retreat. This dynamic is essential to understanding Harriet Powers's embodiment because both are at work.

Powers is present through her talking needle that stitches together her argument, images, and vision of divine action. This medium lends tactility and immediacy to her ideas. Clearly, the quilts are the work of her body, even stained with her blood. At the same time, Powers's patchwork sermons have a conspicuously absent preacher. Her physical absence gives her a heightened presence—much like the apostle Paul, whose letters testified to his bodily existence and made him present to his readers despite his imprisonment.[102] Harriet Powers's quilts are also, like Paul's, inscribed in her "own hand" (Gal. 6:11; 2 Thess. 3:17; Phlm. 19).

Yet in Powers's case, the quilts invoke her presence as well as those of other African American women from centuries past who used quilts to pray, testify, and remember. In this respect, Powers's quilts function as forms of layered address. Like collective utterances, the quilts evoke the voices of African ancestors who used quilts to express spiritual wisdom. And while Powers's quilts are individual works that included machine work, quilting was in some cases a group activity in which not only women but the whole community made creative contributions.[103] By bringing the ancestors into the sermon, Powers imparts a vision of shared authority.

Powers's approach involves drawing on the language of ancestors. Making their histories present involves asserting the ephemeral nature of earthly power on the one hand and remembering the potential for the abuse of power as well. More importantly, invoking the ancestors provides a reminder of the love within which the viewer is held and urges accountability to past and future generations. The ethical imperatives of the message—like the call to heed the warnings of nature, learn the ways of God, and trust in Christ's redemptive work—are amplified by the notion that the ancestors, like the myriad stars in her quilt, are acting as guides and witnesses.

Harriet Powers's quilts have a few pathbreaking features: First, the quilts help us imagine African American preaching outside the frame of aurality. Black sacred rhetoric is not limited to oral discourse. Second, Powers's quilted sermons challenge typical frames of authority by highlighting the significance of inventiveness. Further, Powers's quilts underscore the pivotal role ancestors play in preaching. By quilting her messages, Powers chose a highly expressive medium that African American women have used for centuries to tell stories, testify, and create new possibilities out of fragmentation.[104] In doing so, she expanded the normative understanding of the preacher's voice.

QUESTIONS AND CHALLENGES

The works of Rosie Lee Tompkins and Harriet Powers raise important questions and challenges for contemporary preachers. First, how much latitude do preachers have in moving away from oral discourse? And how might a visual sermon sharpen spiritual perception and enhance a congregation's engagement with the world? Tompkins and Powers emphasize the importance of taking creative liberties. They leap from the literal to the figurative and the abstract, confident that the shift will ultimately nurture believers. The Christian faith, after all, requires the capacity to bracket the existential world and dive into the mythical. At the same time, Tompkins and Powers are attuned to the imagistic nature of preaching. Their images foster a sense of immediacy and illumine universal themes—strategies that are similarly effective in the pulpit. Following their lead involves selecting biblical texts as well as color palettes that illumine them, embracing asymmetry, and doing more depiction and less explanation. They also present models of ethical reflection that do not devolve into ranting and thus avoid some of the coercive patterns that have plagued American preaching.

Christianity aims not merely for cognitive understanding of the gospel but for an experience of grace that recenters how one moves through the world.

Through their quilts, Harriet Powers and Rosie Lee Tompkins sought to facil-itate such an experience. Like all great sermons, their quilts warn, enchant, exhort, and encourage the renewal of the mind (Rom. 12:2). But are there other wordless ways of preaching? What insights emerge if movement and gesture anchor the proclamatory endeavor—if we focus on "the feet of the messenger" bringing good news (Isa. 52:7)? These questions lead us to the next chapter on dance.

3

The Dancer

Dance can be the word in motion, the word made flesh for all to see.
—Nadine George-Graves

When Sister Thea Bowman gave a presentation, she often began by speaking briefly on the topic at hand. Yet to explain why the topic mattered, she turned to song—usually a spiritual. Her operatic singing could tunnel down to the song's essence. Listeners could feel it and see how the truth of the lyrics and melody were being expressed through rocking, swaying, and gesturing. Once she was inside the music, she would invite the listeners to join her. She beckoned them not only into the song but into the dance, and soon the whole group was a dance choir motioning and singing together. Their dance was not about skill or proper technique, nor did it consist of merely acting out the lyrics. It had an integrity and expressiveness of its own. The dance announced Christian freedom, and each participant contributed to the message.

While best known for her singing and advocacy, Bowman was a multitalented artist who gave presentations that involved song, exhortations, mini-lectures, and dance. This combination has resonances with the role of African historians who sing, dance, tell stories, and share wisdom. They are called by a broad range of terms depending on the people group and region but are commonly grouped under the (contested) umbrella terms *griot* or *griotte*.[1] Their consciousness of how orality, musicality, and movement interact is evident in Bowman's presentations.

Sometimes Bowman and her copresenters did all the dancing. Other times she led the audience in dancing. Her use of movement was not ancillary to verbal statements; movement was elemental. She had a different vision of preaching and, as a starting point, assumed that dance was not only capable of communicating the gospel but that it added something essential to Black preaching.

Bowman played with the typical boundaries of preaching in several ways.[2] First, most of her efforts involved exegeting Negro spirituals and revealing how they illumined Scripture and the life of faith.[3] Following the tradition of treating the spirituals as sung sermons, she helped listeners embody the wisdom of the songs and make direct connections to Christian discipleship. Second, while she took the lead, her work with copresenters made the presentations collective utterances and challenged individualism. The communal approach reflected her strong commitment to Black culture and belief that spiritual wisdom is held communally by all the members of the church rather than a resource residing primarily in clergy that is periodically transferred to the laity.

Owing to her respect for the teaching of the Roman Catholic Church, Bowman did not call her presentations "sermons," but she was well aware of their effects. "Women can't preach in the Catholic church," she said, "but I can preach in the streets. I can preach in the neighborhood. I can preach in the home. I can preach and teach in the family. And it's the preaching that's done in the home that brings life and meaning to the Word your priest proclaims in his official ministry in the pulpit."[4] As she searched for ways to share the gospel and be faithful to church tradition, dance would play a vital role. Until her health failed, dance served as a principal language she used to express the good news.

SISTER THEA BOWMAN: A BIOGRAPHICAL SKETCH

Sister Thea Bowman was a celebrated Christian whose life witness has prompted a cause for canonization for sainthood in the Roman Catholic Church. She was born on December 29, 1937, in Yazoo City, Mississippi, to Theon Bowman, a physician who spent his early years in Yazoo City and Memphis, and Mary Esther (Coleman) Bowman, an educator from Greenville, Mississippi. The Bowmans named their daughter Bertha Elizabeth Bowman.[5]

Prior to his daughter's birth, Theon settled in Canton, Mississippi, because the African American community had no doctor. White physicians regularly refused to treat African American residents. The town's labor force consisted largely of sharecroppers, farmers, factory workers, and domestics who could barely afford basic medical care. While the Bowmans did not have a lavish lifestyle, they were comfortable enough to enjoy regular outings for artistic performances.

Having been childless for over a decade before their daughter's birth, Theon and Mary Esther were exuberant parents. Mary Esther memorialized

Bertha's early milestones in a scrapbook—noting that Bertha danced at the circus in October 1938.[6] "Little Birdie," as she was affectionately called, was surrounded by caring older adults who shared songs and stories of faith. She would later describe herself as an "old folks' child," referring not only to the experience of being raised by older parents and their elderly friends but to the ways hearing their songs and stories shaped her religious identity. These elders laid a foundation for her spiritual formation:

> I grew up in a community where the teaching of religion was a treasured role of the elders—grandparents, old uncles and aunts, but also parents, big brothers and sisters, family friends, and church members. Many of the best teachers were not formally educated. But they knew Scripture, and they believed the Living Word must be celebrated and shared. . . . Their methodologies were such that, without effort, I remember their teachings today: songs of Adam, Eve, Noah, Abraham, Moses, Joshua, Miriam, David, Dives, Ezekiel, Daniel, Jonah, John, Mary, Jesus: his birth, his life, his teachings, his miracles, his disciples, his Passion, his glory, his promise to us all of eternal life.[7]

Some of these lessons emerged when she and her family visited their friends' churches: "When I was a little girl in Canton, Mississippi, I went to those old black churches, and I learned what they called the old-time religion. I wanted to grow up so I could be a preacher."[8]

This spiritual nurture she received was essential for a young Black girl growing up in Canton during the 1940s and 1950s, when Jim Crow laws were pervasive and racialized violence was common. During her early years in Canton, a young family friend had to flee the region after retaliating against white aggressors, another young man was shot by police after refusing to say "sir," and Chinese immigrant children were dragged from a patriotic parade during World War II.[9]

In addition, the resources dedicated to public schools for African Americans were woefully insufficient. Committed to helping young Bertha obtain a solid education, the Bowmans enrolled her in Holy Child Jesus School, a newly opened school run by the Franciscan Sisters of Perpetual Adoration from La Crosse, Wisconsin. Bertha thrived at the school academically and personally. She felt the sisters genuinely cared about her and was awed by how they met the needs of impoverished children in the community—wiping their noses, feeding them, and playing with them.[10]

While it may have seemed odd to some, Bertha felt the sisters' model of loving their neighbors was consistent with the emphasis on prayer, simplicity, and service that she was learning from her elders. In June 1947, at age nine, she was baptized at Holy Child Jesus Mission and a day later made her First Communion.[11] Her conversion to Catholicism added more diversity to an ecumenical household. Mary Esther was Episcopalian and Theon was Methodist, but they were both determined to support her spiritual development even as it took unexpected turns.

Still, they were unprepared when at just fifteen, Bertha insisted that her next step would be to the convent. She wanted to move to La Crosse, Wisconsin, and complete high school at the motherhouse of the Franciscans of Perpetual Adoration.[12] Her parents resisted, but Bertha had made up her mind. After reaching an impasse, she stopped eating until they agreed to let her go.[13] Theon made a desperate attempt to get Bertha to join a community comprised largely of Black nuns in New Orleans just a few hours away, but she was unwilling. She felt clear that her call was to the Franciscan Sisters of Perpetual Adoration in La Crosse, Wisconsin, and to the sisters who had nurtured her at Holy Child Jesus School. In 1953, she took the long train ride to Wisconsin accompanied by Sister Lina Pantz. Because African Americans were ordinarily assigned to ride in baggage cars, Sister Lina had to obtain special permission for the pair to ride together in a standard car.[14]

At the St. Rose Convent, she no longer had a room of her own. Now she slept in a large dormitory in a "cell" that, in lieu of walls, had a white curtain that she could pull around her bed for privacy.[15] Living in community brought a more regimented life rhythm. Her days consisted of worship, class, and meals shared with the nearly two hundred sisters living at the convent, none of whom were African American. Bertha was expected to assimilate to the community pattern of prayer and worship, and she did so with little hesitation. This also meant comporting herself along norms that made little room for her culture. There was no room for "whole-body, whole-spirit, whole-voice living," and she learned to subdue her inclinations to dance and sing spontaneously.[16] At home, folks from African Methodist Episcopal, African Methodist Episcopal Zion, Baptist, Episcopal, Methodist, and Holiness churches had regularly interacted. Now she was among only Roman Catholics. Gone also were the African American elders who had enriched her life with story and song. As Theon anticipated, Bertha faced the racism of some members of her new community, but she was determined to win them over with her joyous, energetic spirit.

It is not uncommon for a call to ministry to include a delay that ultimately has an intensifying effect. Bertha faced such a delay in the spring of 1955 when she was diagnosed with tuberculosis. She spent almost a year convalescing at the St. Francis hospital near the convent and the River Pines Sanatorium about 115 miles away.[17] The recuperation period also meant she was unable to matriculate with the friends who started with her. Yet she did not waver and soon entered the novitiate. On August 12, 1956, she took the name "Mary Thea." "Mary" honored the mother of Christ, and "Thea" honored a revered martyr as well as her father, Theon.[18] Two years later "Sister Thea" took her initial vows of poverty, chastity, and obedience, making headlines as the first professed African American member of the Franciscan Sisters of Perpetual Adoration.[19]

She completed her undergraduate studies at Viterbo, which was also affiliated with the Franciscan Sisters of Perpetual Adoration. There, her interests in literature and education grew. After graduation, her first ministry assignment was to teach fifth grade in La Crosse. Some parents initially objected to having their children taught by a Black teacher, but the complaints were quelled when the parents experienced Bowman's warmth and expertise. She delighted her students and their parents and was soon selected to return to Canton to teach at her alma mater, Holy Child Jesus School.

From 1961 to 1965 she relished being back in her hometown. Looking back on the years spent teaching in Canton, Bowman noted that she taught with unusual urgency. She knew what was at stake in educating Black children whose personhood was under near-constant assault. Her teaching had to be done with diligence, attention to the whole person, and Franciscan joy if she was to instill a sense of belovedness and confidence in her students.

Some of the urgency may have also stemmed from an anticipated shift. In 1966, due in part to her literary skill and aptitude as a teacher, she was sent to Catholic University in Washington, DC, to pursue graduate studies in literature. She arrived in Washington at a pivotal juncture, when Black consciousness was shaping life at the university and in the city. For the first time, she found herself engaging with other Black people who had taken religious vows. These interactions led her to think more critically about what it meant to be Black and Catholic. Her room became a salon for discussing faith and race and a place for enjoying newfound friendships. Sister Patricia Chappell remembers coming to one of these gatherings and laying eyes on Bowman for the first time. She happened to be dancing to Aretha Franklin's "Respect."[20]

The web of relationships that Bowman developed at Catholic University affirmed her sense of belonging and strengthened her resolve to embrace a more embodied experience of her faith. On the one hand, she wanted a spirituality that reflected her fidelity to the joyful, nature-loving servanthood of St. Francis and the wisdom of St. Thomas More, who was the subject of her dissertation. At the same time, she needed her spirituality to reflect her ancestors whose ethical commitments had made Catholicism appealing in the first place. She also wanted to help others recognize how cultural diversity was essential to the church's mission.[21] While still in her graduate program,

Bowman gave the first of a series of presentations on Black history and culture. Interest in these presentations sparked, and she continued sharing them when she returned to Viterbo in 1972—this time as a faculty member in the English department.

Determined to honor her own cultural identity in the classroom, she sometimes began class by singing a spiritual. She also started a group called the Hallelujah Singers, a choir that, though composed mostly of white singers, focused on Negro spirituals and gospel music. Her presentations on Black history similarly incorporated songs, stories, and dance.

Eventually she assembled a performance troupe with members from minoritized backgrounds, and together they sang, presented dramas, and danced in and around La Crosse.[22] These presentations resisted the melting pot theory of cultural identity that was popular at the time. Instead she stressed respect for difference. In summer workshops on Black culture and religion, she made presentations alongside members of indigenous communities who shared their histories and cultures and discussed how their traditions communicated spiritual wisdom through dance. Later she studied Winnebago traditions and introduced an indigenous literature class at Viterbo that connected students with members of the local Winnebago community.[23]

Bowman's passion about these matters was not new, but sharing this history and challenging the church to be more inclusive brought out a new dimension of her vocation. Increasingly she functioned as both a teacher and an advocate. Her presentations were occasions for lively worship as well as opportunities to examine the effects of slavery and colonialism. With these twin aims she cast a vision of Catholicism that was hospitable to Black culture. Song, storytelling, and dance served as indispensable tools.

In 1978 Bowman's life took another significant turn. By this time her elderly parents needed more support, so she returned to Canton to care for them. Bishop Joseph Bernard Brunini of the Diocese of Jackson was eager to see her continue advocating for African Americans and other minoritized groups, so he appointed her first as diocesan consultant and then director of the Office of Intercultural Awareness.[24] This role was providential. It gave her the creative freedom and structural support she needed to flourish. Her witness to the community ended up exceeding any title that could have been given. A teacher, catalyst, drum major, and convener, she helped congregants share liturgies and educational resources and helped found the Black Catholic Theological Symposium. She also served as a faculty member for the Institute for Black Catholic Studies at Xavier University of Louisiana, where she taught homiletics. All the while, she continued singing, dancing, and dramatizing Scripture in her presentations.

In her first years back in Canton, she had a calendar full of speaking commitments and could easily spend a third of the year on the road. The work excited her, and she slowed down only in 1984, the year both her parents died and the year she learned that she had breast cancer. Unwilling to give up traveling to give presentations, she began making them between chemotherapy treatments. On January 18, 1988, she gave a presentation in Milwaukee titled "Martin Luther King: Seize the Vision." It would be her last address given from a standing position. Subsequent presentations were made from her wheelchair, and she would increasingly rely on the care and assistance of Dorothy Kundinger, but she prayed that God would help her live vibrantly until she died.

She found that being around other people of faith increased her stores of energy and that singing eased her pain.[25] Nature also brought a sense of serenity that she associated with the ancestors:

> From the spiritual tradition of the black community I learned that we are *all* God's creatures. Creation is a gift God shares with us. We have a responsibility to learn from nature how to live, to observe nature because it houses the lessons of life. We can learn from the way the ant works with his peers, how the bear lives in winter, how the tree grows tall, how the sun rises in fidelity, the way day follows night.[26]

Though frail, she recorded two albums, *Sister Thea: Songs of My People* and *Round the Glory Manger: Christmas Spirituals*, and completed a documentary, *Almost Home: Living with Suffering and Dying*. Unafraid of death because her ancestors had taught her that death was a part of life, she likened herself to Sojourner Truth, saying she was not going to die but go to heaven like a shooting star.[27] What was most important was making a valiant attempt to teach, heal, and exude Christ's joy for as long as she could.

Bowman died at her home early on the morning of March 30, 1990. Thousands traveled to Canton for her funeral, which reflected the energetic liturgies she had helped others cultivate. She was buried in Memphis next to her parents and her uncle, and at her request the words "She tried" were inscribed on her headstone.

After her death, many emphasized her gifts as a singer, preacher, teacher, and advocate, but Joseph M. Davis asserts that dance was indispensable to her ministry. In his memorial poem "Gone—for Glory!" he celebrates how the gospel was announced through her dancing. Davis alludes to a mythic dimension of her dancing that exceeded her physical limitations and death, and he suggests that she continues to dance before the Holy One.[28]

PROCLAMATORY DANCE

Given Bowman's commitment to African and African American cultures, her decision to proclaim through dance is unsurprising. As catechesis, dance provided a means of proclaiming the gospel through a medium Africans use to tell stories, relay history, and unify communities. Dance also offered a holistic alternative to the more literal and cognitive logics that had characterized much of her Catholic formation.

Yet she danced at a time when there was considerable resistance to liturgical dance. Some of the resistance may have stemmed from longstanding associations of dance with paganism.[29] Distrust of the body and a desire to silence expressions of sexuality also prompted objections, though Judith Rock and Norman Mealy note, "The attempt to avoid this 'threat' of sexuality also accounts for the blandness and kinetically impractical costuming of some contemporary church dance. Dance can nurture us spiritually, but it is a contradiction in terms to try to make dances that are more spiritual than physical . . . not unlike trying to create music that is more inaudible than audible."[30]

Neither the influence of paganism nor the sexuality inherent in dance kept it from being an indispensable expressive medium in ancient Jewish culture. It is as "certain" that Jesus "danced as it is that he wore a beard."[31] And more, the "rejoicing" that the Bible emphasizes is foundational to a life of faith. In fact, the terms *rejoice* and *dance* may even be synonymous.[32]

In Bowman's context, an additional hindrance concerned the idealization of the dancer's body. Dancers were often expected to adhere to the European norms of beauty that were reflected in ballet. This rarely attainable body type presented an idolatrous distraction for some worshipers.[33] Similarly, some viewers bristled when women and girls displayed their strength and athleticism. But by defying these norms, dancers could have helped faith communities challenge them and consider how the gospel might offer a more humane frame for thinking about human bodies.

Dance's capacity for communicating the gospel was also considered dubious because of its nonverbal nature. Yet this argument reflects a misunderstanding of dance as well as preaching, which leans heavily on movement, gesture, and presence. These hard-to-quantify nonverbal dynamics shape the meaning-making process more than some preachers would like to admit.[34]

Dance is suasive communication even when it does not take an explicitly narrative form. Movement can be used to retell a biblical story, as in Mikhail Baryshnikov's *The Prodigal Son*, or aid in the interpretive process, as in JoAnne Tucker and Susan Freeman show in *Torah in Motion: Creating Dance Midrash*.[35] Such performances of Scripture reveal that the Word is, like the sacraments, "physically rooted."[36] Dance is, as the Harlem Renaissance dancer-activist Pearl Primus explains, "a language of the body . . . like the transmission of a message from a transcendent sender to a human receiver."[37] A dancer's signs point "to the whole of our existence, just as the word points to our expressive powers as a whole and, in a mythical sense, to God."[38] The tendency in some Christian circles to reduce dance to an aesthetic experience or to inspiration for thought forms deemed higher or purer misses the mark.[39] Dance is a "way of knowing," a form of communicative movement that exceeds function.[40]

There are also important parallels between dance and poetry. As Sondra Horton Fraleigh explains, "Dance uses human movement like poetry uses the word, not factually but imaginatively: that is *imagistically* and in the metaphysically open, nonrestrictive sense of metaphor. Even when a dance denotes something specific, it does so in an open, interpretive way."[41] The mystery, elusiveness, and ephemerality of dance are vital for communicating something as numinous as the gospel. And because a dance has the capacity to carry multiple meanings at once, it can communicate a diunital message— something Bowman stressed: "African people are diunital people, seeking richness of meaning in *apparent* contradiction. They are comfortable with bringing together realities which may appear contradictory or in opposition: for example, body/spirit, sacred/secular, individual/community. They reach toward unification or synthesis of opposites."[42]

At its core, the resistance to proclamatory dance that Bowman faced may have indicated discomfort with the elusiveness of metaphor that anchors the Bible and Christian rituals, such as baptism and Eucharist. And as Robert Frost warns, "Unless you are at home in the metaphor, unless you have had your proper poetical education in the metaphor, you are not safe anywhere. Because you are not at ease with figurative values."[43] He goes on to say that the "attempt to say matter in terms of spirit and spirit in terms of matter" is "the height of all thinking."[44] Inventive thinking—particularly about the patterns of human behavior and the meaning of human life—relies on this facility. Recognizing how the archetypes, symbols, and dilemmas of Scripture are being replayed in contemporary life similarly requires the kind of metaphorical thinking cultivated by dance.

Rather than being insufficiently expressive, dance is a potent communication form. It awakens the kinesthetic realm of perception that involves thinking *and* moving, or as Erin Manning says, "thinking in the moving."[45] For Africanist traditions that understand movement to be integral to spirituality, this union is essential.[46] Witnessing a dancer shift from one form to another can illumine the human capacity for transformation.[47] Of course, the danced sermon involves giving up some control and accepting that, as in the case of traditional preaching, members of the congregation will have different experiences and takeaways. In the case of dance, the affective nature of these experiences may be too fluid for verbal summation. Dancers challenge preachers to consider how affect is shaped by moving outside of a highly literal, cognitive framework.

DANCE AND/AS BLACK PREACHING

For Bowman, Black preaching was not beholden to a Cartesian divide between the mind and the body. Inspired by the dancing of her ancestors, "Thea knew that a genuine spirituality cannot be disembodied, but is embodied, incarnated, in the flesh and blood and bones of a human being."[48] James Cone's influence on her thought is evident. When teaching others to dance the spirituals, she drew on Cone's scholarship, at one point stressing that he said, "I affirmed the reality of the spirituals and blues as authentic expressions of my humanity, responding to them in the rhythms of dance. I, therefore, write about the spirituals and the blues, because *I am the blues* and *my life is a spiritual.* Without them, I cannot be."[49]

The "Thea experience," as her friend Joseph Brown dubbed her presentations, usually commenced with a spirited, percussive rendition of "Old Time Religion," moved into exhortations to pray and to remember one's identity and ancestors, and segued into Jesus' call to serve the church family and the human family.[50] Several spirituals and gospel songs accompanied the exhortations, and listeners were invited to dance, rock, gesture, and sing along in response.

For example, she got people "up and moving" when singing "Joshua Fit the Battle of Jericho" and modeled a shoulder dip when leading "Wade in the Water."[51] The dances she introduced were simple and not designed for mastery; increasing openness to the Spirit was the aim. The dancing continued with different songs and dances from Bowman's repertoire until she turned to "Done Made My Vow to the Lord," the presentation's finale. By its close, listeners "had been named, and then renamed as *children* of God. Without fail, all gathered had been *powered* by the spirit of the ancestors—all were called and cajoled and ordered to sing and dance and move and give other enthusiastic physical response to the word they were sharing."[52] That is to say, they had taken on the shared role of performing the spirituals and telling the biblical story. And as James Cone observes, "To tell the story is to act out with the rhythm of one's voice and the movement of the body, the truth" that grounds one's testimony.[53]

This approach to dance may veer toward treating dance as music visualization—an idea that some modern dance artists reject as reductive.[54] But Africanist traditions tend to treat music and dance as equals. Reflecting on her experience as a choreographer in this vein, Dianne McIntyre concludes that dance involves merging with the music, allowing the body to become an instrument until "there is no difference between the dancer and the music."[55] Together their capacities for truth bearing are heightened.

Similarly, Bowman began with the premise that wisdom is *embodied*. Rather than assuming wisdom only takes the form of abstract thought, she believed it could be communicated through movement. And since she saw this pattern in African and African American history, she was convinced that being open to sharing spiritual wisdom through song and dance was indicative of being "fully functioning"—a term she used repeatedly to convey Black wholeness and capaciousness.[56] Moreover, dance was an essential vehicle for erasing the tapes of internalized racism and embracing one's identity as a child of God. This aim aligns Bowman with Henry Mitchell and Frank Thomas, who stress the importance of erasing old tapes—only their method is aural, and Bowman deconstructs through movement.[57]

Respect for the communicative potential in movement has deep roots in African American preaching. As just one example, William Holmes Borders, the esteemed pastor of Wheat Street Baptist Church in Atlanta who had a significant influence on Martin Luther King Jr.'s preaching, had a pattern of performing biblical scenes—even on one occasion hiding behind the organ and lying on the floor to act out the story of David and Goliath.[58] In this case, his sermon amounted to a performance of the text. As Gennifer Brooks explains, "How the hearers receive the text in all the senses beyond the auditory has great influence on their immediate and subsequent responses to both the text and its sermonic interpretation."[59] To some degree, movement takes precedence over speech by determining receptivity for what is said verbally. The point here is that the body tells the story and mediates truth through movement.

In keeping with this tradition of foregrounding movement and gesture, a dancer could function as an "icon" of the gospel, a mirror reflecting what is in the heart, or embody an ephemeral word as evangelist, teacher, prophet, or priest.[60] These are not merely metaphorical terms but reflections of the dancer's actions, intentions, and reception. Bowman's approach is consistent with this view. She treated the dancer as a bearer of what she called the "true truth," a truth that crackles like lightning, yielding a flash of clarifying light and energy.[61] Joseph Brown argues that Bowman used dance, gesture, and movement "as the syllabus of her teaching, lecturing, and performing before and among all her various audiences" and that this rhetorical strategy gave her audience an experience of Black wholeness "for the duration of her instruction (just as Baby Suggs makes her audience *whole* and *healed* for the time of her preaching and dancing)."[62] In both cases, dance provides an immersive experience of the gospel that stretches the imagination as movement releases the body's wisdom.[63]

Dance also has a catalytic dimension. Its kinetic charge emphasizes the performative aspect of the word. Teresa Fry Brown alludes to this dynamic in her essay "The Action Potential of Preaching." Brown explains that the "impulse of the word of God permeates the personal and communal walls or barriers by stimulating a change in one's negative charge—lack of faith, doubting faith, or need to reinforce personal belief—by introducing a positive charge—faith, acceptance, or belief."[64] Proclamatory dance follows a similar logic. Dance mediates àṣẹ—a Yoruba concept signifying "the power to make things happen."[65]

Bowman was well versed in the ways various African cultures used dance to eulogize, tell stories, and convey history. These approaches reveal high expectations for the formative value of dance for both dancer and witness. And more, an ethical response on the part of the spectator is assumed.[66] Dance is a visible announcement of the ethical values expressed in the music; dance incarnates these values by dialoguing with the music.[67] The dancer is presumed to hold the power to "transform the observer's consciousness" and stir embryonic internal resources.[68] This realm of spiritual knowledge cannot be accessed as easily through abstract argument. Often it is only after the swaying of muscles and bones and the consequent elevation of the heart rate that divine clarity emerges, suggesting a correlation between intentional physical movement and sharpened spiritual perception.

Clearly, Bowman had a high view of the proclamatory power of dance. Before her cancer progressed, she regularly danced in presentations. She danced while singing certain spirituals and gospel songs and performed mimetic dance. For example, when teaching "Old Time Religion" to children, she sometimes paired it with a jubilant dance that involved raising both arms above the head, waving them, and turning around in a circle.[69] Narrative dance was similarly vital to her work, leading her on one occasion to retell the wedding of Cana story by framing it in a New Orleans Mardi Gras context.[70] She also choreographed dance for liturgy and sang spirituals alongside dancers who helped stretch and illumine the meaning of the songs.[71] While there may seem to be a clear line between dancer and spectator in these cases, the line is blurrier than it might seem. According to Pearl Primus, dance is a medium that erases the line between dancer and viewer, creating an environment where there are "no observers—all are in the arena."[72] Langston Hughes notices this phenomenon when reflecting on one of Primus's performances: "Every time she leaped, folks felt like shouting. Some did. Some hollered out loud. . . . The way she jumped was the same as a shout in church."[73] In other words, the dancer and the audience became one; the choreography illumined the human condition rather than merely the dancer's individual prowess.

Yet for the purposes of thinking about dance as preaching, the most intriguing example of Bowman's use of dance concerns communal dance—the dance she would first model and then perform along with the audience when singing spirituals. On these occasions, her dancing reflects the Yoruba concept in which the "dancer seeks to receive the power of the divine, for the sake of the community."[74] This emphasis on collectivity was critical for Bowman, who felt community was elemental to Black spirituality.[75]

As one might expect, Bowman loved the audibly communal nature of Black preaching. Evans Crawford explores this dimension in *The Hum: Call and Response in African American Preaching*, where he describes call-and-response as "participant proclamation" and notes that, rather than preceding from a more transactional premise in which the preacher imparts insight to the listeners, Black preaching prizes and seeks to elicit the community's shared wisdom.[76] At its best, Black preaching summons the shared wisdom that already exists and makes this common knowledge more palpable. Bowman's communal dances turned on a similar ethos. Moving together was a way to witness to one another about shared beliefs. And dancing together has both a literal, visible dimension and a more numinous one because communal dance tends to increase perception of the ineffable.[77]

Further, the components of corporate dance—following another's lead, blending together, releasing and resuming—shape collective unconscious and have a dialogical flavor.[78] In *And We Shall Learn through the Dance*, Kathleen Turner emphasizes the dialogical nature of antiphonal movement.[79] Her study of the ring shout and the use of dance among enslaved African Americans led her to describe the dancing community as a *griot*:

> The entire community joined in and the effect was a communal awareness of the ever-sustaining presence of God as deliverer in their midst. The community of worshippers all became the central *griot* and this afforded them opportunities to reflect, build, and strengthen one another's faith, to press forward in their present state of slavery.[80]

Two aspects of Turner's argument stand out: First, individuals were not left to their own devices; dance weaves the individual into a whole—into a community, a tradition, and a shared domain of wisdom. Second, through communal dance, the community becomes a wisdom-bearing *griot*, jointly engaged in announcing divine possibilities. Rather than focusing on a singular prophet, a community of prophets enflesh truth together.

Moreover, Veta Goler observes that the ring shout involved syncopated stomping that kept the body grounded, giving dancers "a full experience of the power and beauty of their bodies, and a calling forth from within the strength of the spirit."[81] And while the dance itself was ephemeral, the effects were longstanding. The memory of dance tends to linger in the body long after movement stops. The choreographed phrase becomes part of one's kinesthetic vocabulary. That is to say, dance becomes part of one's being and shapes the energy and presence one exudes.

ANNOUNCING JOY

Another key feature of communal dance concerns joy. As a Franciscan, Bowman saw "contagious joy" as a charism.[82] She once greeted a priest by saying she enjoyed his sermon, only to be rebuked. The priest was insulted by the idea that his sermon might be enjoyed and urged a more solemn disposition when listening to sermons.[83]

Black preaching presents a different homiletical stance that foregrounds joy. One might root this joy in the belief that an omnipotent God acts on one's behalf.[84] Experientially, joy might erupt among worshipers as a sign of the Holy Spirit's energizing presence in the congregation. For Henry Mitchell, infectious joy bubbles up when some of the congregation's "felt needs" are addressed and when the biblical text is "etched by ecstasy on the heart of the hearer."[85] Or to quote Frank Thomas, joy is the ether emitted when listeners "experience the *assurance* of grace (the good news) that is the gospel of Jesus Christ."[86] As part of her definition of preaching, Gennifer Brooks stresses "offering the gathered community an opportunity to celebrate and claim the love of God in Jesus Christ."[87] She goes on to explain that "explicit good news is an important element in every sermon and in every act of preaching as it enlivens, awakens, and energizes preacher and people for joyful living in a troubled world. . . . Preaching is thus a celebrative act of God's people, which helps to shape and define the ongoing life of the gathered community."[88]

Bowman's approach was consistent with all these views, particularly the emphasis on the enlivening, energizing, and "joyful living" expressed by Brooks. But Bowman emphasized a kinesthetic dimension of joy, seeing it as a dynamism that manifests not only through speech but also through movement. Her version of communal dance announced and enacted jubilee. To use a New Testament term, dance was a form of *kerussein*, of heralding or making a proclamation of good news.[89] Through dance she declared release from the death grip of the past and proclaimed the freedom and joy accompanying God's reign.

In cultural contexts that idolize control, joy tends to be misunderstood and undervalued. It should come as no surprise, then, that Bowman's joy was occasionally misread. She knew that a lively performance had the potential to misdirect an audience's attention by pointing to the performer rather than to the deeper truth that performer was trying to share, and she sometimes feared that listeners were merely entertained by her song and dance. Those fears were not unfounded. Some listeners were overwhelmed by her presentations or felt they veered into minstrelsy—particularly when she assumed the persona of an old lady.[90]

For the most part, Bowman seems to have anticipated and accepted such resistance and misunderstanding as unavoidable byproducts of preaching the gospel. Plus, her approach would inevitably rile those who preferred the more staid programs and liturgies that were common in Roman Catholic churches at the time. She faced resistance with belief in the integrity of her message and method, seeing them as gifts from her ancestors.[91] This is not to say that she understood ancestral traditions to be beyond critique—indeed, she generally found that one's beliefs were strengthened through the humility and openness that critique prompted. But she felt the faith of her ancestors had been tested in the crucible of slavery and its aftermath and proven reliable. Her ancestors not only had been sustained but also were equipped to face the precarity and mystery of life with joy.

Like many of her African American listeners, Bowman saw the ancestors as "repositories of communal wisdom," and joy was an instrumental dimension of the faith her ancestors had bequeathed.[92] As an "old folks' child," she had an ethical commitment to the ancestors that undergirded her preaching. Her faith tied her to previous generations similar to the way the apostle Paul suggested that Timothy's faith had come from his grandmother, Lois, and mother, Eunice (2 Tim. 1:5). In this respect, Bowman was very much an heir who sought to teach others the joyous tradition she had received.

The lessons on finding and guarding joy were myriad. She credited elders and ancestors for teaching her how to bask in the beauty of nature, how to face the challenges of life and death, how to persevere, and how to live without fear. They also passed on a history of praying and believing that infused her singing of the spirituals and dancing. When teaching spirituals, she urged listeners to dance along with them.[93] "Our music is an experience that marshals the forces of the body to become part of it," she explained.[94] She was convinced that the ancestors "planted solutions to problems" and healing in the music.[95]

Bowman felt that the elders' defiant joy and commitment to self-definition enriched their approaches to scriptural interpretation. She had a pattern of sharing their wisdom when she was explaining the meaning of biblical texts. For example, during a commemoration of Jesus' presentation at the temple, Bowman said,

> It seems to me that our ancestors had a "Mary and Joseph way of looking at things." . . . Most often they were the only ones who

recognized the presence of God in black life. They didn't need the approval of somebody else to know that we, too, are made in the image and likeness of God. . . . Just like our ancestors, we got to hold on to a "Mary and Joseph kind of faith."[96]

She made a similar homiletical move when exploring a text from Deuteronomy about the blessings associated with obeying God. After noting how Moses instructed his community that observing divine laws would result in wisdom and intimacy with God, she follows with a rhetorical question: "Isn't that what your Mama told you? or your grandmother, aunt, or whoever mothered you in the Spirit?"[97] Elevating these ancestral voices was a means of holding fast to the faith that aided communal and cultural survival.[98] And for Bowman, dance was an essential part of this catechesis and a means through which the faith was articulated. "Didn't they [the ancestors] tell you that faith and values must be expressed, must be celebrated, must be lived in song and dance and story?"[99]

Bowman taught that, though dead, the ancestors have an ongoing presence. Illuminating their influence was a critical task of African American preaching because the listener was deemed to be "an extension and expression of their lives."[100] Dance was especially suited to facilitate this union between the living and the dead. As John Miller Chernoff suggests in *African Rhythm and African Sensibility*,

> Symbolically, the drum is the "voice" of the ancestors, those who watch over the moral life of a community, and proper drumming and dance are founded on a sense of respect and gratitude to the ancestors for the continuity of the community which uses music and dance to restructure and refocus its integrity as a source of strength in the lives of its members. The elders, to put it most simply, participate best because they know more dead people, and their drumming and dancing will communicate and contribute their greater awareness of the deepest moral forces which can serve to bind the living community. African music and dance are art forms which permit them to demonstrate and express this wisdom for all to see.[101]

In multiple African cultural contexts, Chernoff observes that leadership requires demonstrating regard for the ancestors—a regard some chiefs display by dancing in front of their communities.[102]

In Bowman's African American context, dance announced the ancestors' legacy of overcoming fear and put worshipers in touch with the joy and freedom the ancestors are presumed to experience in paradise. Dancing unearths the ancestors' testimonies of living with faith. Further, a danced reflection on these testimonies does not leave the congregation in the same place where it started; its members are empowered to face the demands of the present by remembering the faithful witness of the ancestors. And here it is important to note that African American preaching is anchored not only in discrete discursive messages but also in the memory of the lived faith of ancestors.

PROPHETIC DANCE

Clearly, Bowman's approach to proclamatory dance rooted faith communities in African American history and fostered experiences of freedom and joy. But Bowman's vision of dance was not focused on aesthetics alone; her vision was also political. She hoped to enact a Christian ethical framework through dance. In this regard, one can draw parallels between Bowman's understanding of dance and that of Pearl Primus, the Harlem Renaissance dancer-activist who performed "electrifying" protest dances like "Hard Times Blues" at anti-fascist political rallies during the 1940s and performed pieces like "Strange Fruit," which prompted picketing and FBI surveillance.[103] Bowman shared the belief that dance communicated ethical and political ideas. She did not believe preaching could be apolitical because of the need to advocate for the poor and the oppressed. The protest demonstrations she was most familiar with were largely danced testimonies of the *imago Dei* that consisted of rhythmic, syncopated marching, circling around a speaker or monument, and swaying and rocking to a cappella song. This rhetorical blend of song, dance, movement, and spectacle evokes Miriam's prophetic song and victory dance that announced God's power and testified about Israel's escape from Egypt (Exod. 15:20–27).

One song that Bowman regularly included in her presentations was "We Shall Overcome." When leading this song, she emphasized an embodied method of singing. "Folks call it primitive strength and energy. It has to come from the bottom of your feet, from the pit of your stomach, from your heart as well as your head. It has to come from all the times when somebody beat you down."[104] She also had a pattern of insisting that the group members come close enough together to lock arms while singing. She explicitly linked the group's locked arms and swaying in the present with civil rights demonstrations of the past. On January 17, 1988, Bowman gave an address honoring Martin Luther King Jr. for the Milwaukee Commission on Community Relations. As usual, her address incorporated song and dance, and she instructed the choir members beforehand on how to lock arms for "We Shall Overcome": "Lock those arms and move with me. When we were down south during the marches, the people would lock those arms, so that when the dogs came, when the billy clubs came, so that when the rifle butts came, when the tear gas came, nobody would get lost and nobody would get hurt."[105]

Swaying with locked arms was similarly important to her in September 1989, when she gave a presentation at a concert for people living with AIDS in Minneapolis. Signaling the choir to sing "We Shall Overcome," she addressed the audience:

> Please cross your right arm over your left and clasp your neighbor's hands. That means you are going to have to move closer together, and that's part of the program. It's so that when the dogs come, when the bullets come, when the tear gas comes, and when the billy clubs come, and when the tanks come, when the rocks and bricks come, nothing or no one can separate you from your brother, your sister, your father, your mother, your child. . . . We sing this song in solidarity with our brothers and sisters who are singing it in Japan, in China, in South Africa, in Guatemala, in Nicaragua, in Northern Ireland, all over these United States, wherever men and women and children take a stand for freedom and for justice and for love.[106]

It is not an overstatement to say that Bowman treated "We Shall Overcome" as a song that required communal dance to effectively make its announcement of the will to be free.

This understanding of "We Shall Overcome" is woven into her famous 1989 address "To Be Black and Catholic," given before an assembly of the United States Catholic Bishops at Seton Hall University:

> What does it mean to be black and Catholic? It means that I come to my church fully functioning. That doesn't frighten you, does it? I come to my church fully functioning. I bring myself, my black self, all that I am, all that I have, all that I hope to become, I bring my whole history, my traditions, my experience, my culture, my African American song and dance and gesture and movement and teaching and preaching and healing and responsibility as gift to the church.[107]

She went on to challenge the church's leaders to learn from Black culture and remember that catholicity requires respect for the gospel's expression in different cultures. Her message climaxed with an invitation to the bishops to sing "We Shall Overcome," in which she encouraged the bishops to claim the lyrics as one claims a creed. And because she believed the song needed to be danced as well as sung, she instructed the bishops to move together and lock arms as civil rights demonstrators. As in prior cases, moving together was not just about proximity but about crossing arms, joining hands, and rocking in unison. Moving together meant allowing their gestures to announce a faith-centered commitment to justice even as they sang about it.

By the time she gave the "To Be Black and Catholic" address, Bowman's mobility was extremely limited. One observer noted that the "frailty of her gestures were also part of her preaching that day."[108] Despite her limited movement, the power of the communal dance still spoke volumes, as Marie Augusta Neal makes clear: "When I reflect on Thea Bowman, her life and work, the first thought I have is she made the bishops dance."[109] Neal goes on to say, "For some of them it was a reluctant participation and some may have felt even a little discomfort, but they danced and sang: "We shall overcome someday."'[110] The joint movement made for a memorable announcement of solidarity to the other bishops gathered in the room and to the thousands who subsequently watched the recording of the address. The gestures were not ancillary; they were "the terms by which" Christian solidarity was expressed.[111]

QUESTIONS AND CHALLENGES

Sister Thea Bowman's story raises important questions about the nature of preaching. First, instead of a more abstract vision of truth, what might it mean to foreground a kinesthetic understanding? What kind of intervention would that make in the mind-body dualism that so often hinders Christian preaching? And if the aim of preaching is to help listeners incarnate a message, might dance have unique capacities for facilitating this process? Bowman challenges preachers to think not just about the ears and minds of listeners but also about their bodies. *Bodies* receive and discern truth. For many people, the body is a space of seemingly unrelenting captivity. Reaching the inner pool of despair— shaking and jiggling it to prove its finiteness—often requires more than cognition; it requires a form of preaching that incorporates movement. Truth is, as Jawole Willa Jo Zollar observes, "articulated . . . in our bodies as well as our stories."[112] Knowing this, Sister Thea Bowman treated the sermon as a holistic genre that seeks to reintegrate mind and body while communicating the gospel.

This reintegration has a collective dimension. In addition to an individual dancer who bears spiritual wisdom through movement, Bowman stressed that the gospel is proclaimed by a congregation dancing in unison. Such communal movement edifies and announces the reality of God's reign, hinting at the Spirit's presence in their midst. Further, dancing the truth in this way and interpreting biblical stories as they were canonized in the spirituals and gospel songs of African and African American ancestors unites the living and the dead. Strengthening this bond is critical. The danced word has been censored due to the legacy of slavery, and much is at stake in its recovery. Dance is a central paradigm for African American sacred rhetoric and a critical vehicle through which the gospel is passed.

Sister Thea Bowman's work reveals how the performative or outward aspects of sacred dance are propelled by an equally active inner life. How might preachers demonstrate more appreciation for the lively inner worlds of their listeners? How might the sermon genre shift when plumbing those inner worlds becomes the preacher's priority? I explore these questions in the next chapter, where I examine the correlations between the sermon and the spoken meditation.

4

The Intercessor

Mystics, trying to tell us of their condition, often say that they feel "sunk in God like a fish in the sea." . . . Yet prayer is above all the act in which we give ourselves to our soul's true Patria; enter again that Ocean of God which is at once our origin and our inheritance, and there find ourselves mysteriously at home.

—Evelyn Underhill

When Howard Thurman gave a meditation, he got straight to the point. No chatty introduction. No anecdotes to warm up the listener. He spoke with slow deliberation, freighting each syllable with meaning, and within a sentence or two, he would plunge the listener into a lush interior world:

> There is in every person an inward sea, and in that sea, there is an island and on that island is an altar and there stands guard over that altar the angel with the flaming sword. And nothing can get by that angel to be placed on that altar unless it has the mark of your inner authority upon its brow. And what gets by the angel with the flaming sword and is placed on your altar on your island in your sea becomes a part of what a friend of mine calls the "fluid area of your consent"— the center of your consent. And what becomes the center of your consent is your connecting link with the Eternal.[1]

More than merely charting this inner journey, Thurman's meditations provided safe carriage. In just two or three paragraphs, he could bracket the empirical world and all its pressures long enough to quicken awareness of God's abiding presence. This awareness in turn yielded a taste of true freedom.

Howard Thurman's gifts as a pastor, preacher, and spiritual writer brought considerable acclaim during his life and contribute to his continuing popularity. While his life and work have generated a great deal of scholarly interest, less attention has been focused on the significance of his meditations, though they were published in several volumes, including *Meditations for Apostles of Sensitiveness* (1947), *Deep Is the Hunger* (1951), *Meditations of the Heart* (1953), *The Inward Journey* (1961), and *The Mood of Christmas* (1973). Meditations precede sermons in Thurman's sermon compilations *The Growing Edge* (1956) and *Temptations of Jesus* (1962). Designed to focus the mind and attune the heart for worship, the meditations usually played a preparatory and auxiliary role to sermons that took place in formal worship services. Yet packed as the meditations were with spiritual insight, they could stand alone as condensed or compressed sermons or function as devotionals geared toward shaping daily living. According to Thurman scholar Walter Earl Fluker, Thurman's ministry focused largely on helping the nation find its soul.[2] His meditations played a critical role in this endeavor.

HOWARD THURMAN: A BIOGRAPHICAL SKETCH

A trusted guide on spiritual life and celebrated author, pastor, and teacher, Howard Thurman was born on November 18, 1899, in Daytona Beach, Florida. He was raised by his parents, Alice Ambrose Thurman and Saul Solomon Thurman, and his maternal grandmother, Nancy Ambrose, who had been enslaved until young adulthood. Alice and Nancy were active church members, but Saul was not. The character of his faith was unique—a kind only understood by God—and Saul felt church attendance could harm him spiritually, that he might *lose* his soul if he joined the church.[3] Instead, Saul nurtured his spirit with long periods of silence while gazing out at nature.[4]

An early tragedy shook Thurman's world and relationship with the church. When Thurman was seven, his father, who typically left for two weeks at a time to lay railroad tracks along the Florida coast, returned home earlier than expected. Feverish and exhausted by an advanced case of pneumonia, he could barely breathe or walk. For five difficult days, Thurman and his mother cared for Saul in their home, but despite their efforts, Saul died. Young Howard was distraught.

His sorrow was compounded shortly afterward as it became clear that the family's pastor refused to officiate at Saul's funeral because he had not been a member of the church. Through persistence, Nancy Ambrose managed to arrange a church funeral; an itinerant preacher, Sam Cromarte, presided. Adding to the family's anguish, Cromarte's message condemned Saul. "I listened with wonderment, then anger, and finally mounting rage as Sam Cromarte preached my father into hell," Thurman remembered. "This was his chance to illustrate what would happen to 'sinners' who died 'out of Christ,' as my father had done."[5] After this traumatizing experience of preaching, Thurman became estranged from the church and, like his father, found his connection with God through nature. He found friendship in the woods, nightfall, the ocean, the river, and a beloved oak tree.[6] Indeed, the natural world served as the context for his earliest religious experiences and would go on to be foundational to his spiritual life.[7]

At twelve, Thurman found his way back to the church, though some quibbling ensued when he presented himself to the deacons for church membership. When questioned, Thurman said, "I want to be a Christian."[8] This response was deemed insufficient evidence of a completed conversion until his grandmother intervened.[9] Despite these two early negative experiences of church, Thurman came to relish it. In the fellowship of the faithful, he learned two critical lessons: that his words and actions were consequential and that living with ethical intentions was vital.

His intellectual and moral development accelerated in the fall of 1919 when he enrolled in Morehouse College. Several faculty members played instrumental roles in his formation, including the college president, John Hope; its dean, Samuel Howard Archer; and two professors, Benjamin E. Mays and E. Franklin Frazier. While he majored in economics, Thurman developed an affinity for philosophy as an undergraduate and eagerly listened to good preachers. In addition to the sermons given by Morehouse faculty, he was moved by Hugh Black of Union Theological Seminary and Fifth Avenue Presbyterian Church, whom Thurman heard during a summer in New York.[10]

Having discerned a clear desire to become a pastor, Thurman went on to Rochester Theological Seminary. Rochester was a place where he thrived, made friends, and grew as a scholar and preacher. The seeds for lifelong reflections on race and spirituality were already germinating. In his service as a guest preacher and lecturer during these years, race was a consistent theme. Upon graduation, he married Kate Kelley of LaGrange, Georgia, and became pastor of Mount Zion Baptist Church in Oberlin, Ohio, where he would serve for two years.

The congregation was a nest for him. He had for years felt uncomfortable praying in public, but his self-consciousness subsided. He also found a creative outlet in the sermon series that he held on Sunday evenings. The conversations that grew out of the sermons connected him with the intellectual community at Oberlin College and strengthened his relationship with church members. In addition, two memorable pastoral care experiences refined his approach to ministry. The first involved an elderly man who faced a spiritual crisis. Decades earlier, while enslaved, he had been severely beaten due to a false accusation. A Good Samaritan tended to his wounds and helped him escape to Ohio, but rather than savoring his freedom, he was consumed by anger. During a pastoral visit he described himself as "kept alive by hatred."[11] Sensing the depth of the man's struggle, Thurman listened rather than offering to pray or trying to resolve the situation. Over the course of weeks, he made periodic visits to check in on the man. On one of these subsequent visits, the man was ecstatic, telling Thurman, "It happened last night! It happened!"[12] Days later, the man died.

Not long afterward, Thurman was sent to Steubenville, Ohio, to visit a church member who had been hospitalized after a car accident. The parishioner had been a passenger in a car driven by her brother. When Thurman arrived at the hospital, a nurse explained that the driver had not survived the accident and that his parishioner was too weak to handle the shock of the news. During their pastoral visit, Thurman read Scripture and prayed. As their visit came to an end, she asked, "How is my brother? Is he dead?" Following the nurse's guidance, he offered words of assurance: "No, he is not dead. He is here in the hospital"; however, he felt tormented by this response and was unable to preach and lead worship in his usual way.[13]

His sermon that Sunday consisted of sharing a story about a Roman soldier who lies to protect the life of a Jewish boy (from Henry Van Dyke's *The Other Wise Man*) and then sharing "in naked detail" what had occurred in Steubenville.[14] The congregation's response to his message was resounding, and his reflections on the Van Dyke story later became part of a meditation, "To What Loyalty Are You True?"[15]

Both pastoral care experiences had a softening effect on him, making him more transparent and emotionally available. Buoyed by the knowledge that the congregation appreciated his willingness to wrestle with the complexities of life, his confidence increased, and he felt freer to embrace the unique contours of his own spirituality. His comfort praying in public increased to the point that he could be overcome by a "full tide of emotions" as he sensed the weight of God's love. Preaching also changed for him. Rather than focusing on teaching the faith, his preaching was "almost entirely devoted to the meaning of the experience of our common quest and journey." This shift had an ecumenical dimension. A Chinese Buddhist listener once told Thurman, "When I close my eyes and listen with my spirit I am in my Buddhist temple experiencing the renewing of my own spirit."[16]

Thurman's interest in mysticism and the philosophy of religion bloomed. He resigned from his pastorate at Mount Zion and began a period of independent study with the Quaker scholar Rufus Jones at Haverford College in January 1929. The time with Jones was brief—less than a year—but proved pivotal in shaping Thurman's theological framework. When he accepted a joint teaching appointment at Morehouse College and Spelman College the following year, he took this renewed focus on mysticism and philosophy of religion with him. At Morehouse and Spelman, Thurman was an innovative teacher who was willing to forego textbooks and instead contemplate essential life questions. He invited Morehouse students to sit in a circle on the floor while eating peanuts rather than conduct a more formal class seated at desks.[17] The joy and energy of this time plummeted in 1930 when his wife, Katie, who had been ill for years, suddenly died. The shock left him at sea.

Thurman went to Europe for the summer and came back certain about his vocation as a pastor and teacher. In 1932, he married Sue Elvie Bailey, a friend he had met years ago, whose love touched him at his "center" and "made the whole world new."[18] That year he also accepted a position at Howard University, where he served as professor of theology and later dean of Rankin Chapel. His imprint on the life of the school and on the spiritual lives of students was tremendous. A tour-de-force of a preacher, Thurman delivered sermons that affirmed the dignity of human life—and specifically Black life. He began writing a weekly meditation for the congregation and would continue this practice for decades.[19] The meditations underscored the personhood of his listeners, assuring them that they were not beholden to the crushing and caustic opinions of a white supremacist culture.

In September 1935, Thurman went on a pilgrimage of friendship to India, Burma (now Myanmar), and Ceylon (now Sri Lanka) that would change his life. The tour lasted several months and was sponsored by the World Student Christian Federation and Student Movements of India, Burma, Ceylon, and the United States. During the trip, he had a short but transformative encounter with Mahatma Gandhi that deepened his already profound curiosity about other faiths. The colonialism and hierarchy he saw also put racial hierarchy and segregation in the United States in a broader context. Inspired in part by his experiences during this trip, Thurman would later write *Jesus and the Disinherited*, which explored the themes of fear, deception, hate, and love and framed the gospel as a resource for resisting oppression. The book also reveals the chasm between what Thurman calls the "religion of Jesus" and the distorted Christianity that undergirds white supremacy.[20]

In 1943, Thurman accepted a call to be the copastor of San Francisco's Church for the Fellowship of All Peoples, the first intentionally interracial and intercultural church in the United States.[21] The church was located in an area where large numbers of Japanese citizens had been forcibly removed and incarcerated due to Roosevelt's Executive Order 9066. There were over a thousand congregants consisting largely of African American, Asian, and white members. At Fellowship Church, Thurman was surrounded by a community that shared his curiosity, zeal, and love of experimentation. Worship included not only hymns and formal prayers but also visual art, "creative quiet," drama, dance, and meditation.[22] On Sundays the services centered around sermons that combined "instruction, guidance, inspiration, conviction, dedication, and challenge—in an enveloping all-embracing Presence."[23] Usually structured in a series, his sermons allowed listeners to explore a given theme in depth over several weeks.

Through Fellowship Church, Thurman sought to serve local activists by providing the spiritual refreshment, courage, and clarity needed by "individuals who were in the thick of the struggle for social change."[24] This aim involved renewing the activists' feelings of belovedness, fostering a connection to the broader world and creation, and helping them grasp the importance of their role in the broad sweep of human history. He wanted this spiritual nourishment to have a holistic effect on the person, feeding the mind, spirit, and, perhaps most importantly, the will. Urging these activists to get more involved in justice work would not suffice. After all, they were already engaged in the throes of that work. His intervention was to provide an opportunity for them to reflect on their labor, to consider the short-term and long-term stakes, and to recommit with new creative resources. The paradoxes, polarities, absurdities, and complicated historical dynamics that complicated the activists' decisions could be named and explored.[25] Ideally, the worship experience would cultivate perceptive, disciplined prayer lives— the kind that could deepen their resolve.

By helping people move out of spectator mode, the church "provided a place, a moment, when a person could declare, 'I choose!'"[26] Reflecting back on that time, Thurman stressed that "there can never be a substitute for taking *personal responsibility* for social change. The word 'personal' applies both to the individual and to the organization—in this instance, the church."[27] Worship cultivated this responsibility and fostered what Miles Yates calls an "inner accord" with God, the sense that the "leaven" of God's "greatness is enfolded in our littleness." [28] Thurman believed such knowledge equipped people to live out their Christian convictions. He would go on to play a similar supporting role for civil right leaders who were not active members of Fellowship Church; these included James Farmer, Jesse Jackson, Vernon Jordan, Martin Luther King Jr., Bayard Rustin, and Whitney Young.[29]

In 1953, after nine years of ministry at Fellowship Church, Thurman accepted a call to serve as dean of Marsh Chapel and professor of spiritual disciplines and resources in the Graduate School of Theology at Boston University.[30] The invitation came with the hope that he would recreate the broad spiritual vision he had cultivated at Fellowship Church and adjust it for a university setting. Within his first three weeks, the liturgy was rearranged to foreground a period of meditation: the choir sang the first verse of a hymn a cappella, a meditation period followed, and then the congregation sang the remainder of the hymn. Thurman described the meditation period as "the heart of the total experience of worship." For him, the movement from meditation to prayer "blended as one movement of experience in the presence of God. . . . Sometimes the whole experience would be a prayer. At other times I would move from the depths of my reflection, and the next thing I knew I would hear myself talking to God. They were not two separate experiences; there was no boundary."[31]

His approach satisfied a deep thirst among listeners. Boston University's radio station, WBUR, broadcast the sermons live and aired them again on Sunday evenings. Requests for interviews and invitations to preach and lecture abounded. He even began sharing messages on a weekly television show, *We Believe*. The show required adjusting to the lack of a live audience and working with tighter time constraints. Most messages were under fifteen minutes. Despite some struggles with the administration, the friendships he made through the show and as a pastor enriched his time at Boston University and made it one of the more dynamic periods of his life.[32]

Thurman retired from Boston University in 1965 and returned to San Francisco to serve as founder and chairman of the Howard Thurman Educational Trust. The trust focused on religious, educational, and literary causes, and his work involved preaching, lecturing, and fundraising. As was his custom, he immersed himself in this work, continuing until health issues required him to slow down. Thurman died at his home on April 10, 1981, at age eighty-one. He was lauded for being a luminary with a host of achievements. "But more than anything else," Luke Powery observes, "what is compelling about Thurman, even with all of his accolades, is that he was a genuine human being. . . . He was human."[33] The wonder he found in being human kindled his words and shaped his legacy.

MEDITATIVE VENTURES

Like his many books and sermons, Thurman's meditations have a timeless quality and play an important role in his legacy. They offer condensed versions of his most significant teachings on the life of prayer and reveal the wonder of the human spirit. The term *meditation* has a broad spectrum of meaning, including arranged silence, marinating on a specific Scripture passage, attempting to clear the mind, surveying the conscious thoughts of the mind, or otherwise focusing one's attention on the divine. Thurman's approach involved cordoning off a specific time to offer short readings or reflections aloud that were punctuated by brief silences. While his content would vary, he centered on the nature of God and human existence. The reasoning dimension of the mind was active during the meditations, yet more than anything else the meditations were occasions to dwell in God, to commune and relish the divine presence and the wonder of being human. And though meditations could bear fruit—like a sharpened awareness of God's will in a given circumstance or a sensation of inner calm—attaining this fruit was not the primary objective. Meditation was not an *acquisitive* venture; dwelling in God's presence was an end in itself.[34] Like Mary in Luke 2:19, listeners were encouraged to treasure truth and ponder it in their hearts.[35]

The meditations Thurman composed and shared in worship were modes of intercession that reflected his attempt to pray for his congregation at their point of deepest need. A fusion of petitionary prayer and sermon, the meditation was a vehicle through which he named their unspoken longings for courage, self-knowledge, and divine perspective. To use a Quaker phrase to describe Thurman's posture toward the congregation, he was "holding them in the Light."[36] His words and intentional silences reveal this holding to be a slow endeavor. One might compare Thurman's meditation to a pause during which the soil of the mind is aerated. Thurman loosens the negative tapes and secular notions of personhood that beset the listeners and enables them to absorb their identities as "God's children" as his enslaved ancestors understood the term.[37] That is to say, he made it clear that the individual is not wholly limited to time and circumstance, that there is within human identity an eternal dimension that connects the living and the dead.

Thurman usually structured his meditations in a paragraph or two, though he would add to these if he could do so while keeping the message concise. Most of his meditations were under six hundred words and could be read aloud in fewer than seven minutes. Careful about word choice, he used language that was at once evocative and simple, aural but also formal. Even when his message was light or humorous, the language carried a certain gravitas. Edward K. Kaplan, a literary scholar attuned to religious aspects of human experience, aptly compares Thurman's meditations to poems due to their elegant language and depth.[38] One part of the poetic quality stems from the nonagonistic tone—a pattern of using story, *māšāl*, or parable, images, and questions to provoke reflection while being careful to ensure that the reflection process is still largely self-directed. Dharma talks often have this character because the listener's inner world is usually treated with high regard. This experience of listening differs from simply yielding to a preacher's argument. Similarly, in Thurman's case, meditations are not so much arguments but invitations to ruminate.[39]

Another part of the poetic quality stems from the way his words open both affective and cognitive meaning.[40] His opening lines, for example, are brief and provocative, speaking to mind and emotions: "Thou art with me."[41] "There is ever a thin line which separates courage from cowardice."[42] "Again and again we seek to escape from the struggle of life."[43] "It is often very difficult to make up one's mind."[44] Occasionally he starts with a question instead: "Are you a reservoir or are you a canal or a swamp?"[45] "How well do you get along with people?"[46]

Despite Thurman's gifts with language, Patrick Clayborn convincingly argues that Thurman's communication turns less on a high view of the power of speech and more on a prelingual understanding of communication.[47] In other words, the shared experience of God determines the efficacy of the words, and the Spirit orchestrates the communication process. In this regard, pauses are as instrumental as words in shaping consciousness and receptivity. Like Thurman's words, his pauses have varying flavors—demonstrating curiosity, wonder, or delight in some cases, or allowing the meaning of words to blossom in the mind.[48]

After opening, he quickly builds momentum and launches the listener into an inner galaxy. Despite the often dramatic nature of the odyssey, Thurman felt the aim of his meditations was more modest: he sought to clear mental distractions and focus the mind. This way listeners could bring prayerful attention to worship and be open to the songs, sermon, and prayers. Ideally this shift in disposition would also facilitate a wide-ranging openness to life overall. And while Thurman sometimes turns to Scripture, he avoids dense or definitive explications of texts, instead offering a short line or phrase that steeps in the heart of the listener. Scripture functions more as a mirror or as water to slake one's inner thirst.

Clearly, conversion in the traditional sense is not the objective, though the meditations are geared toward converting consciousness and readying listeners for divine encounter.[49] The shift Thurman facilitates is one of deepened perception. As Pamela Burnard argues, "Perception, in arts as well as in sciences, is different from simple 'reception' (as in the process of registering stimuli from an external reality). Perception is very much an active shifting of our own attention to the world, as in the original Latin 'ab-tension'; that is, to draw something or somebody towards."[50] And as Leslie Paul suggests, perception is a holistic process. While we know with the intellect, understanding or perception "demands the co-operation of all the powers of the mind or being—feeling, intuition, will, and so forth."[51]

The meditations have a healing effect in that they plumb the listeners' interiority, enabling them to see their own depth. In the hands of another, such a process could be jarring, but Thurman is gentle. While the meditations point to dormant fears, they also maintain a respectful distance (often through metaphor) and keep the listener at the helm.[52]

Nature plays a critical hermeneutical role in enabling listeners to see themselves with fresh eyes. The human struggle for life might, for example, be compared with a tree struggling to grow above the timberline.[53] Or life after tragedy might be examined through the metaphor of the seed of the jack pine, which is more often released from the cone amid the heat of a forest fire.[54]

Whatever the metaphor, the driving underlying question is "How will you live?" Helping the listener claim power when life seemed to present no options was essential for Thurman. He even described freedom as a sense of "alternative."[55] Yet particularly for African American listeners, it was necessary to underscore the freedom to reconstruct one's personhood and sort through the toxic ideas and internalized racism that inhibited self-recognition. In this respect, Thurman's meditations were designed to decolonize the mind by enlarging listeners' view of themselves. Acknowledging the white power structure without getting consumed by it, Thurman deftly placed his emphasis on the individual journey toward a fuller life. This approach gave him the freedom to focus on individual self-worth. As Luke Powery explains, Thurman knew "being a human being" involved more than "living a racialized life."[56] To be clear, Thurman did not advocate colorblindness or the erasure of cultural particularity; he gestured "toward humanization" in a way that acknowledged the "reality of racialization."[57] He wanted his listeners to face the dehumanizing truth of racialization while claiming fuller lives as children of God.

In fact, nurturing an individual's self-recognition as a beloved child of God and as a vital part of the created order proves foundational to Thurman's work. He helps his listeners sift their motives and weigh their desires in light of the larger purpose of human life. Self-loathing and misdirected strivings are often revealed as a consequence.[58] The meditations were not simply constructed to help listeners feel good about themselves; they were designed to hold up a mirror and facilitate an incisive gaze.

One might assume the brevity of the meditations would preclude depth, but the opposite is true. Brevity sharpens the message and helps Thurman sift out all that is unnecessary. Much like a poet, he foregrounds life's contradictions and in doing so reveals the heroism of spiritual life—the valiant efforts at what may be an unresolvable conflict, the longings that will require enormous labor, the need to accept crushing limitations. Avoiding platitudes, he dives into the mire of everyday life and goes directly to the area of tension. And rather than resolving dilemmas, he sees them as bound up in the cosmic struggle of good and evil. His role is to knead the questions like dough and trust that such pressure will have a beneficial effect. Ultimately, Thurman illumines the listener's unity with other humans, the creation, and God—all ends that fit well under the umbrella of Christian edification.

SEED OF A SERMON

What's challenging is discerning what distinguishes Thurman's meditations from his sermons. Two key distinctions concern length and performance. The meditations are considerably shorter than most of his sermons—even the shorter ones broadcast on *We Believe*. And as far as performance, he seemed to inhabit his sermons more by giving them more volume and vocal intonation. Apparently, he also gestured for emphasis. Recordings of his sermons sometimes include tapping on the pulpit and other sounds of movement. His vibrant delivery reflects his view that a sermon should have a "smell of ammonia about it."[59] This ammonia is manifested through passionate surges as well as through equally dramatic "meditative pauses" that prompt moments of intense reflection.[60]

The similarities between the meditations and sermons abound. Both are geared toward the human "quest for meaning, for significance, and for intentional living."[61] Like the sermons, the meditations brim with "homiletic insight."[62] Thurman uses both meditations and sermons to help listeners become more conscious of their thinking and develop a supple, expectant disposition that is consistent with Christian faith. In truth, some of the content in his meditations appears in sermons, suggesting a fluid boundary between the two. Perhaps most important is Thurman's consistency in using both the meditation and the sermon as a "diffractive prism," or a mode of "doing" that reframes the world and our roles in it.[63] That dynamism, which Teresa Fry Brown describes as "the action potential of preaching," centers and illumines the soul.[64]

Many of the principles Thurman valued in sermons apply to his meditations as well. He described a sermon as the "distillation of the thinking, reading, observation, brooding and meditation of the preacher" and suggested that it stirs listeners to live faithfully.[65] Thurman created a file, "Notes on Homiletics Course," that outlines some of his elemental assumptions about the nature and purpose of preaching. While undated, his references, including one to "President Johnson," presumably Mordecai Wyatt Johnson, who served as Howard University's president from 1926 to 1960, suggest the course was prepared for Howard University students.[66] Thurman names the challenge of addressing the human condition, encouraging preachers to discern the "felt need," define the struggle, and offer promising solutions rooted in experience.[67] What he wants is to have the people's prayers and longings named and taken seriously in the sermon. This approach respects the dignity of the human struggle and the need for prayerful, theologically informed reflection that will undergird the soul's journey with God. Stressing that preaching is an intellectual endeavor requiring reading across many disciplines, he urges his students to study in order to avoid "preaching scraps, trash."[68]

The emphasis on "felt need" comes up later in Henry Mitchell's *Black Preaching: Recovery of a Powerful Art,* where Mitchell describes felt need as elemental to call-and-response: "Black preaching at its best has remained focused on problems that people confront daily and feel real needs in meeting. . . . The Black preacher has had to give strength for the current day's journey, the guidance and vision for extended survival in an absurdly trying existence."[69]

For Thurman, the felt need is addressed through a "trunkline utterance, a basic idea" or core theme expressed in a sentence.[70] The trunkline utterance organizes and anchors the energy of the message much like Samuel DeWitt Proctor's "thesis" and Thomas G. Long's focus and function statements.[71] Along this line, Thurman urges preachers to develop clear intentions for what they will say and what the desired outcome will be.[72] But key to the effect is the emphasis on a transcendent experience that enables listeners to see themselves in a truer light and discern the aiding presence of God. In other words, the ends Thurman sought were cosmic, involving awakening awareness of the mystery and wonder of life and the significance of ethical action. Preaching spoke both to the present and to the eternal.

Notably, Thurman addresses felt need through argument, and while he seeks to speak to the whole person—and this would necessarily involve cognitive and emotional dimensions—he explicitly cautions against "exploiting peoples' emotions" and getting "people all worked up only to go home and to get their dinner." He even cautions preachers not to rely too heavily on the emotional climate of the worship service.[73] Clearly, avoiding coercion is a primary concern. In his own approach he maintains a degree of distance from the listeners, explaining, "When I get up to speak, I do not try to get a concerted positive or negative mood from the audience. I struggle with an idea. I must be true to the spiritual insight with which I am working. When I am speaking, I am not conscious of my audience. I have taken them in before I get up to speak."[74] Despite his own method, Thurman stresses that he thinks it is better to be conscious of the listeners, provided one can avoid exploiting them. The intoxicating effects of the power relationship between preacher and listener were of particular concern. He worried that preachers underestimated the ego temptations that could come with being on a pedestal—that having a glowing reputation, even if short of fame, could distort a preacher's self-perception and sense of vocation if that preacher were not careful.[75] He warns of the dangers of prominence, lamenting that influential preachers can easily "become brutes."[76]

One of the more striking conclusions Thurman makes in his "Notes on Homiletics Course" concerns his vision of excellent preaching. "The greatest preaching," Thurman explains, "is what takes place when the people in your congregation are as conscious of the presence of God as they are unconscious of the preacher. And the greatest preaching is done when the preacher is able to be transparent to the truth."[77] This statement would certainly seem to apply to his meditations with equal force.

SINKING INTO SACRED TIME

The notion that one can become unconscious of the preacher and have a more direct divine encounter suggests an expanded experience of place and time. Thurman repeatedly stressed the human ability to imagine life outside of the places and events that would seem to define one's life.[78] And he believed that as beings able to taste eternity within time, humans held latent powers of perception. Prayer and proclamation activated those latent powers, yielding a fresh outlook on the world and one's purpose within it.

Effecting a shift in perception and somehow loosening the grip of time served as twin aims of Thurman's meditations. Noting that members of the congregation come to worship with distracted minds, he suggests pastors offer a reading that will focus their concentration.[79] Yet he is quick to root this strategy in traditional practices of Black preaching, noting that in lieu of a reading, Black preachers of prior generations achieved similar ends by lining hymns to foster an atmosphere of worship.[80] By bracketing the immediate pressures of life, Thurman's meditations served at once as moments of proclamation and respite. Under the canopy he created, listeners could pause and examine their lives. His meditations function as moments of spiritual and psychological refuge in which the ultimate meaning of human life takes the foreground and the relentless demands of everyday life are quieted. This pause provided a space for contemplation and divine union—both direly needed in social climates permeated by oppression.

The time Thurman carved out had a sacramental quality because it provided sabbath. Mentally and emotionally exhausted listeners could rest in God's presence and gain an enlightened view of themselves and the world surrounding them. By the meditation's close, they had been brought to an internal wellspring. And here it is important to note that the wonder of the meditation time was not limited to the few minutes when Thurman's voice could be heard. The benefits extended into the future as listeners acted on the truths they had heard and forged an identity that was not rooted solely in temporal concerns. The meditations charged life choices with meaning.

As Leslie Paul, a theologian Thurman revered, argues, "Everything matters, every deed, every act, every life has significance."[81] Paul goes on to argue that Christian conviction involves believing "the track of a person's life through time cannot be an episode without meaning beyond time, unconnected with the ultimate significance of the universe, that it is not wiped out and all done with, and the person's responsibility along with it, by the circumstance of death, but is carried forward into what is beyond time, eternity."[82]

In addition to blurring the boundaries between the temporal and eternal, sacred time suggests that the empirical world does not reveal all of reality. As Paul puts it, there is "a reality standing behind the reality signalled to us by our senses," though that belief does not require dismissing or devaluing the value of the material world.[83] So, in short, a new mode of perception ensues, leading listeners to attend to the visible and the invisible.

Paul's views on time also resonate with Thurman's teachings on immortality. In his discussions of the spirituals, he stresses that his ancestors had an "authentic belief in personal immortality" that is expressed in songs like "Were You There When They Crucified My Lord?" and "We Are Climbing Jacob's Ladder."[84] The end of their earthly lives did not mark a definitive termination of life; it gave them "another quality of being," making them "at one with moonrise and starlight."[85] The activity of the ancestors shaped his consciousness profoundly. Feeling their presence while on a ship, Thurman recounts, "From my cabin window I look out on the full moon, and the ghosts of my forefathers rise and fall with the undulating waves. Across these same waters how many years ago they came!"[86] And more, he hopes his own words will communicate the ancestors' wisdom, that "their children will hear their Voice above the present conflict."[87] The aim of channeling their wisdom was not limited to his lectures on the spirituals but carries over more subtly in sermons and meditations when the partition between the living and the dead is lifted.

SILENCE

Silence plays an instrumental role in this channeling process. Inspired in part by his experiences in Quaker worship, Thurman assumed silence was dense with meaning and was convinced it could have different flavors depending on the moment. The challenge was to be sensitive enough to discern its subtleties and avoid squandering it. He thought those who respected silence could be borne up by it, transformed into gateways for the Spirit. On a practical level, he saw silence functioning as something like a divine catalyst.[88] Intentional moments of silence could help listeners absorb ideas, debate them internally, or develop anticipation for answers to questions raised in the meditation. Brief silences also cultivated a feeling of union with God and other worshipers.

On a deeper level, silences slowed thinking and fostered shared consciousness. Immersed in such silences, Thurman felt a cosmic oneness. "I was no longer I, Howard Thurman, but I blended with the people there, and when the thing was over I came back to myself. Three times in a Quaker meeting, others have been thinking exactly what I was thinking, and anticipated me by a few seconds in getting up to say it."[89] This capacity for losing one's ego long enough to become one with other worshipers and explore new dimensions of the soul were the fruits of the meditations. Strengthened internally and externally, the individual was ready to engage Scripture, act ethically, and continue seeking out the ways and will of God. In short, the meditations had clarifying and integrating effects and paved the way for faithful living.

The silence surrounding and flowing through Thurman's meditations also had a prophetic dimension. Here it is helpful to draw on Abraham Joshua Heschel's explanation about the relationship between sacred time and the prophetic word: "Holiness in space, in nature, was known in other religions. New in the teaching of Judaism was that the idea of holiness was gradually shifted from space to time. . . . The emphasis on time is a predominant feature of prophetic thinking. 'The day of the Lord' is more important to the prophets than 'the house of the Lord.'"[90] Heschel believes sanctity is "a quality" humans create,[91] and explains, "A special consciousness is required to recognize the ultimate significance of time."[92] Helping people discern the eternal weight of each moment was primary for both Heschel and Thurman, and Thurman was convinced silence was essential in helping people appreciate it.[93]

For Thurman, the sculpting of sacred time involved finding a space beneath speech and beneath the dogma of Christianity where the soul could encounter the living God. Thurman was skilled at digging beneath cerebration to a layer of truth that sits under creedal formulas.[94] He believed truth functioned less as an abstract phenomenon and more as an encounter.[95] This encounter-based understanding of truth has a strong biblical foundation and manifests as a glimpse or an elusive experience of truth.[96] While listeners gain only a glimmer of truth through their encounters, that glimmer is nonetheless formative in awakening a greater call to listen for the Spirit's continual leading and, in turn, witnessing to one's convictions. Experiencing this stirring, this dynamism, is an essential dimension of prophetic speech that frees listeners from rigid religious or denominational categorization and enables individuals to savor the divine presence. Thurman's approach reveals his concern for the prayer lives of his listeners and his hope that worship would enrich their spirituality.

Evelyn Underhill (1875–1941), a friend of Rufus Jones and a spiritual teacher with whom Thurman was very familiar, similarly used retreat meditations to help listeners pray. While her meditations were significantly longer than Thurman's and often took place over the course of a weekend, she structured her messages around periods of quiet and focused on a central theme like courage, growth, or generosity. She spent less energy explaining Scripture and focused instead on the nature of Christian life. Her intent was to focus adoring attention on God and to help people shift to a disposition of trust, delight, and rest in God or, in other words, to recognize that they are held by God. Mindful that an experience like this could lead a person to "stand aside, feeling pure and agreeable to God," Underhill was careful to urge the listener toward action—to go "right down into the mess" of the world and emanate love there.[97] All these objectives required a sacramental experience of time, which she marked through periods of silence and by encouraging retreatants to hear her addresses as food for their own reflection time with God, which formed the heart of the retreat. By decentering her meditations and emphasizing the importance of their own prayers, the time and space of the retreat was cordoned off. "A retreat is your time *with Him*, for facing realities in His light, for thinking in His presence. It is an opportunity to be like the simple but devoted old man who was once asked how he prayed, and quietly replied: 'We look at one another.'"[98]

Thurman did not usually have the cocoon of a weekend retreat in which to situate his meditations and instead worked within the space of a Sunday morning worship service. Yet he held a similar aim of opening the listeners to the quiet splendor of the divine presence.[99] For him, this entailed carving out a haven for a few minutes when the mind could be focused on the life of prayer and trusting that the flashes of insight that emerged would have ripple effects on the lives of the listeners and on the lives of the people surrounding them.

SAGELY AUTHORITY

Thurman was convinced that preaching had an effectiveness that exceeded human comprehension and that the proclaimed word made impressions on listeners apart from their acquiescence to it. While Thurman valued the expression of agreement through traditional call-and-response in preaching, during his meditations he was more focused on entering the listeners' internal dialogue. This goal has implications for the mode of authority he embodied. He evidenced a respect for the often-subtle work of the Holy Spirit and an understanding that the Spirit's healing work often takes place by degree rather than all at once. Evelyn Underhill encouraged people of prayer to remember the "persistent sandpaper by which so much of His work on the soul is done."[100] Thurman seemed to concur. His authority did not rest on his ability to excite the listeners but on the power of the Spirit to soothe the listeners through a single insight that elevated their perspectives on life and enabled more vibrant living to become possible.

Thurman offers a model of sagely authority. His messages were focused and delivered with confidence, but he did not envision himself as superior to his listeners and suggested that any preacher who did was an infidel.[101] On this issue, he explains, "As sure as my name is Howard Thurman and I am black and weigh 203 pounds, you can not help people when you feel that out of one order of life and being you have come, and that they have come out of another, and that they do not have what you have."[102] Nor does Thurman condescend to the listener with trite answers to life's complex moral dilemmas. Instead, he dives into them, coming to conclusions slowly, if at all.

Allowing ideas to percolate served as a clear strategy in helping listeners own and probe their faith.[103] The Christianity Thurman sought to nurture was not puréed; it required earnest consideration. Here it helps to turn to insights from Miles Yates, an ascetical theologian whom Thurman esteemed: "'Consider' is from the Latin *cum*, with, and *sidus*, a star or constellation. It actually means 'observing, looking up to the stars together.'"[104] Drawing on this understanding of consideration that seems consistent with Thurman's, the proclaimed word encourages listeners to gaze and ponder life's dilemmas without expecting an instant conclusion. An unhurried scrutiny emerges—a form of scrutiny that attends not only to immediate circumstances but also to the mysteries of the universe and the long view of human history.

In addition, Thurman's approach suggests he was mindful of the privilege of speaking into another's inner life and fundamentally respected the listener's unique experience and moral agency. Rather than foregrounding explanations or points, he foregrounds curiosity about the nature of life and the challenges of living from an ethical compass. Clues from Scripture as well as literature, history, and the natural world are appreciated for the light they shed on life, but the underlying enigma remains. Thurman's authority is grounded in his honesty about life's complexity and incongruities.

On another level, as a sage, his approach reflects a pattern of elevating everyday decisions and putting them in an eternal context. This reframing reveals the significance of seemingly mundane choices and underscores the listener's agency.[105] The overall effect is revelatory. He peels back illusions and emphasizes the meaning of the listener's life. For example, in "The Need for Approval," he reflects on the anxiety surrounding external approval: "It is a searching question: from whom do I seek approval and why? Why is this person or that person's approval important to me? Why? Why? Why?"[106] After saddling the listener with this question and prompting reflection on the past and present reasons for approval-seeking, he turns to Scripture for a cosmic angle on the issue. "If God be for us," he asks, "*who* can be against us?"[107] Thurman goes on to posit that our longing for approval reveals a deeper hunger for God and that a person's security and self-respect ultimately stem from being in union with God and the universe.[108]

Overall, the tone in his meditations carries both intimacy and immediacy, yielding the sense that one has listened to a sage but also to a friend who is equally engaged in sorting out life's myriad struggles. His is not a power over his listeners, but a power that grows out of sensitivity, out of having experienced the human condition and the action of the Spirit. Thurman speaks as a spiritual companion and a pilgrim who is still absorbed in the mystery of God. Every insight he gains about the soul's journey is treasured but accepted as a fragment. Consequently, his spiritual wisdom does not function as a basis for elevating himself above listeners who, like him, are also engaged in an ongoing search.

Convinced that his wisdom flowed from God rather than his intellect alone, Thurman tried to keep the divine channel open, and humility was essential in this regard. And more, he sought to bring his full self to the meditations so that he, too, could experience the grace he hoped to mediate to his listeners.

KEY INSIGHTS AND QUESTIONS

Thurman's meditations provide layers of spiritual nourishment. The content of his meditations mirrors what is found in his sermons concerning what it means to be human, the telos of human life, lessons from the natural world, and the ways of God. Shunning tidy answers, he gravitates toward dilemmas that cannot be fully resolved, and he reflects on themes that strengthen the human will for ethical living. The meditations give listeners occasions to examine life's immediate concerns through the lens of the ultimate without getting bound up with moralism or personal scruples. While brief, his meditations suspend time and space to give listeners a respite and emphasize the beauty of their inner lives. The capacity to think beyond the pressures of everyday life yields an increased sense of power to shape reality rather than simply respond to it. In short, Thurman's meditations put listeners in touch with their mortality while also stressing their freedom to live as agents of grace and change.

Thurman's meditations raise important strategic questions about preaching. First, when does our speech *about* God hinder intimacy with God, adding an unnecessary layer of distance? If encouraging this intimacy is one of the central aims of preaching, watching this dynamic seems crucial. Another issue is dogma. When does dogma clutter preaching, serving as an obstacle to divine encounter? What proportion of a sermon ought to consist of dogma?

A final issue is wonder. What role ought the cultivation of wonder play in preaching? Thurman's sense of wonder is contagious, propelling his meditations as well as his sermons. He uses wonder to deepen reflection and take the contradictions and mysteries of life seriously. His approach also hints at the parabolic nature of preaching and suggests it is an inherently elusive venture. This elusiveness is the focus of the next chapter.

5

The Parabler

For if anything is true of black women, it is how consistently they have (deliberately, I suspect) defied classification.

—Toni Morrison

By 1993, Toni Morrison was met with a thundering ovation whenever she approached a rostrum to give a lecture. What usually followed was a reverent silence, the kind reserved for clairvoyance rather than mere celebrity. The quiet held questions that a century ago may have filled church pews: What makes genuine faith turn venomous and poison the soul? Can one move forward without a reason for living? And if so, how? What living horrors are worse than death? What are the aims of human life? Morrison's calm, warm voice was the first answer to these questions. The second and subsequent answers were woven into her prose—so elegant it rivaled poetry. In her lectures, she dove into the paradoxes, contradictions, and absurdities of life, attentive both to the continuing grip of the past and the possibilities for newness. The clarity of her moral compass and depth of her wisdom on the human condition made her a modern-day Qoheleth. And much like Ecclesiastes, her novels carry "a strange mixture of piety and impiety, belief and disbelief, wide-eyed wonder and cynical world weariness, orthodoxy and heresy . . . all strung together in a single structure."[1]

Though biblical sages had various roles, one important aspect was literary. Their writings explored "creation, justice as cosmic and social order, retribution, theodicy, the suffering of the righteous, the nature and character of God, and moral behavior."[2] Drawing on insights from their ancestors as well as from observation and experience, they developed keen understandings of the human condition.[3] Though there is often a clear shared mission between the prophets and the sages, some important distinctions shape the reception of their words.[4] The prophet wants people to "hear, decide, and obey," while the sage "summons them to understand and to learn."[5] The prophet's theology is largely vertical or theocentric, centered on the words of Yahweh as indicated in the prophetic formula "Thus speaks Yahweh."[6] By contrast, the sage's theology is more horizontal and anthropocentric, because sages could focus on either secular or religious matters and were encouraged to study their own tradition as well as the wisdom of other peoples and nations.[7] In doing so, sages leaned heavily on literary devices such as allegory, debate, and parable or *māšāl* to communicate wisdom. The sage provides an apt frame for thinking about Toni Morrison as a wise woman whose writings examine the riddle of life.

Morrison's creative works are legion and span multiple genres. Though also a playwright, librettist, children's author, and essayist, she earned most recognition as a novelist. She insisted on making her novels aural experiences, describing language as consequential and eventful, but she nevertheless bridged the gap between the page and face-to-face encounter with numerous public readings and speeches.[8] The framing for these addresses varied but included commencement and convocation speeches, tributes, meditations, and "remarks"—a nebulous category that, as in some African American church traditions, typically involves short exhortations and words of commendation. The aims of Morrison's speeches varied with context, but overall those speeches reveal her as a valiant witness and sage.

And while a number of Morrison's addresses illumine her role as sage, one stands out: the Nobel Laureate Lecture on Literature given on December 7, 1993. The lecture has remarkable hybridity and has been described in sermonic terms.[9] The fact that it focuses on a parable, interprets that parable by alluding to Scripture, and emphasizes self-examination and ethical action justifies sermonic comparison. But more, this address offers vital insight on the edifying role of ancestral wisdom and its significance in African American preaching.

MORRISON THE WITNESS

While known for maintaining her privacy, Morrison relayed the broad contours of her life story in multiple interviews. Yet certain biographical details concerning her vocation and its evolution stand out. Chloe Ardelia Wofford, who would later become known publicly as Toni Morrison, was born on February 18, 1931, in Lorain, Ohio. Her father, George Wofford, was a shipbuilder and steelworker who spent his early years in Cartersville, Georgia, before moving to Ohio. Ella "Ramah" Wofford (née Willis), Morrison's mother, had moved to Ohio from Greenville, Alabama, as a child. The couple married in Lorain and had five children: Lois, Chloe, Robert (who died shortly after birth), George, and Raymond.

Morrison spent a considerable amount of time with the maternal side of her family, including her grandparents, John Solomon and Ardelia Willis. She also had memories of her great-grandmother, Millicent MacTeer, whose entry into a room commanded so much respect that her male relatives would rise from their seats.[10] Morrison attributes this response to her great-grandmother's role as a midwife—a revered role in African American communities.[11] Midwives did more than deliver children and offer medical care; they often functioned as spiritual advisors. Working on the boundaries between life and death positioned them as intercessors and as stewards of cultural wisdom.

Growing up in Lorain alongside immigrants from Czechoslovakia, Hungary, Italy, Poland, Romania, Scotland, and Yugoslavia made Morrison aware of the cultural significance of language.[12] At home, she became conscious of African American linguistic patterns, noticing that "when something terribly important was to be said, it was highly sermonic, highly formalized, biblical in a sense, and easily so," and family members "could move easily into the language of the King James Bible and then back to standard English, and then segue into language that we would call street."[13]

Faith formation played an important role in Morrison's childhood. She was schooled in superstitions, myths, ghost stories, and her mother's practice of interpreting dreams.[14] Her family attended Greater Saint Matthews African Methodist Episcopal Church, where her father became an officer and her mother and brother sang in the choir. Morrison describes her mother's singing voice as exceptional and remembers that people traveled long distances to hear her solos. Skilled in many genres, Ramah Wofford's singing was, according to Morrison, "a way of speaking" that revealed her state of mind as she moved through the day.[15] Later a similar musicality would propel her daughter's writing.

Scripture reading and song shaped the worship services at Greater Saint Matthews, but other members of her family were having a different experience as Roman Catholics. Morrison sometimes worshiped with these relatives. Initially a close relationship with a cousin was a primary motivation, but at some point there was an internal shift. The combination of story, drama, and ritual increasingly appealed to her, and she converted to Catholicism at age twelve, taking the name Anthony (after Saint Anthony of Padua) at her baptism.[16] She would give this baptismal name more significance by urging classmates who struggled to say "Chloe" to call her "Toni" instead.[17] Later, Morrison would speak of the unifying dimension of the Latin Mass and relish in the call to linger with the passion and contemplate the life that emerges after death.[18] Coupled with the abiding influence of her mother's singing, the Catholic Church's mysteries and symbols laid a spiritual foundation for Morrison that proved durable even as her formal affiliation with organized religion shifted.

Morrison attended Howard University in Washington, DC, where she studied literature and classics. Eager to embody texts as well as read them, she thrived as one of the Howard Players, an acclaimed theater group. She graduated in 1953 and continued studying literature in a master's program at Cornell University, graduating in 1955. Several years of teaching followed, first at Texas Southern University in Houston and then back at her beloved Howard. In 1958, she married Harold Morrison, an architect, and soon had two sons, Harold Ford Morrison and Slade Morrison, both of whom she had baptized in the Catholic Church. The marriage ended in 1964, and Morrison moved to Syracuse, New York, to accept a position as a textbook editor with the L. W. Stringer Company. When Stringer was subsequently acquired, she moved to New York to work for Random House.

Morrison's gifts as an editor proved formidable. As one of only a few African American editors at major publishing houses at the time, she supported her authors through critique as well as fierce advocacy. She worked with writers who exposed clichéd representations of African American life: Muhammad Ali, Toni Cade Bambara, Lucille Clifton, Angela Davis, Henry Dumas, Leon Forrest, Gayl Jones, and James Alan McPherson. Morrison also shepherded *The Black Book* (1974), a foundational text that brings readers into an archive of African American history through selected primary source materials.[19] Whatever the form, helping writers bear witness to the range of Black experience and longing energized her.

Despite the demands of editing, she made time to write early in the morning before her children awoke, and as early as 1966 she was seeking a publisher for a work in progress of her own that later became *The Bluest Eye* (1970). She soon finished her next novel, *Sula* (1973), which was nominated for the National Book Award. When "the Sisterhood," a circle of Black women writers, began meeting monthly in New York, Morrison joined June Jordan, Ntozake Shange, Alice Walker, and several other esteemed women who listened to one another and offered critique. By this time, however, her imprint on the canon was clear. *Song of Solomon* (1977) earned the National Book Critics Circle Award. Her subsequent novels, *Tar Baby* (1981), *Jazz* (1992), *Paradise* (1997), *Love* (2003), *A Mercy* (2008), *Home* (2012), and *God Bless the Child* (2015) also elicited wide praise and commercial success. *Beloved* (1987) won the 1988 Pulitzer Prize. Despite the public recognition, she suggested her books had sacred origins: "I don't want to sound too mystical about it, but I feel like a conduit, I really do."[20]

Not confined to the novel, she branched into other forms, writing a short story, "Recitatif"; a play, *Dreaming Emmett*; and librettos in collaboration with Richard Danielpour. She and her son Slade wrote several books for children inspired by Aesop's fables. In addition, she produced a body of nonfiction concerning African American studies and American literary studies, including texts such as *Race-ing Justice, En-Gendering Power: Essays on Anita Hill, Clarence Thomas, and the Construction of Social Reality* (1992), and *Playing in the Dark: Whiteness and the Literary Imagination* (1993).

During much of this time, Morrison's fiction writing paralleled her career as a teacher. In 1983, she accepted a post at the State University of New York at Albany as the Alfred Schweitzer Chair in Humanities. She also taught at Bard, Yale, and Rutgers before joining the faculty at Princeton University in 1989 as the Robert F. Goheen Professor in the Humanities, where she taught until 2006. At Princeton, she taught courses in the humanities, creative writing, and African American studies. Intrigued by interdisciplinary work and eager to work across genres, she instituted the Atelier program, a collaborative learning model that linked students with accomplished artists such as Richard Danielpour, Yo-Yo Ma, Bernice Johnson Reagon, Toshi Reagon, Peter Sellars, and Hua Wenyi.

From the early 1990s through the 2010s, she was showered with honors and awards. In addition to the Nobel Prize for Literature, Morrison received the Légion d'Honneur (2010), the Presidential Medal of Freedom (2012), the National Hawthorne Medal (2000), the National Book Foundation Medal for Distinguished Contribution (1996), and the Chianti Ruffino Antico Fattore International Literary Prize (1990). The Toni Morrison Society was founded in 1993 to study and support scholarship on her work.

As one might expect, Morrison's literary work prompted a tremendous public response. Though she was not without her critics, she received a river of gushing praise. Some fans wrote to thank her for brief conversations on the street or to let her know they drove by her house hoping she would step outside. Teachers wrote to reflect on the experience of ushering students into her novels, and readers wrote from as far as Thailand, Spain, France, and Ghana to express their gratitude. In addition to notes of thanks, they sent CDs, recipes, birthday and Mother's Day greetings, book manuscripts, and poetry. For example, in gratitude for *Song of Solomon*, one reader composed a poem with some of Morrison's most memorable lines and images.[21] When fire destroyed her home, she lamented the loss of photographs, her sons' report cards, artwork, and a jade plant she had nurtured for decades.[22] Friends and readers wrote to express their condolences.

One has to wonder what effect such adulation had on Morrison's psyche given its intensity and how sustained it appears to have been over multiple decades. Whatever the impact, the devotion suggests she was seen as a spiritual guide as well as an intellectual. As a keeper of African American ancestral wisdom, she was held in a level of regard that paralleled that of her midwife great-grandmother, Millicent MacTeer. This role as sage undergirded and amplified the other formal titles Morrison held.

As early as 1976 her work, whether fiction or nonfiction, tended to focus on moral imagination. In a piece titled "Moral Inhabitants" given at a symposium hosted by the Lutheran Church of America to celebrate the nation's bicentennial, she recounts a series of racist statements made by prominent American political and military leaders and concludes, "Our past is bleak. Our future dim. But I am not reasonable. A reasonable man adjusts to his environment. An unreasonable man does not. All progress, therefore, depends on the unreasonable man." She goes on to encourage her listeners to take more responsibility for the country's lack of resolve: "We are the moral inhabitants of the globe. To deny this, regardless of our feeble attempts to live up to it, is to lie in prison." Yet, unwilling to give the world's mysterious cruelty the last word in her address, she stresses that there is a twin "mystery of beauty, of light, the canary that sings on the skull" and that grace is "wholly free and available to us."[23]

During the succeeding decades, her speeches and lectures addressed race, history, globalization, and politics, though largely in connection with art's role in catalyzing a more humane world. Art, Morrison asserts, encourages us to move "into bearing witness to the world as it is and as it should be."[24] This moral imperative led her to become an ardent supporter of Barack Obama's 2008 presidential campaign and write opinion pieces criticizing the racism and nationalism that proliferated during the 2016 presidential election.

Morrison died on August 5, 2019, at age eighty-eight. The work she left behind reveals a profound grasp of history, a love for African American culture and humankind, and a commitment to sharpening moral imagination. Moreover, Morrison's works functioned for many as forms of spiritual nourishment. She fed her readers and listeners the manna of self-knowledge and ancestral history, both of which have the effect of cleansing and suturing the wounds of slavery and colonialism.

LITERARY SAGE

Morrison's voice as a novelist informs her reception as a lecturer, so before turning to her Nobel lecture it is important first to comment on some of the goals that ground her creative writing. Rather than pursuing her art for the sake of pleasure alone, Morrison makes it clear that her writing is driven by an ethical agenda and a strong sense of what fiction "ought to do."[25] Her aims are to explore African American cultural wisdom, hoping to "clarify the roles that have become obscured," "identify those things in the past that are useful and those things that are not," and offer content that nourishes and inspires her readers.[26] Naturally these tasks require engaging the imagination in edifying ways.[27] In keeping with the etymology of "edify" (*aedes*, Latin for "temple"), she is creating a shelter of meaning where the mind can abide and where endangered cultural principles can be incubated.[28] Much like Flannery O'Connor, who described converting readers or trying to "prove the existence of the supernatural" as "low motives," Morrison is interested in the drama of human life and what it shows us about agency, forgiveness, self-determination, and love.[29]

EMBEDDING SERMONS IN A NOVEL

Morrison's novels *Beloved* and *Paradise* include memorable sermons offered by characters.[30] In *Beloved* readers get an early hint about the significance of the proclaimed word when Sethe, the novel's protagonist, thinks back on a word uttered by the preacher at her child's funeral: "Beloved."[31] The word is chiseled on a headstone and into Sethe's consciousness. Over the course of the novel, that chiseled word becomes a sermon in itself, continually opening to new and deeper layers of meaning.

Yet the central preacher in *Beloved* proves to be Baby Suggs, holy, Sethe's mother-in-law. Like Sethe, Baby Suggs, holy is inspired by a historical figure— Mary Garner, an enslaved woman of deep faith who, along with her husband, Simon; son, Robert; daughter-in-law, Margaret (often called "Peggy"); and four grandchildren escaped with a large group of others from Kentucky to Cincinnati, Ohio, on January 27, 1856. Once the Ohio River was frozen, the family rode over the ice in a sleigh hitched to two horses.[32] The family was pursued and their enslavers were at the door when Margaret killed her three-year-old daughter, Mary (who may have been the elder Mary's namesake) and attempted to kill her other three children, Thomas, Samuel, and Priscilla. When Morrison read about the family while editing *The Black Book*, she was struck by the fact that Mary Garner witnessed the murder and attempted murder of her grandchildren and "neither encouraged nor discouraged her daughter-in-law,—for under similar circumstances she should probably have done the same."[33] That haunting line revealed the moral quandary slavery presented and the central dilemma *Beloved* explores.

In the novel, Baby Suggs's tender touch and soothing voice counsels Sethe after the murder. "Lay em down, Sethe. Sword and shield. Down. Down."[34] Even though decades of overwork had warped and wearied Baby Suggs's body, her soft, wise voice proves to be just the balm needed by Sethe and others in Cincinnati's Black community. Unconstrained by formal ecclesiastical structures, she is free to love her community with abandon:

> Accepting no title of honor before her name, but allowing a small caress after it, she became an unchurched preacher, one who visited pulpits and opened her great heart to those who could use it. In winter and fall she carried it to AME's and Baptists, Holinesses and Sanctifieds, the Church of the Redeemer and the Redeemed.[35]

When the weather allowed, Baby Suggs preached outdoors in an area called "the Clearing," which was at once open, or unobstructed and enclosed by a thicket of trees.[36] The Clearing seems to correspond with the Hush Arbors where the enslaved worshiped. By emphasizing the openness of the Clearing, Morrison also provides a link to the broad spaces that God gives to the faithful as a refuge after delivering them from suffering: "He delivered me from my strong enemy, and from those who hated me. . . . He brought me out into a broad place; he delivered me, because he delighted in me" (Ps. 18:17, 19). "Out of my distress I called on the LORD; the LORD answered me and set me in a broad place" (Ps. 118:5).

Whether in church or in the solace of the Clearing, the community receives something more from Baby Suggs than the typical sermon. Her preaching consists of bearing her heart to the listeners, of expressing her yearnings for them in word and gesture. And perhaps even more striking, her preaching is part announcement, part invitation, and part call—a calling forward, that is, a summoning of the listeners that collapses the distance between speaker and audience in order to facilitate a more intimate sacred encounter.[37] In this vein, as one who calls, Baby Suggs signifies the feminized depiction of Wisdom who calls in Proverbs 1:20, 24; 9:3; and particularly 8:1–4:

> Does not wisdom call,
>   and does not understanding raise her voice?
> On the heights, beside the way,
>   at the crossroads she takes her stand;
> beside the gates in front of the town,
>   at the entrance of the portals she cries out:
> "To you, O people, I call,
>   and my cry is to all that live."

Like Wisdom, Baby Suggs's voice is not limited to "the sacral sphere of the sanctuary."[38] Her message resounds in the forest, giving it an Edenic quality as her words take root in the heart of each listener. Surrounded by all that greenness, the human capacity for newness and growth, for slowly evolving and continually finding divine light, is writ large. Spatially and rhetorically, the sermon is an occasion for expansion.

In addition to her setting, the form of Baby Suggs's preaching similarly reflects insight on the needs of souls battered by experiences of enslavement and its continuing effects on subsequent generations. Just before preaching, she utters a silent prayer of illumination, sets her walking stick aside, and begins by calling her listeners into themselves. And in a phrase reminiscent of Jesus' "Let the little children come to me" in Matthew 19:14, Baby Suggs begins by calling the children forward: "Let the children come!"[39] This work of self-collection first involves inviting children to laugh, then calling the men forward to dance, and finally calling the women forward to weep. Once heard by themselves and one another, inner portals open, freeing women to laugh and dance, men to weep and laugh, and children to weep and dance as desired. Together, with the trees and sky as witnesses, they bare their souls. Their hearts are also readied to receive the next part of Baby Suggs's incarnational message.

What follows is not a scolding or a message that exalts them above others. Neither is it a reflection on divine transcendence: "'Here,' she said, 'in this here place, we flesh; flesh that weeps, laughs; flesh that dances on bare feet in grass. Love it. Love it hard.'" The call is to cherish themselves in the face of hostility, to love their own bodies—seeing goodness deep within as well as without, to cultivate their own imaginations, and be generous toward themselves.[40]

What Baby Suggs offers is a window into the community's own beauty and wholeness, and both are essential to healing. She closes her exhortation by moving out of the verbal, instead using her dancing body to communicate the remainder of her message while the community sings.[41] Baby Suggs's message blesses and reintegrates body, mind, and spirit. Her regard for the listeners and vision for their flourishing are inescapable. Clearly, for Baby Suggs preaching is not an exchange between an expert or luminary and the laity, and it is certainly not an exchange between superior and subordinate. Something purer takes place. Preaching consists of a human-to-human encounter, a moment when one human beholds others in the light of God. Using her method as a homiletical template, one evaluates the sermon on the basis of its capacity to illumine what it means to be human, what it means to be reliant on other humans, the natural world, and God.

And further, the efficacy of Baby Suggs's message is not determined by the immediate balm it offers alone, but by the way it reverberates in the memory of the listeners.[42] Nine years later during a crisis of loneliness, the sermon offers Sethe passage to a light-filled place in her mind that makes it easier for her to face the challenge of daily living. The verdancy of the message over time suggests its divine origin even though the preacher herself proves vulnerable to despair and dies shortly after preaching so lovingly. Ultimately, in *Beloved*, Morrison offers a story in which a sermon enacts a lasting vision of human flourishing.

In another narrative example drawn from the novel *Paradise*, Morrison gives her readers two adjacent images of sermons at a small-town wedding. The guests who wait in anticipation have dressed in a bright spectrum of color and have breathed joyous energy into the sanctuary. Thirsting for a word that will speak to the miracle of love and the importance of this particular union for the town, with hearts open, they look up into the face of Rev. Senior Pulliam. Immune to the happiness in the room, he offers a bitter message that verges on blasphemy: "You do not deserve love regardless of the suffering you have endured. . . . You can only earn—by practice and careful contemplation—the right to express it and you have to learn how to accept it. Which is to say you have to earn God." The preacher's venom keeps dripping. "Love is not a gift," he says, "It is a diploma. . . . God is not interested in you." He closes with a cold blessing on the "pure and holy."[43]

If the telos or ultimate end of all preaching is love, and if the facility for sharing love is the measure by which all homiletical rhetoric is tested, Pulliam's message is an anti-sermon.[44] His words cultivate spiritual bondage by instilling fear, denying grace, and overall inverting the wild generosity of the gospel. Ultimately, his is a chthonic message.

To be clear, the problem at the heart of Pulliam's message is not in the insistence on challenge or discipline—both of which are vital homiletical tools—but in his proclamation of a loveless, graceless deity who is unconcerned about humankind, "who is interested only in Himself."[45] These are the words of an apostate preacher who not only fails to read the joy of the moment but fails in his fundamental role of tending the souls in his care during the course of the sermon. While Pulliam adheres to the superficial criteria of a sermon because he shares a message offered by a cleric in a liturgy for the instruction of those gathered, the message has a contaminating effect due to his withered theology and corrupted motives. Rather than being an occasion when human longing is satisfied by a word of grace, the experience is one of methodical and malicious withholding.

Rev. Richard Misner, by contrast, has a deep regard for grace. He overhears the message that has been preached by Pulliam and, to mitigate the harm to the listeners, takes an oak cross off the wall in the rear of the church. Then he stands, silently holding the cross before the listeners, unphased by the clock.[46] He hopes they can absorb the pure love coming through the symbol and pouring forth from his own heart. This response by Misner is a bona fide sermon. It reveals that, apart from the words spoken, a sermon has semiotic force; it is a sign that mediates divine grace and shields listeners from evil.

In each case above, Morrison's readers overhear sermons.[47] That is to say, truth is mediated indirectly through the engagement with the characters. The indirection gives listeners space to take in the story and come to their own conclusions about the implications for their lives. So when Morrison's characters preach, they help the novel fulfill certain ends—namely, the depiction of healthy and unhealthy visions of authority and the communication of spiritual nourishment to the reader.

NOVEL AS SERMON

In addition to creating scenes in which readers overhear sermons, Morrison participates in the sermon genre through her use of the novel as a whole. David Z. Wehner reads Morrison's novel *Song of Solomon* as a meditation on the meaning of rebirth for African Americans given the distorting and deathly influence of whiteness.[48] As the novel unfolds, the protagonist, Milkman Dead, discovers that certain refusals of his inherited worldview are necessary if he is to find true wholeness or, in Morrison's words, "learn to live this life intensely and well."[49] The novel's christological references suggest that resurrection becomes possible only after shedding the acquisitive individualism with which he has been indoctrinated.[50] Overall, the novel prompts reflection on what a full and vibrant life entails for African Americans. Yet Morrison stresses that spurring reflection is only part of her goal: "I want my fiction to urge the reader into active participation in the nonnarrative, nonliterary experience of the text, which makes it difficult for the reader to confine himself to a cool and distant acceptance of data."[51] Morrison's aim is edification. Ultimately, *Song of Solomon* functions as a "conversion narrative outside the Christian paradigm."[52]

Framing the novel as a conversion narrative coheres with a long history of using the novel for sermonic ends. Zora Neale Hurston, for instance, used the novel as a sermonic tool in a number of works, but chiefly *Their Eyes Were Watching God* (1937), which is propelled in part by a grandmother's thwarted desire to preach: "Ah wanted to preach a great sermon about colored women sittin' on high, but they wasn't no pulpit for me. . . . Ah said Ah'd save de text for you."[53] She passes the text to her granddaughter, Janie, whose testimony of self-definition functions as the novel's central epiphany narrative. Janie's prophecy about Black women's agency creates a disciple in Pheoby, a friend who feels "ten feet higher" after listening and is determined to live differently.

Through the act of bearing witness, Janie evolves as well. At the novel's end, she "called in her soul to come and see."[54] These words echo Jesus calling the disciples to "come and see" in John 1:39.

Though Morrison makes it clear that Hurston was not an influence on her until well after her own voice had developed, other writers have preached through novels. Almost a century before Hurston, Harriet Beecher Stowe's novel *Uncle Tom's Cabin* was written in the shadow of the pulpit that she, as a woman and layperson, could not access in her denominational tradition—a situation that at least on the surface reflects that of Morrison as a professed Catholic. Stowe shared the zeal of her father, Lyman Beecher, and her brother Henry Ward Beecher, both noted preachers, and asserted that she preached through literature. In his study of *Uncle Tom's Cabin*, David Reynolds observes that Stowe functioned as a lay preacher in personal letters. In an 1829 letter to her brother George, she explicitly accepted the mantle: "It is as much my vocation to preach on paper as it is of my brothers to preach viva voce."[55]

German nuns used letters to exhort one another and give spiritual counsel to clergy and political leaders during the fourteenth century, so Stowe was not alone in using this approach.[56] Yet after seeing a vision of a tortured slave, she was inspired to write and found the novel to be a fitting medium for her preaching vocation.[57] In *Uncle Tom's Cabin: Or Life among the Lowly*, and *A Key to Uncle Tom's Cabin* (1853), she recasts nineteenth-century America into a scene for dilemmas depicted in Scripture: Canada was heaven and the Ohio River was the Jordan River that the escapees sought to cross.[58] These depictions were so vivid and the core narrative so arresting that Bible sales increased in response.[59]

More than an author of sentimental fiction, Stowe became something of a revivalist who sought to convert her listeners through her pulpit-page.[60] Charles Campbell even suggests that Stowe may have been a precursor of the New Homiletic, which emphasized narrative preaching.[61] Though limited by the lens of white motherhood, Stowe used her novel to sensitize readers to the plight of enslaved mothers. [62] She invited readers to identify with Eliza, an enslaved mother seeking to escape to Canada with her son, Harry:

> If it were *your* Harry, mother, or your Willie, that were going to be torn from you by a brutal trader, to-morrow morning,—if you had seen the man, and heard that the papers were signed and delivered, and you had only from twelve o'clock till morning to make good your escape,—how fast could *you* walk? How many miles could you make in those few brief hours, with the darling at your bosom,—the little sleepy head on your shoulder,—the small, soft arms trustingly holding on to your neck?[63]

Eliza's story is framed by those of other enslaved mothers who would rather see their children die than live in bondage. In stories that foreshadow Margaret Garner's situation, an unnamed mother jumps into the Red River with her infant in arms, and Cassy, another distraught mother, poisons her newborn son after the sale of two older children.[64] Individually and collectively these stories function as exempla—as sermon illustrations—designed to appeal to the reader's (presumably Christian) conscience. Each tormenting narrative points to the notion that Christian charity demands abolition.

Drawing connections between Stowe's work and Morrison's, Cynthia Wolff argues that Harriet Beecher Stowe's labor in *Uncle Tom's Cabin* is "completed" in Morrison's *Beloved*.[65] Morrison's questions, however, are more layered and daring, considering the social implications of infanticide in the context of enslavement as well as the spiritual consequences for subsequent generations. Further, she plumbs these issues with a syncretic vision of African American spirituality. For example, an African cosmology features prominently in the novel. In *Toni Morrison's Spiritual Vision: Faith, Folktales, and Feminism in Her Life and Literature*, Nadra Nittle argues that the character Beloved may symbolize the *abiku*, a Yoruba term for young children who die before puberty and can be repeatedly reborn, causing cycles of emotional pain for their parents.[66] Similarly, when Beloved appears pregnant with hair consisting of vines or fish, Nittle suggests she is a manifestation of "the Orisha Yemaya" who "is associated with fertility, water, and all sea life."[67] With such images, Morrison foregrounds an African diasporic worldview. Like the biblical sages who draw on multiple wisdom traditions, Morrison makes Yoruba wisdom central to the meaning-making process.

Beloved has been aptly described by Kathleen Marks as an apotropaic text—a text that reflects on evil with the purpose of warding off evil.[68] One might think of the novel as an exorcism that summons wickedness in order to purge it and enable a fresh and more balanced life experience. Using mythology, "the first speech of the soul," the novel seeks "to achieve a clearing and an atonement"—tasks best understood as "soteriological."[69] So while tragic elements play a primary role, they are designed to facilitate the kind of bountiful life that can emerge only after focused discernment. One must distinguish that which is "fruitful, potential, and unitive from what is fallow, ill-conceived, and injurious."[70] In other words, the novel attempts to weed and aerate the reader's imagination so that new life becomes possible. Indeed, the love Baby Suggs preaches about remains beyond the community's reach until this weeding and aeration takes place.[71]

As an apotropaic sermon, *Beloved* has a dual effect. On the one hand, it clears by illuminating that which is shrouded—namely, the ancestors who died in the Middle Passage and under the brutality of chattel slavery to whom the novel is dedicated. At the same time, the novel clears the "debt of pain" bequeathed by these ancestors for the sake of communal wholeness and freedom.[72] Some cultural fragments of the past should be named, explained, and then rejected in order to move out of the death grip of the past. This double clearing animates *Beloved*, making it an apotropaic sermon that, in the words of Kathleen Marks, "enacts a benediction" while also "in a sense saying, 'Get thee behind me, Satan' in its rejection of the glamour and pomp of an evil persisting power."[73] This twofold effect of benediction and eschewing evil is also evident in biblical apotropaic texts like Psalm 91.[74]

Moreover, this moral clarity, this insistence on probing good and evil, reveals Morrison's proclamatory aim. She assumes the task of moral instruction and does not fear taking on a preacherly tone. Morrison occasionally even elicits resistance for these approaches—much like traditional preachers.[75] Such resistance underscores that the proclamatory elements exist and are readily recognizable, even if some readers seek a different kind of literary experience.

PROCLAMATORY ATTRIBUTES OF MORRISON'S NOVELS

A few deliberate features of Morrison's work support this novelistic view of the sermon. The first concerns language, which for Morrison is a means of fashioning a narrative framework within which existential questions can be examined. Language, she argues, should "limn the actual, imagined and possible lives of its speakers, readers, writers" and illumine a path to meaning.[76] Language also contributes to the function of the novel, and Morrison stresses that a novel should be formative: "It should have something in it that enlightens; something in it that opens the door and points the way. Something in it that suggests what the conflicts are, what the problems are. But it need not solve those problems because it is not a case study, it is not a recipe."[77] The aims Morrison articulates are consonant with those of many preachers.

She similarly values the performativity of language. Aurality plays an essential role in this regard, and she tries to make her novels sonic experiences. Her language, she explains, "should try deliberately to make you stand up and make you feel something profoundly in the same way that a Black preacher requires his congregation to speak, to join him in the sermon, to behave in a certain way, to stand up and to weep and to cry and to accede or to change and to modify—to expand on the sermon that is being delivered."[78]

One strong counterargument for those who see no overlapping area between the vocations of the novelist and the preacher concerns audience.

Reading a novel is a solo venture. When one listens to a sermon, one ought to understand that one is part of a community of listeners. Yet while Morrison honors the respite and depth of wisdom that are fostered by the solitary aspect of reading, the dynamic she seeks to set up is not solely between author and reader; the intent is for the reader to turn inward and then outward.[79] The world created by the novel places the reader in the role of ethical agent in a broader social milieu. Faithful living in the broader world is the expected consequence.

Morrison laments that her work is often compared to that of writers like James Joyce and William Faulkner—not because she does not respect their works, but because she felt her work ought to be examined and critiqued on its own terms and examined on the basis of its fidelity to African American culture.[80] Given her spiritual and didactic aims, performative language, and communal focus, a homiletical frame may contribute to the process of examining her work on its own terms. Whether through specific sermons featured in her novels or novels understood as sermons in their entirety, Morrison participates in the sermon genre by authoring sermons.

MORRISON THE PARABLER

Morrison's 1993 Nobel lecture similarly has homiletical dimensions, revealing her as a sage who stewarded ancestral wisdom through story, riddle, and metaphor.[81] This address sits on the border between sermon and lecture. First, it is a face-to-face encounter because it was shared before a live audience. Second, she focuses on a parable, a rhetorical device in which one idea is illumined by being "cast beside" another, often through a tale, allegory, riddle, or metaphor.[82]

In Morrison's parable, a wise woman—in this case old, African American, blind, and the daughter of slaves—lives on the edge of town. Her home on the periphery suggests she has the keen perception of an outsider, perhaps even that of a seer. A few young people approach her with a puzzle. "'Old woman,'" one of them says, "'I hold in my hand a bird. Tell me whether it is living or dead.'"[83]

The question falls on weary ears. Years of isolation have taken a toll on the old woman. Hearing only a taunt in their question, after a long silence she throws the question back at the youth. "It is in your hands," she says.[84] That is to say, whether the bird is living or dead, the young people with their cruel game are responsible. Frustrated, the youth voice their outrage. "Why didn't you reach out, touch us with your soft fingers, delay the sound bite, the lesson, until you knew who we were?"[85] Set aside your ego, they seem to say, and share your wisdom with us, however imperfect it may be. Reveal something about the beauty, horror, and challenge of being human. Then, responding to their own hunger and the old woman's, they begin a story about slaves en route to an unclear destination, their predicaments only hinted at by the image of "placenta in a field" and bodies anxious for food, warmth, and deeper sustenance.[86]

Softened by the story, the old woman reciprocates their gesture of connection. "I trust you now. I trust you with the bird that is not in your hands because you have truly caught it," she says. "Look. How lovely it is, this thing we have done—together."[87]

HOMILETICAL ELEMENTS

Morrison stresses the world-shaping power of language by sermonizing on a parable.[88] A few homiletical elements are worth noting. First, the tower of Babel (Gen. 11:1–9) plays a key role. Morrison places this allusion in the middle of the talk and uses it to consider language's capacity to help us achieve paradise. While her treatment of Genesis 11 is spare, she makes it clear that humans need the generosity, humility, and wonder that tend to emerge when studying another language. In Morrison's hands, Scripture provides a lens for reading the human condition.

Though Morrison does not proselytize, her message does have some religious scaffolding. The reference to Genesis serves as one example. Another is more deeply embedded. In earlier drafts of her address, she has a different opening:

> "Once upon a time there was an old woman. Blind but wise." Or was it an old man? A guru perhaps or a mullah. Possibly a rabbi. Or a griot soothing restless children. In any case, I have heard this story in a number of versions from the lore of many lands.[89]

This parable, she seems to suggest, is a unifying one and is not owned by or its meaning dictated by any single religious tradition or history of interpretation. The listener has a level of authority in shaping the meaning, too, and this provides for a more receptive and less reductive hearing. Elsewhere Morrison stresses the community-forming nature of myth—implying that myth is not the fashioning of a story by one interpreter but a collective endeavor. "A myth is whatever concept of truth or reality a whole people has arrived at over years of observation," she explains. "It must be the collective creation of—and acceptance by—hordes of anonymous people."[90] She insists on opening the field of interpreters.

A second homiletical element concerns the approach to truth. Morrison's approach has much in common with Søren Kierkegaard, who though aiming to create Christian disciples through his writings, emphasized the indirect apprehension of truth.[91] Kierkegaard was convinced that indirect communication turned the addressee inward, requiring one to take more responsibility for meaning making. In keeping with the Latin sense of authorship that involves prompting growth, Kierkegaard functioned like a midwife, helping the reader labor and give birth to personal meaning.[92] Similarly, by design Morrison's parable places the bulk of the interpretive task in the listener's lap. Truth is not predigested and divvied out; the listener must mull over the message to discern its character and weight.

For Morrison, storytelling, in this case parable, provides a means of exploring moral imagination while avoiding the "nonlanguage of command."[93] Sermons have long had a disciplinary function, often serving to issue commandments and elicit obedience to Scripture, the preacher, communal norms, and God without also providing sufficient insight on the layered and contextualized nature of texts, the intrinsic limitations of the preacher, the faith community's history of sometimes falling short, and the Holy One's bafflingly enigmatic ways. Morrison's approach explores communal values while holding on to a critical degree of ambivalence. She is eager to examine that which is beneficial as well as that which is dross.

Along this line, Morrison minimizes explanations that are driven by a white gaze. She preferred to plant a seed that would continually germinate in the mind over an extended period. Her method involves raising questions and reflecting on why they matter instead of answering them outright. By exploring what is at stake in a question, she helped her audience plumb ideas. This meant pondering, pushing back, and testing limits and possibilities. Afterward listeners were better equipped to recognize and transcend broken norms and juxtapose warped visions of themselves with new ways of being. As Bernice Johnson Reagon explained in a letter of gratitude, Morrison showed African Americans ways to move toward reinvention and self-definition, ways to plumb new depths of agency and self-discovery.[94]

SLOW PATH TO TRUTH

The epiphanies Morrison fosters require percolation: "I don't want to give my readers something to swallow. I want to give them something to feel and think about, and I hope that I set it up in such a way that it is a legitimate thing, and a valuable thing."[95] Her method presents a stark contrast to preaching that seeks instant acceptance without serious or extended contemplation.

This demand for immediate and complete assent is often more reflective of consumer advertising culture than an understanding of faith development, which tends to build slowly and cumulatively as new insights are weighed alongside personal and communal experiences.

Jonathan Sacks, an Orthodox rabbi, suggests that rather than always being immediately apparent, biblical truth often takes time and experience to recognize.[96] Because it has a divine source, truth cannot be fully grasped by humans. So, as Ockert Meyer explains, it is mediated through traces and glimpses. These partial and progressive experiences of truth nevertheless have an uncanny sufficiency when slowly absorbed. Truth can even have an efficacy that complements and exceeds abstract theological statements, as Meyer makes clear:

> Perhaps therefore the best sermons that I have listened to—the ones that I can remember, without necessarily being able to remember a single word—are those that I can remember, not for what they said to me but what they did to me, not for what I took from them, but how they took hold of me, not for what I saw in them, but what they saw in me. Or again in the words of Kierkegaard, "You cannot have truth in such a way that you catch it; but only in such a way that it catches you."[97]

ALIGNING WITH JESUS' METHOD

Morrison's commitment to slow, penetrating apprehension of truth seems to be in sync with Meyer's experience. This approach also has much in common with Jesus' method of using parables. While often taking narrative form, Jesus' parables, according to C. H. Dodd, consisted of "a metaphor or simile drawn from nature or common life, arresting the hearer by its vividness or strangeness, and leaving the mind in sufficient doubt about its precise application to tease it into active thought."[98] Some, like Adolf Jülicher, argue that each of Jesus' parables has a single point, but the broader consensus suggests a spectrum of meaning all under the umbrella of his mission.[99] Jesus' parables leave listeners with a puzzling sense that the world as they know it is off-kilter and create a longing for God's new alternative. Aptly described as "worldly" and "secular," Jesus' parables express his wild love for the world.[100] As Richard Lischer puts it in his study of New Testament parables, "To interpret a parable is to meet Jesus."[101]

Of course, one critical distinction between Jesus' method and Morrison's concerns mission. Jesus' parables form part of the corpus of the Synoptic Gospels and, though often opaque, clarify his unique identity. By contrast,

Morrison's parable stands alone. Hers is not explicitly framed by christological mission (though some listeners might with due effort make such a connection). The primary similarity between Jesus' approach and Morrisons's involves the use of parable to illumine the nature of truth. And as Richard Lischer makes clear, Jesus' "parables do not enshrine a body of truths but suggest a *method* of approaching and experiencing the truth."[102] This method is particularly fitting for exploring the mysteries, precarities, and absurdities of human life in a secular setting.

Parable also requires loosening one's grip on the kataphatic approach to Christian theology (which consists of making definite assertions about God) and leans more toward the apophatic way—saying less and being mindful that God defies and exceeds any description or explanation humans can conceive. As C. Clifton Black argues, "Christian preaching lies in that middle ground between sheer kataphrasis and pure apophrasis, at the intersection of Affirmation Avenue and Disavowal Drive."[103] Morrison's parable occupies this middle ground. It resists resolution. A response is demanded but not in the form of an "Amen." What is called for is an answer encompassing the whole of one's life, living with the truth in an ongoing way so that it shades moral obligations to God, self, and others.[104]

PRACTICAL AND AESTHETIC IMPLICATIONS

Morrison's parable reflects African American aesthetics. In her fictional writing, these features include aurality and the use of a chorus to reveal communal perspectives, even if that community consists of the natural world. In *Tar Baby*, for example, the communal voice emerges when "the trees hurt, fish are afraid, clouds report, and the bees are alarmed."[105] Elemental to her aesthetic is a communitarian ethos that still makes room for contrarian perspectives. In addition, she emphasizes self-definition, improvisation, functionalism, and, in keeping with the spirituals, a little turbulence or irresolution; the audience must live with some unanswered questions.[106] Supernatural phenomena also play a critical role, often through magic or superstition. Dual allegiances to the realms of the visible and the invisible fund an expansive and inventive worldview.

Yet above all, central to Morrison's aesthetic is the presence of an ancestor who provides spiritual nourishment in the form of a link to the past.[107] This presence may be mediated indirectly, as through the flowers and trees in *Beloved* that symbolize ancestral folk wisdom and cultural healing practices.[108] Or the ancestor may have a more explicit presence, as in the case of the old wise woman in the parable. Either way, the ancestor's wisdom reframes the present and has a "benevolent, instructive, and protective" influence.[109]

In emphasizing the role of ancestors, Morrison points to a crucial dynamic in African American preaching. Ancestral wisdom, whether implicit or explicit, is critical to cultivating a strong moral compass and a vibrant faith. Ancestors shape sermonic space and contribute to its gravity. Their influence is vital because Black life often involves increased vulnerability and a sense that one is living in the shadow of death.[110] Addressing the spiritual needs of people who feel an ongoing sense of precarity is an essential aspect of Black preaching.

Ancestral wisdom can undergird African American preaching in multiple ways. First, it creates a bridge between the conscious and the unconscious by revealing the edges of the temporal realm. Listeners are invited to see the empirical world as one part of the cosmos rather than the whole. Linear time is bracketed and enfolded into the lushness of sacred time—a realm where the ongoing communion with the ancestors becomes perceptible. There is, of course, an affective dimension at work here because remembering elicits the mutual care between the living and the dead, and along with that mutual affection comes insight. In other words, revelations, impressions, and way-opening ideas often emerge or crystallize as the curtain between the visible and invisible worlds is lifted. Ultimately, this heightened perception animates and propels the preaching endeavor.

At the level of theology, ancestral wisdom fuels reflection on the paradoxes and absurdities of Black life, often resulting in a healthy mix of skepticism and rugged hope. Ethically, reflecting on the witness of the ancestors brings up memories of their individual and collective sacrifice for subsequent generations and a consequent present-day obligation to live in the light of those sacrifices. This means becoming a faithful ancestor oneself and demonstrating fidelity to God and to past, present, and future generations.

As for hermeneutics, relating biblical texts to the documented experiences of African American saints or those depicted in myth or folklore, whether for introductory purposes or for comparison, contrast, or amplification, can help listeners experience Scripture as part of their own story. Through such cultural grafting, Christian identity does not subsume or erase cultural identity but reveals its significance. In *Black Preaching: The Recovery of a Powerful Art*, for example, Henry Mitchell notes that some preachers have a pattern of quoting their "parents, grandparents, and great-grandparents," and he compares this method of sharing ancestral wisdom with "the Hebrew oral tradition, which spoke of the deity as 'God of Abraham, Isaac, and Jacob.'" A vital link to the past is strengthened when a preacher probes Scripture "for what Grandma would reach into the Bible for" given the demands of the contemporary moment.[111] The interpretive strategies, logics, ethics, and longings of the ancestors are more likely to become embedded in the sermon as a result. Methods will vary depending on the particulars of a given congregation, occasion, or biblical text, but purposeful attention to the ancestor paves the way to a response from the listeners that is, in Morrison's words, "visceral, emotional," and "intellectual."[112]

Intentional focus on the ancestors may also have a corrective impact on preaching by imbuing a sacral energy to sermons. Religious language has withered under the pressures of media, polarization, and market-driven immediacy. Morrison laments that religious language has been "forced to kneel before the denominator that is most accessible, to bankrupt its subtlety, its mystery in order to bankroll its effect" and to sacrifice its "ambiguity, depth, and moral authority."[113] Fidelity to the ancestors can function as a check on these tendencies.

To be clear, preserving the ancestors' legacy is not the primary purpose of preaching. Summoning their presence is, however, a means of developing a culturally informed and humane vision of Christianity despite the wreckage of Christian colonialism. The ancestors offer reminders of what gives life true meaning and purpose, superseding the cheap, consumer-driven images of human life that saturate contemporary life. By carrying the memories of the witness of the ancestors, listeners tap into that part of themselves that is not beholden to the empirical world alone but is equally tied to the realm of the invisible.

Conclusion

Preaching with the Ancestors

> I regard African-American sermons as a paradigm of the structure of ambivalence that constitutes the black person's relationship to American culture and apprenticeship in it.
>
> —Hortense Spillers

In this book I have attempted to provide an atypical peek into the history of African American preaching by peering through the lenses of genre fluidity and fidelity to the ancestors. Curiosity has propelled my analysis, but so has a certain ambivalence about preaching that stems from the fact that, at least for the enslaved, antebellum sermons often functioned as violent disciplinary tools that caused psychological and spiritual harm. One cannot help noticing the number of accounts in which slave owners preached to people enslaved to them, to people enslaved to others, or to white congregations. In some cases, they preached immediately before or immediately after inflicting violence. Rev. John Sella Martin reports that a Presbyterian minister beat an enslaved man named Flanders to death and went straightaway to church to preach, using the homicide as a sermon illustration.[1] Another clergyman went to church and preached a sermon all the while knowing a young woman was tied to a post to be tortured by him upon his return.[2]

I raise these accounts not just to point out the brutality and hypocrisy that sometimes corrupted antebellum preaching but also to think about what it means to pick up the practice of preaching today in light of this history and in light of the fact that preaching remains susceptible to many forms of manipulation and control. The violence of the past is not over; it just seeps out in more subtle ways. The history of African American preaching indicates the valiant and largely successful attempt to counter the legacy of violence by making sermons spaces of spiritual nourishment rather than occasions for abuse, though those of us who are LGBTQ+ listeners, women listeners, and/ or living with disabilities sometimes feel the limits of these efforts.

On those occasions when I worry about the harm caused by preaching, my hopes are buttressed by the belief that there is more going on than is visible to the outward eye. I am convinced that sermons are spheres where the living and the dead mingle, much like they do in Communion or Eucharist when all the saints are gathered together. A sermon can be an encounter with the ancestors, rooting the listener's spiritual story into a longer communal history of faith and reminding the people of the larger spiritual family of which they are a part.

One obvious question that arises is how in such a fast-paced world do we maintain ties to the ancestors that are not merely nominal? Social media and online worship have changed preaching. The energy and pace are higher, the demand for simpler, easily digestible content has increased. Such content often requires less of a relationship between the preacher, listener, and faith community and a minimal sense of the past. In many cases, preachers feel pressure to defer to external norms of relevance. Larger social and economic forces—particularly in the United States—operate in ways that tend to alienate us from spirituality unless we approach it as a means of enhancing our participation in market systems. Hartmut Rosa, a German sociologist and political scientist who has thought extensively about the implications of acceleration on contemporary society, writes about the need for "oases of sustenance" amid the alienation of the modern world.[3] Drawing on Charles Taylor, he speaks of the need for humans to become more "porous" and to become "embedded in a *stream of life*" that includes visible and invisible realms.[4] Preaching can play this role, and African American preaching may be particularly disposed to do so, given the history of honoring ancestors.

I find the artist Betye Saar instructive on this front. One scholar describes Saar's work as "drenched in memory and past—in 'the realm of departed ancestors.'"[5] Saar imagines Black culture extending over time-space barriers, attributing the power of her work to what she calls "cumulative consciousness," which includes the recent past, the "nostalgic past" of her mother and aunt's lifetimes, and the ancient past—going even to the beginning of time. She is also inspired by visions, dreams, and contemplating the future.[6] What I find intriguing is Saar's sacramental understanding of time, her suggestion that the world is shaped by the ongoing activity of ancestors. Her vantage point seems fitting for those who see anamnesis as an essential dimension of preaching.

To be clear, the turn to the ancestors is not a stewing in the pain of the past; nor is it a strictly retrospective move. The turn to the ancestors reflects a belief that they have gifts to offer for the present moment. Listening for the ancestors is a way of acknowledging the web of love and wisdom in which we are held. That web includes the testimonies, strategies, perspectives, and prayers of those who lived and died under the weight of oppression and now live outside the grip of empire. Though fallible, they gleaned a vision of God and "of divine force working in the captive situation to free it."[7] They gleaned an angle on human worth that was not rooted in money, political power, external notions of beauty, or any other kind of acquisition but was grounded in tenderness, collectivity, and intimacy with the earth. Any understanding of spirituality or human freedom is faulty without such a foundation.

A few points of emphasis are in order. First, when drawing on the wisdom of ancestors, whether as part of performing biblical interpretation, explaining theology, or distilling ethical imperatives, the preacher should not presume to speak for the dead. That approach could too easily devolve into manipulating, mischaracterizing, or otherwise forgetting that when discussing the ancestors one is handling the sacred. Rather than presuming to speak for the ancestors, a better approach would involve finding ways to use quotation, folklore, or symbols (performative or otherwise) that enable the ancestors to speak for themselves. This humbler posture appreciates the ancestors' power to speak to the present moment on the one hand, while acknowledging the limits of our own perception.

Next, recognizing the presence of ancestors in sermonic space also requires respecting their limitations. Reading their witnesses through the lens of nostalgia or idolization is a failure to see who they are now, who they were, and what horizons framed their lives. Instead, preachers should consider the trajectory of their thought and explore the present-day faith practices that might be considered extensions of their faith practices. In other words, the practice of seeking and drawing on ancestral wisdom should not result in dwelling in the past or reliving traumatic experiences. Above all else, the ancestors bequeath insight that energizes, buoys, and broadens perspective. Their legacy inspires informed engagement in the present rather than retreating from its demands.

DISCERNMENT QUESTIONS FOR PREACHERS

Some ongoing questions for preachers, whether in traditional pulpits or other spaces, follow. Rather than simply doing what they did, how does our preaching build on the values of our ancestors faithfully? When does preaching go astray from the models we've inherited or the values that undergird those models, or when might proper adherence to form cloak betrayal of their ethics? And how does our memory of the ancestors provide a framework for addressing current social problems?

There are also implications for understanding divine revelation. An individual's sacred dialogue with God is informed by God's prior interactions with one's faith community and climaxes when that community brings eternity into time.[8] If part of the preacher's role is to guide a congregation as they live in history and help them discern God's hand in it, how might leaning on the witness of ancestors aid in this process?[9] How might their witness be drawn on to equip congregations to face the many uncertainties of the future?

The six sages featured in this book provide starting points for thinking through these questions. Each person held a high view of the ancestors and expressed this through genre-bending sermons that glorified God and highlighted issues of authority, embodiment, and the ephemeral nature of the preached word.[10] Walking along the homiletical shoreline involved moving in and out of the typical framework for sermons and revealing the genre's complexity and continuing evolution. In their own ways, they underscore the gospel's tendency to break molds and loosen the rigidity of long-held standards. At the same time, their approaches make room for a different posture of believing. Song, dance, quilting, meditations, and parables are holistic genres that simultaneously accommodate doubt and paradox, urging people toward a vision of faith that consists of more than a set of doctrinal propositions.

The inner lives of these preachers birthed unique ways of expressing spiritual wisdom through hybrid forms that, though largely illegible on the surface, ultimately expanded the sermon genre. The issues of genre and legibility bring to mind a famous legal case concerning a last will and testament. Cecil George Harris was a Canadian farmer who, in a moment of duress after a tractor accident, expressed his final wishes for the distribution of his assets by carving a statement with a knife onto a tractor fender. He died two days later, and the portion of the tractor fender with Harris's intentions was included in his case file. In addition to the Harris case, other "holographic" or handwritten wills have been inscribed on bedroom walls, furniture, eggshells, and napkins, to name just a few examples.[11] Each situation is unique and demands reflecting on the testator's circumstances and intentions as well as the aims of the law. Judges ask, What is it about the person's situation that led to this manner of expressing their final wishes? A similar question can be asked concerning sermons. In fact, this parallel has *already* been framed and treated as foundational for thinking about the history and continuing practice of preaching: "What is it about the *gospel* that demands this particular expression?"[12]

The preachers I have focused on seek to express the gospel in ways that are consistent with the approaches of their ancestors, whose culturally prized methods of wisdom-sharing and self-definition were often prohibited under the conditions of slavery and maligned long afterward. These methods point to the ongoing life of the ancestors, testifying to their spiritual triumph. And while I have focused on African American preaching, there are other cultures that reverence ancestors and see them as having an important role in Christian preaching. By exploring our similarities and differences, we could make important contributions to a decolonial homiletic.

Homiletical whiteness infects assumptions about which voices matter and how content ought to be arranged, and it devalues the interplay of body, culture, and time that often contributes to the vitality and integrity of Black preaching.[13] If the sermon is to be a site of expansion, of discovering God, neighbor, self, and earth, if it is to be a site of healing, wonder, and fruitful debate, then preaching will need a deeper communion with the ancestors. They can provide the accountability and energy needed to enrich our vision of spiritual thriving.

Mahalia Jackson, Rosie Lee Tompkins, Harriet Powers, Thea Bowman, Howard Thurman, and Toni Morrison provide a compass for us. Their genre-bending sermons do what all sermons should do: lay the groundwork for a new world.[14] No task is more daunting or more necessary. But thankfully the ancestors are still speaking.

Notes

Introduction

1. Jason C. Bivins, *Spirits Rejoice! Jazz and American Religion* (New York: Oxford University Press, 2015), 32.
2. Pauli Murray, "Collect for Poplarville" and "For Mack C. Parker," in *Dark Testament and Other Poems* (Norwalk, CT: Silvermine, 1970), 38–39.
3. Pauli Murray, *Pauli Murray: Selected Sermons and Writings*, ed. Anthony B. Pinn (Maryknoll, NY: Orbis, 2006), 207.
4. Isaiah 20:1–3; Jeremiah 27–28.
5. Beverly Mayne Kienzle, "Typology of the Medieval Sermon and Its Development in the Middle Ages: Report on a Work in Progress," in *De l'homélie au sermon: Histoire de la prédication médiévale, actes du colloque international de Louvain-la-Neuve*, ed. Jacqueline Hamesse and Zavier Hermand (Louvain-la-Neuve: Institut d'études médiévales de l'université catholique de Louvain, 1993), 86.
6. Donyelle McCray, *The Censored Pulpit: Julian of Norwich as Preacher* (Lanham, MD: Lexington/Fortress Academic, 2019), 27.
7. C. Clifton Black, *The Rhetoric of the Gospel: Theological Artistry in the Gospels and Acts*, 2nd ed. (Louisville: Westminster John Knox, 2013), 119.
8. Black, 148.
9. Fred Moten, *In the Break: The Aesthetics of the Black Radical Tradition* (Minneapolis: University of Minnesota Press, 2003), 1.
10. James H. Cone, *God of the Oppressed* (New York: Seabury, 1975), 17.
11. David C. Driskell, "Some Observations on Aaron Douglas as Tastemaker in the Renaissance Movement," in *Aaron Douglas: African American Modernist*, ed. Susan Earle (New Haven, CT: Yale University Press; Lawrence, KS: Spencer Museum of Art, University of Kansas, 2007), 91.
12. Jacques Derrida, "The Law of Genre," trans. Avital Ronell, in *Acts of Literature*, ed. Derek Attridge (New York: Routledge, 1992), 227.
13. Kurt Buhring, *Spirit(s) in Black Religion: Fire on the Inside*, Black Religion/Womanist Thought/Social Justice Series (Cham, Switzerland: Palgrave Macmillan, 2022), 37.
14. This book is in conversation with Alyce M. McKenzie's scholarship on wisdom preaching—particularly *Preaching Biblical Wisdom in a Self-Help Society* (Nashville: Abingdon, 2002)—and Kenyatta R. Gilbert's scholarship on the sage in African American preaching in *The Journey and Promise of African American Preaching* (Minneapolis: Fortress, 2011).
15. Malan Nel, "Preaching, Truth-Sharing, and 'Eager to Prophesy'" (paper, *Societas Homiletica*, Budapest, Hungary, August 14, 2022).

16. Kenyatta Gilbert observes that the sagely voice in African American preaching "is the most overlooked, primarily due to Black religious practices that are preoccupied with the ethos of contemporary culture, which ascribes greater worth to present-future preaching interests." Gilbert, *Journey and Promise of African American Preaching*, 14.

17. Mahalia Jackson and Evan McLeod Wylie, *Movin' On Up* (New York: Avon, 1966), 29.

18. Barbara A. Kaminska, *Pieter Bruegel the Elder: Religious Art for the Urban Community* (Leiden: Brill, 2019). A recent text that explores the relationship between preaching and art forms such as fashion, film, and architecture is Sunggu A. Yang's *Arts and Preaching: An Aesthetic Homiletic for the Twenty-First Century* (Eugene, OR: Cascade, 2021).

Chapter 1: The Singer

1. Mahalia Jackson and Evan McLeod Wylie, *Movin' On Up* (New York: Avon, 1966), 29.

2. Mahalia Jackson, "Mahalia Jackson: Childhood Memories," in *The Mahalia Jackson Reader*, ed. Mark Burford (New York: Oxford University Press, 2020), 27.

3. Jackson, 27.

4. Jackson's birthdate has been contested, but Mark Burford argues convincingly that her birthdate is October 26, 1911. Mark Burford, *Mahalia Jackson and the Black Gospel Field* (New York: Oxford University Press, 2019), 44–49.

5. Burford, 36.

6. Burford, 38, 42.

7. Burford, 41.

8. Burford, 50.

9. Burford, 42.

10. Burford, 49–50.

11. Mahalia Jackson, *I Sing Because I'm Happy*, with songs recorded, annotated, and compiled by Jules Schwerin (Washington, DC: Smithsonian Folkways Records, 1992).

12. Johari Jabir, "On Conjuring Mahalia: Mahalia Jackson, New Orleans, and the Sanctified Swing," *American Quarterly* 61 no. 3 (2009): 658. Jabir stresses that in addition to the blues, Jackson's music was informed by Black folk religion (651, 654, 657).

13. Clay Gowran, "Gospel Singing Queen Lonely, Sad as a Child: Croons to Doll to Start Life," *Chicago Tribune*, July 31, 1955, 12.

14. Burford, *Mahalia Jackson and the Black Gospel Field*, 65.

15. Horace Boyer, *The Golden Age of Gospel* (Urbana: University of Illinois, 2000), 86.

16. Burford, *Mahalia Jackson and the Black Gospel Field*, 67.

17. Burford, 88.

18. Jackson and Wylie, *Movin' On Up*, 66.

19. Burford, *Mahalia Jackson and the Black Gospel Field*, 225.

20. Jules Schwerin, *Got to Tell It: Mahalia Jackson, Queen of Gospel* (New York: Oxford University Press, 1992), 15. This early insistence did not last throughout her career; she would later accept payment by check.

21. Schwerin, 15.

22. Schwerin does not note the exact date of this incident, but it appears to have been in late 1955 or early 1956. His biography on Mahalia Jackson is less of a detailed historical narrative and more of an artistic portrait. His oral history of Jackson on *I Sing Because I'm Happy* includes accounts of police harassing the African American community in New Orleans.

23. Schwerin, *Got to Tell It*, 15–16.
24. Schwerin, 17.
25. Jackson and Wylie, *Movin' On Up*, 119.
26. Jackson and Wylie, 119.
27. Jackson and Wylie, 122.
28. "With King as its voice, the Civil Rights Movement became a Word of God movement, and the Word, exactly as it is portrayed in the New Testament, became a physical force with its own purposes and momentum." Richard Lischer, *The Preacher King: Martin Luther King Jr. and the Word That Moved America* (New York: Oxford University Press, 1995), 12.
29. Jackson and Wylie, *Movin' On Up*, 122.
30. Jackson and Wylie, 124.
31. Burford, *Mahalia Jackson and the Black Gospel Field*, 369.
32. Burford, *Mahalia Jackson Reader*, 413.
33. Jackson and Wylie, *Movin' On Up*, 104.
34. Peter Feldman, "Mahalia," in Burford, *Mahalia Jackson Reader*, 249.
35. While this note is only suggestive, several scholarly works must be mentioned. Martha Simmons offers a thorough discussion of the chanted sermon in "Whooping: The Musicality of African American Preaching Past and Present," in *Preaching with Sacred Fire: An Anthology of African American Sermons, 1750 to the Present,* ed. Martha Simmons and Frank A. Thomas (New York: W. W. Norton, 2010), 864–84, and Braxton Shelley provides a meticulous study of the correspondence between gospel music and preaching in *Healing for the Soul: Richard Smallwood, the Vamp, and the Gospel Imagination* (New York: Oxford University Press, 2021). Equally vital are Evans Crawford and Thomas H. Troeger, *The Hum: Call and Response in African American Preaching* (Nashville: Abingdon, 1995); Gerald L. Davis, *I Got the Word in Me and I Can Sing It, You Know: A Study of the Performed African-American Sermon* (Philadelphia: University of Pennsylvania Press, 1985); Barbara A. Holmes, "Christ, Coltrane, and the Jazz Sermon: Preaching a Love Supreme," *African American Pulpit* 6 (Fall 2003): 10–14; Kirk Byron Jones, *The Jazz of Preaching: How to Preach with Great Freedom and Joy* (Nashville: Abingdon, 2004); Henry H. Mitchell, *Black Preaching: The Recovery of a Powerful Art* (Nashville: Abingdon, 1990); Luke A. Powery, *Dem Dry Bones: Preaching, Death, and Hope* (Minneapolis: Fortress, 2012); Jon Michael Spencer, *Sacred Symphony: The Chanted Sermon of the Black Preacher* (Westport, CT: Greenwood Press, 1987); Frank A. Thomas, *They Never Like to Never Quit Praisin' God: The Role of Celebration in Preaching* (Cleveland: United Church Press, 1997); and William Clair Turner Jr., "The Musicality of Black Preaching: Performing the Word," in *Performance in Preaching: Bringing the Sermon to Life*, ed. Jana Childers and Clayton Schmit (Grand Rapids: Baker Academic, 2008), 191–209.
36. Amos N. Wilder, *Early Christian Rhetoric: The Language of the Gospel* (Cambridge, MA: Harvard University Press, 1971), 6.
37. Gardner C. Taylor, *The Words of Gardner Taylor: Special Occasion and Expository Sermons*, vol. 4, ed. Edward L. Taylor (Valley Forge, PA: Judson Press, 2004), 141.
38. Braxton Shelley explores the inner workings of this process in his study of the vamp in Shelley, *Healing for the Soul.*
39. C. Clifton Black, *The Rhetoric of the Gospel: Theological Artistry in the Gospels and Acts*, 2nd ed. (Louisville: Westminster John Knox, 2013), 131, 157. Similarly, speaking

from a contemporary context, Jared Alcántara stresses repetition: "*Remember that repetition and restatement are your friends, not your enemies.* . . . In speech, words disappear; they are ephemeral. They need to be repeated and restated." Jared E. Alcántara, *The Practices of Christian Preaching: Essentials for Effective Proclamation* (Grand Rapids: Baker Academic, 2019), 118.

40. These two musical traditions are not easily separated and have a joint influence on preaching. James H. Cone, *The Spirituals and the Blues: An Interpretation* (New York: Seabury 1972); Otis Moss III, *Blue Note Preaching in a Post-Soul World: Finding Hope in an Age of Despair* (Louisville: Westminster John Knox, 2015).

41. Alyce McKenzie, *Preaching Biblical Wisdom in a Self-Help Society* (Nashville: Abingdon, 2002), 35.

42. Kenyatta R. Gilbert, *The Journey and Promise of African American Preaching* (Minneapolis: Fortress, 2011), 14. Gilbert connects the sagely voice with lay preaching. The sage also resonates with John McClure's description of the preacher as "a community narrator, telling the church's faith story as one who is in Christ." McClure makes it clear that the preacher's narration includes Wisdom literature along with stories of God's miraculous action. John S. McClure, *The Four Codes of Preaching: Rhetorical Strategies* (Minneapolis: Fortress, 1991), 96.

43. McKenzie, *Preaching Biblical Wisdom in a Self-Help Society*, 21. Diane Jacobson explains that there are several different understandings of biblical wisdom: "Wisdom can be defined as the literature found in specific books (Proverbs, Job, and Qoheleth, as well as Sirach and Wisdom of Solomon), as one or more movements in history (from sage to scribe), as a set of ideas (learned from observation, experience, and tradition), or as a cultural way of thinking (much as our current society is defined by scientific thinking even by nonscientists). Each of these ways of thinking about what wisdom is has its own set of pitfalls." Diane Jacobson, "Wisdom Language in the Psalms," in *The Oxford Handbook of the Psalms*, ed. William P. Brown (New York: Oxford University Press, 2014), 149.

44. Clay Gowran, "Language No Bar as Mahalia Sings," *Chicago Tribune*, August 14, 1955, 16.

45. McKenzie, *Preaching Biblical Wisdom in a Self-Help Society*, 25, 28.

46. McKenzie, 25.

47. W. Ralph Eubanks, "I Will Move On Up a Little Higher: Mahalia Jackson's Power to Witness through Music," in *Can I Get a Witness? Thirteen Peacemakers, Community Builders, and Agitators for Faith and Justice*, ed. Charles Marsh, Shea Tuttle, and Daniel Rhodes (Grand Rapids: Eerdmans, 2019), 199–200.

48. Eubanks, 200.

49. Eubanks, 201. Mikhail Bakhtin is one theorist whose work scaffolds conversational preaching. Marlene Ringgaard Lorensen, *Dialogical Preaching: Bakhtin, Otherness, and Homiletics* (Göttingen: Vandenhoeck & Ruprecht, 2014).

50. Willie Jennings, "When Mahalia Sings: The Black Singer of Sacred Song as an Icon," in Burford, *Mahalia Jackson Reader*, 198.

51. Jabir, "On Conjuring Mahalia," 656, 664.

52. Jabir, 656.

53. Jabir, 656.

54. Mahalia Jackson, interview by Studs Terkel, WFMT, 1956, Studs Terkel Radio Archive, Chicago History Museum, https://studsterkel.wfmt.com/programs/mahalia-jackson-discusses-her-affinity-gospel-music-and-singing.

55. Danielle Goldman, *I Want to Be Ready: Improvised Dance as a Practice of Freedom* (Ann Arbor: University of Michigan, 2010), 5.

56. According to Alyce McKenzie, "A wisdom focus in preaching yields an egalitarian relationship between preacher and hearer that confers the same title on both speaker and listener: sage." McKenzie, *Preaching Biblical Wisdom in a Self-Help Society*, 35.
57. Letty Russell, *Church in the Round: Feminist Interpretation of the Church* (Louisville: Westminster John Knox, 1993), 67. Russell distinguishes authority of purpose from that stemming from "clerical privilege." Christine Smith suggests that "authority" is an ill-fitting term for preaching given the intimacy involved. Rather than relying on authority or one's license to speak, she urges focusing on credibility and authenticity instead. Christine M. Smith, *Weaving the Sermon: Preaching in a Feminist Perspective* (Louisville: Westminster John Knox, 1989), 47.
58. Henry H. Mitchell, *Black Preaching: The Recovery of a Powerful Art* (Nashville: Abingdon, 1990), 97. Luke A. Powery explores the relationship between the sermon and the Negro spiritual in *Dem Dry Bones: Preaching, Death, and Hope* (Minneapolis: Fortress, 2012), 22–23.
59. Jackson, "Mahalia Jackson: Childhood Memories," 27.
60. Gowran, "Language No Bar as Mahalia Sings," 16.
61. "Mahalia Jackson Gospel Song Diva," *New York Amsterdam News*, October 7, 1950; Burford, *Mahalia Jackson Reader*, 247.
62. Merriam-Webster, s.v. "perform (*v.*)," accessed September 8, 2020, https://www.merriam-webster.com/dictionary/perform.
63. Ruthanna Hooke explains, "To call preaching a performance highlights the fact that it is a practice with a particularly acute tension between the practicing self and the faith that is practiced." Ruthanna Hooke, *Transforming Preaching* (New York: Church Publishing, 2010), 32, 35.
64. Burford, *Mahalia Jackson Reader*, 317n7.
65. Burford, *Mahalia Jackson and the Black Gospel Field*, 242.
66. While there was a period in 1955 when she struggled with her weight amid a series of health issues, on the whole Jackson seems to have been confident, trusting her body and relishing in her gift of making music. Burford, 378–79.
67. Gowran, "Language No Bar as Mahalia Sings."
68. Burford, *Mahalia Jackson and the Black Gospel Field*, 261.
69. Braxton Shelley notes that due to the popularity of contemporary gospel music at the time, Jackson's turn to the spirituals reflects a deliberate choice. Conversation with Braxton Shelley, 1 November 2023.
70. McClure, *Four Codes of Preaching*, 57–58.
71. John Frow, *Genre*, 2nd ed. (London: Routledge, 2015), 11.
72. Frow, 27; Jacques Derrida, "The Law of Genre," trans. Avital Ronell in *Acts of Literature*, ed. Derek Attridge (New York: Routledge, 1992), 227.
73. Cheryl Townsend Gilkes, "Shirley Caesar and the Souls of Black Folk: Gospel Music as Cultural Narrative and Critique," *African American Pulpit*, Spring 2003, 13.
74. Quoted in Jared E. Alcántara, *Learning from a Legend: What Gardner C. Taylor Can Teach Us about Preaching* (Eugene, OR: Cascade, 2016), 65.

Chapter 2: The Quilter

1. Rosie Lee Tompkins, *Untitled*, 1970s with embroidered Scripture added mid-1980s; quilted by Irene Bankhead, 1997; found and repurposed hand- and machine-embroidered fabrics, decorative trim, crocheted doilies, velveteen, shisha mirror embroidery, cotton thread embroidery, and cotton muslin backing; 102 by 92 inches. Photographed by Ben Blackwell. Lawrence Rinder and

Elaine Y. Yau, with a contribution by Horace D. Ballard, *Rosie Lee Tompkins: A Retrospective* (Berkeley: University of California Berkeley Art Museum and Pacific Film Archive, 2020), plate 7, page 38.

2. Gladys-Marie Fry, *Stitched from the Soul: Slave Quilts from the Antebellum South* (Chapel Hill: University of North Carolina Press, 2002), 1.

3. Charles L. Campbell, *The Scandal of the Gospel: Preaching and the Grotesque* (Louisville: Westminster John Knox, 2021), 2.

4. Carolyn Mazloomi, *Spirits of the Cloth: Contemporary African American Quilts* (New York: Clarkson Potter/Publishers, 1998), 28, 127, 182.

5. Elaine Y. Yau, "The Craft and Art of Rosie Lee Tompkins," in Rinder and Yau, *Rosie Lee Tompkins*, 14–15.

6. Tompkins's grandmother was apparently known by "Lovely Bell" and "Lovely Prince." Yau, "Craft and Art of Rosie Lee Tompkins," 17, 20.

7. Yau, 15.

8. Eli Leon, *Something Pertaining to God: The Patchwork Art of Rosie Lee Tompkins* (Shelburne, VT: Shelburne Museum, 2007), 2.

9. Ron DeArman, interview by author, January 26, 2023; Pamela Blake, interview by author, January 26, 2023.

10. Ron DeArman, interview by author.

11. Major C. White, "Missionary Work of the Highest Order," *Pacific Union Recorder* 74, no. 48 (1975): 1.

12. Yau, "Craft and Art of Rosie Lee Tompkins, 16.

13. Leon, *Something Pertaining to God*, 6.

14. Leon, 6.

15. Yau, "Craft and Art of Rosie Lee Tompkins," 21.

16. Leon, *Something Pertaining to God*, 2, 13, 29.

17. Roberta Smith, "The Radical Quilting of Rosie Lee Tompkins," *New York Times*, June 29, 2020, https://www.nytimes.com/interactive/2020/06/26/arts/design/rosie-lee-tompkins-quilts.html.

18. Leon, *Something Pertaining to God*, 10.

19. Horace Ballard also suggests that the pseudonym makes space to honor the women who added the batting and backs to her tops—Irene Bankhead, Willia Ette Graham, and Johnnie Alberta Wade. Horace D. Ballard, "Rosie Lee Tompkins/Sacred Structures" in Rinder and Yau, *Rosie Lee Tompkins*, 45–46.

20. Yau, "Craft and Art of Rosie Lee Tompkins," 14.

21. Rosie Lee Tompkins, *String* (1985), quilted and reconstructed by Willia Ette Graham (1985), velvet, velveteen, and chenille backing. Photographed by Sharon Risedorph. Rinder and Yau, *Rosie Lee Tompkins*, plate 16, page 69. Nancy Humphrey Case, "Quilts with Divine Inspiration," *Christian Science Monitor*, May 24, 2007, 19, https://www.csmonitor.com/2007/0524/p19s01-hfes.html.

22. Leon, *Something Pertaining to God*, 1.

23. Yau, "Craft and Art of Rosie Lee Tompkins," 21.

24. Yau, 21.

25. Rosie Lee Tompkins, *Untitled*, c. 2002, cotton, printed cotton, polyester, canvas, knit velour, polyester fleece, wool, polyester knit, polyester double knit, cotton embroidery, and buttons; 104 by 145 inches. Photographed by Ben Blackwell. Rinder and Yau, *Rosie Lee Tompkins*, plate 51, pages 138–39.

26. Ballard, "Rosie Lee Tompkins/Sacred Structures," 41.

27. Rosie Lee Tompkins, *Untitled*, c. 2002, cotton polyester bedsheet, cotton embroidery, and drapery hooks, 68 by 71 inches. Photographed by Ben Blackwell. Rinder and Yau, *Rosie Lee Tompkins*, plate 52, pages 140–41.

28. Roberta Smith, "Radical Quilting of Rosie Lee Tompkins."

29. Rosie Lee Tompkins, *Untitled*, c. 1996, found and repurposed cotton T-shirts, found and repurposed silk or polyester neckties, cotton knit, acrylic yarn, cotton embroidery, polyester knit, and polyester backing; 61 by 71 inches. Photographed by Ben Blackwell. Rinder and Yau, *Rosie Lee Tompkins*, plate 44, pages 124–25.

30. Rosie Lee Tompkins, *Untitled*, c. 2005, quilted by Irene Bankhead, 2008; cotton or cotton polyester, cotton embroidery and cotton flannel backing; 20½ by 29½ inches. Photographed by Ben Blackwell. Rinder and Yau, *Rosie Lee Tompkins*, plate 63, pages 158–59.

31. Laura U. Marks, *The Skin of the Film: Intercultural Cinema, Embodiment, and the Senses* (Durham, NC: Duke University Press, 2000), 162–63.

32. Marks, 162.

33. John Frow, *Genre*, 2nd ed. (London: Routledge, 2015), 27.

34. Richard Lischer, "Why I Am Not Persuasive" *Homiletic* 24, no. 2 (1999): 14; Amos N. Wilder, *Early Christian Rhetoric: The Language of the Gospel* (Cambridge, MA: Harvard University Press, 1971), 21.

35. While Wilder stresses that hearing is the "primary" mode of Christian rhetoric, he acknowledges the importance of vision as a medium for divine encounter. He also adds, "The New Testament speaks of the divine apprehension in terms of all the senses, not only hearing and sight but touch and smell." Wilder, *Early Christian Rhetoric*, 11, 21.

36. Rinder and Yau, *Rosie Lee Tompkins*, plate 44, pages 124–25; plate 51, pages 138–39.

37. Peter Kline, *Passion for Nothing: Kierkegaard's Apophatic Theology* (Minneapolis: Augsburg Fortress, 2017), 35.

38. Kline, 35.

39. Judith Butler, *Precarious Life: The Powers of Mourning and Violence* (London: Verso, 2004), 28–29, 44.

40. Frow, *Genre*, 27; Jacques Derrida, "The Law of Genre," trans. Avital Ronell in *Acts of Literature*, ed. Derek Attridge (New York: Routledge, 1992), 227.

41. Frow, *Genre*, 14.

42. In keeping with Regenia Perry, I have maintained the substance of Powers's quotation while shifting away from the use of dialect, since in this case it reflects an early twentieth-century racist convention of quoting African Americans in dialect. Regenia A. Perry, *Harriet Powers's Bible Quilts* (New York: Rizzoli International and St. Martin's Press, 1994); Lucine Finch, "A Sermon in Patchwork," *Outlook Magazine*, October 28, 1914, 493; and Gladys-Marie Fry, "'A Sermon in Patchwork': New Light on Harriet Powers," in *Singular Women: Writing the Artist*, ed. Kristen Frederickson and Sarah E. Webb (Berkeley: University of California Press, 2003), 87.

43. Harriet Powers's name is listed as "Harriett" on her headstone and in some scholarship.

44. Fry, "Sermon in Patchwork," 87.

45. Laurel Thatcher Ulrich, "'A Quilt unlike Any Other': Rediscovering the Work of Harriet Powers," *Writing Women's History: A Tribute to Anne Firor Scott*, ed. Elizabeth Anne Payne (Jackson: University of Mississippi Press, 2011), 96.

46. Kyra E. Hicks, *This I Accomplish: Harriet Powers' Bible Quilt and Other Pieces* (n.p.: Black Thread Press, 2009), 38; Ulrich, "Quilt Unlike Any Other," 96.

47. Ulrich, "Quilt Unlike Any Other," 96.

48. Ulrich, 96.

49. Gladys-Marie Fry, "Harriet Powers: Portrait of a Black Quilter," in *Missing Pieces: Georgia Folk Art, 1770-1976*, catalog of an exhibition organized by Anna Wadsworth (Atlanta: Georgia Council for the Humanities and Whittet & Shepperson, 1976), 17.

50. Ulrich, "Quilt Unlike Any Other," 85.

51. Fry, "Harriet Powers: Portrait of a Black Quilter," 19.

52. Fry, 19.

53. Fry, *Stitched from the Soul*, 89. Smith later wrote an eighteen-page letter recounting Powers's descriptions and including her own amplifications. Perry, *Harriet Powers's Bible Quilts*.

54. Fry, "Harriet Powers: Portrait of a Black Quilter," 19.

55. Ntozake Shange, *For Colored Girls Who Have Considered Suicide When the Rainbow Is Enuf: A Choreopoem* (New York: Scribner, 1997), 63. Along this line, Lisa Thompson reflects on the need for exhortations that not only announce God's intervention but "help people sustain hope in the absence of divine intervention or while waiting on divine intervention." Lisa L. Thompson, *Ingenuity: Preaching as an Outsider* (Nashville: Abingdon, 2018), 152.

56. According to a January 28, 1896, letter that is believed to have been authored by Powers, Powers attended the Atlanta Cotton States and International Exposition on December 26, "Negro Day." Hicks, *This I Accomplish*, 38; Ulrich, "Quilt Unlike Any Other," 105.

57. Booker T. Washington, "Atlanta Exposition Speech," transcript of speech delivered in Atlanta on September 18, 1895, Library of Congress, https://blogs.loc.gov/teachers/2011/07/booker-t-washington-and-the-atlanta-compromise.

58. Washington, "Atlanta Exposition Speech"; Ulrich, "Quilt Unlike Any Other," 104–5.

59. Ulrich, "Quilt Unlike Any Other," 87.

60. Finch, "Sermon in Patchwork," 493–95.

61. Fry, *Stitched from the Soul*, 89.

62. Ulrich, "Quilt Unlike Any Other," 102.

63. Mazloomi, *Spirits of the Cloth*, 14–15.

64. Ulrich, "Quilt Unlike Any Other," 91–93.

65. Michelle Cliff, "'I Saw God in Myself and I Loved Her/I Loved Her Fiercely': More Thoughts on the Work of Black Women Artists," *Journal of Feminist Studies in Religion* 2, no. 1 (1986): 25, 32–33; Marie Jeanne Adams, "The Harriet Powers Pictorial Quilts," *Black Art: An International Quarterly* 3, no. 4 (1979): 24–27.

66. Susan Earle, "Harlem, Modernism, and Beyond: Aaron Douglas and His Role in Art/History," in *Aaron Douglas: African American Modernist*, ed. Susan Earle (New Haven, CT: Yale University Press; Lawrence, KS: Spencer Museum of Art, University of Kansas, 2007), 27; Richard J. Powell, "The Aaron Douglas Effect," in *Aaron Douglas*, 60.

67. David C. Driskell, "Some Observations on Aaron Douglas as Tastemaker in the Renaissance Movement," in Earle, *Aaron Douglas*, 91.

68. The continual practice of reading signs sometimes had profound effects. Ted Smith explains that John Brown's attention to semiotics had a strong influence on

his ethical framework. Brown "believed some events or people (types) prefigured others that fulfilled them (antitypes). Brown was constantly trying to discern the typologies at work in his time." Ted A. Smith, *Weird John Brown: Divine Violence and the Limits of Ethics* (Stanford, CA: Stanford University Press, 2015), 157.

69. Perry, *Harriet Powers's Bible Quilts*.
70. Fry, *Stitched from the Soul*, 89.
71. David Buttrick, *Homiletic: Moves and Structures* (Philadelphia: Fortress, 1987), 23.
72. Buttrick, 27.
73. Perry, *Harriet Powers's Bible Quilts*.
74. Adams, "Harriet Powers Pictorial Quilts," 20.
75. Ulrich, "Quilt Unlike Any Other," 97.
76. Fry, *Stitched from the Soul*, 85.
77. Harriet Powers, handwritten descriptions accompanying *Pictorial Quilt*, 1895–1898, Museum of Fine Arts, Boston.
78. The cause of the darkening is unclear, but forest fires and pollution may have been factors. Fry, *Stitched from the Soul*, 89.
79. Fry, 91.
80. Richard Lischer, ed., *The Company of Preachers: Wisdom on Preaching, Augustine to the Present* (Grand Rapids: Eerdmans, 2002), 33.
81. Miriam Gill, "Preaching and Image: Sermons and Wall Paintings in Later Medieval England," in *Preacher, Sermon, and Audience in the Middle Ages*, ed. Carolyn Muessig (Leiden: Brill, 2002), 155; Rosemary Woolf, *Art and Doctrine: Essays on Medieval Literature*, ed. Heather O'Donoghue (London: Hambledon Press, 1986), 57.
82. Woolf, *Art and Doctrine*, 57.
83. Mario Vargas Llosa, *The Storyteller*, trans. Helen Lane (New York: Farrar, Straus, and Giroux, 1989), 244.
84. Aelred of Rievaulx suggests a similar method of meditating by immersing oneself in biblical scenes. Aelred of Rievaulx, *Treatises, Pastoral Prayer*, with an introduction by David Knowles (Kalamazoo, MI: Cistercian Publications, 1995), 81.
85. Henry H. Mitchell, *Black Preaching: The Recovery of a Powerful Art* (Nashville: Abingdon Press, 1990), 63–72.
86. Ulrich, "Quilt Unlike Any Other," 89.
87. Fry, *Stitched from the Soul*, 84.
88. Cleophus J. LaRue, *The Heart of Black Preaching* (Louisville: Westminster John Knox, 2000), 14–15.
89. Adams, "Harriet Powers Pictorial Quilts," 16.
90. Ulrich, "Quilt Unlike Any Other," 93. Ulrich also notes that while Bryan's approach is more geometric, Powers's approach is more representational and narrative.
91. Fry, *Stitched from the Soul*, 65.
92. Christine M. Smith, *Weaving the Sermon: Preaching in a Feminist Perspective* (Louisville: Westminster John Knox, 1989), 46–47.
93. Clarence E. Hardy III, "Fauset's (Missing) Pentecostals: Church Mothers, Remaking Respectability, and Religious Modernism," in *The New Black Gods: Arthur Huff Fauset and the Study of African American Religions*, ed. Edward E. Curtis IV and Danielle Brune Sigler (Bloomington: Indiana University Press, 2009), 18–19.
94. Maude Southwell Wahlman, *Signs and Symbols: African Images in African-American Quilts* (Atlanta: Tinwood Books, 2001), 65.
95. Thompson, *Ingenuity*, 19.

96. Pauli Murray, *Pauli Murray: Selected Sermons and Writings*, ed. Anthony B. Pinn (Maryknoll, NY: Orbis, 2006), 190.

97. Joseph Sittler, "Imagining a Sermon," in *The Company of Preachers: Wisdom on Preaching, Augustine to the Present*, ed. Richard Lischer (Grand Rapids: Eerdmans, 2002), 332.

98. James A. Noel, "African American Art and Biblical Interpretation," in *True to Our Native Land: An African American New Testament Commentary*, ed. Brian K. Blount (Minneapolis: Fortress Press, 2007), 73.

99. Smith, *Weaving the Sermon*, 47.

100. Ruthanna Hooke and Lisa Thompson offer reflections on the meaning of embodiment in preaching. Ruthanna B. Hooke, *Transforming Preaching* (New York: Church Publishing, 2010), 38; Thompson, *Ingenuity*, 91–94.

101. David Appelbaum, *Voice* (Albany: State University of New York Press, 1990), xi, 9.

102. Donyelle McCray, *The Censored Pulpit: Julian of Norwich as Preacher* (Lanham, MD: Lexington/Fortress Academic, 2019), 60.

103. Fry, *Stitched from the Soul*, 69–82.

104. Noel, "African American Art and Biblical Interpretation," 77.

Chapter 3: The Dancer

1. For example, the Mandinka refer to them as *jali*, the Wolof use the term *gewel*, and the Mossi refer to *bendere*. Since ethnicity and regional differences affect these roles, lumping them under the term *griot/griotte* can be misleading. Thomas A. Hale, *Griots and Griottes: Masters of Words and Music* (Bloomington: Indiana University Press, 1998), 10. Hale offers a history of the term *griot*.

2. Christian Koontz, "Rhetoric in the Service of the Real," in *Thea Bowman: Handing on Her Legacy*, ed. Christian Koontz (Kansas City, MO: Sheed & Ward, 1991), 59.

3. Luke Powery describes spirituals as sung sermons, and Sister Thea uses a similar approach. Luke A. Powery, *Dem Dry Bones: Preaching, Death, and Hope* (Minneapolis: Fortress, 2012), 21–23.

4. Thea Bowman, *Sister Thea Bowman, Shooting Star: Selected Writings and Speeches*, ed. Celestine Cepress, FSPA (Winona, MN: Saint Mary's Press, 1993), 76.

5. Charlene Smith and John Feister, *Thea's Song: The Life of Thea Bowman* (Maryknoll, NY: Orbis, 2009), 19.

6. Smith and Feister, 20.

7. Quoted in Smith and Feister, 25–26.

8. Bowman, *Sister Thea Bowman, Shooting Star*, 76.

9. Smith and Feister, 28–30.

10. Smith and Feister, 36.

11. Smith and Feister, 26.

12. Smith and Feister, 37.

13. Smith and Feister, 37–38.

14. Smith and Feister, 41.

15. Smith and Feister, 46.

16. Smith and Feister, 53.

17. Smith and Feister, 64.

18. Smith and Feister, 71.

19. Smith and Feister, 74.

20. Sister Patricia Chappell, SNDdeN, "Sister Thea Bowman: Faithful Life, Powerful Legacy, Continuing Lessons" (Dahlgren Dialogue, Georgetown University Initiative

on Catholic Social Thought and Public Life, Washington, DC, May 3, 2022), https://catholicsocialthought.georgetown.edu/events/sister-thea-bowman.

21. In addition to learning about other cultures, Sister Thea argued for Christian ecumenism and challenged Roman Catholics to deepen their respect for other faith traditions. She similarly argued for an inclusive vision of Christ's cosmic love and stressed that this love was not limited to celibates or heterosexuals. Bowman, *Sister Thea Bowman, Shooting Star*, 95, 108–9.

22. Bowman, 83.

23. Smith and Feister, *Thea's Song*, 145.

24. Bowman, *Sister Thea Bowman, Shooting Star*, 83.

25. Joseph A. Brown, *A Retreat with Thea Bowman and Bede Abram: Leaning on the Lord* (Cincinnati: St. Anthony Messenger Press, 1997), 49; Bowman, *Sister Thea Bowman, Shooting Star*, 127.

26. Bowman, *Sister Thea Bowman, Shooting Star*, 114–15. She goes on to express her need to share the earth's resources with the millions of struggling people who cannot yet fathom the dangers associated with the ozone layer, acid rain, contaminated waste, or deforestation. She also suggests her ancestors taught about the importance of caring for creation long before the environment became a central issue for contemporary ethicists and theologians (116).

27. Maurice J. Nutt, *Thea Bowman: Faithful and Free* (Collegeville, MN: Liturgical Press, 2019), 119. Nell Irvin Painter suggests this line about going to heaven like a shooting star was not in fact spoken by Sojourner Truth and is instead one of many statements attributed to Truth for theatrical purposes. Nell Irvin Painter, *Sojourner Truth: A Life, a Symbol* (New York: W. W. Norton, 1996), 265.

28. Joseph M. Davis, "Gone—for Glory!" in *Thea Bowman: Handing on Her Legacy*, ed. Christian Koontz (Kansas City, MO: Sheed & Ward, 1991), 20.

29. Chrysostom expressed concern about pagan influences on Christian dance. Margaret Fisk Taylor, *A Time to Dance: Symbolic Movement in Worship*, ed. Doug Adams (Austin: Sharing Co., 1980), 79–80.

30. Judith Rock and Norman Mealy, *Performer as Priest and Prophet: Restoring the Intuitive in Worship through Music and Dance* (San Francisco: Harper & Row, 1988), 97–98.

31. Martin H. Blogg, *Dance and the Christian Faith: A Form of Knowing* (London: Hodder and Stoughton, 1985), 5.

32. Blogg, 10.

33. Pat Moore, "Liturgical Dance Reviews Mixed," *La Crosse Tribune*, February 14, 1975, 5.

34. Teresa L. Fry Brown, *Delivering the Sermon: Voice, Body, and Animation in Proclamation* (Minneapolis: Fortress, 2008), 76–77.

35. JoAnne Tucker and Susan Freeman, *Torah in Motion: Creating Dance Midrash* (n.p.: Open Road Media, 2014).

36. Rock and Mealy, *Performer as Priest and Prophet*, xx.

37. One of Primus's collaborators, Linda Spriggs, adds, "Everyone now says 'dance is a language,' but Pearl said it with a particular meaning about the way the intensity of movement telegraphs people and culture." Peggy Schwartz and Murray Schwartz, *The Dance Claimed Me: A Biography of Pearl Primus* (New Haven, CT: Yale University Press, 2011), 146, 227.

38. Sondra Horton Fraleigh, *Dance and the Lived Body: A Descriptive Aesthetics* (Pittsburgh: University of Pittsburgh Press, 1987), 171–72.

39. Kathleen S. Turner, *And We Shall Learn through the Dance: Liturgical Dance as Religious Education* (Eugene, OR: Pickwick Publications, 2021), 43. Turner explores the scholarship of Maxine Greene.

40. Turner, *And We Shall Learn through the Dance*, 55; Jennifer Donohue Zakkai, *Dance as a Way of Knowing* (Los Angeles: Stenhouse, 1997), 20.

41. Fraleigh, *Dance and the Lived Body*, 171.

42. Thea Bowman, "The Gift of African American Sacred Song," in *Lead Me, Guide Me: The African American Catholic Hymnal* (Chicago: G.I.A., 1987), [9].

43. Robert Frost, "Education by Poetry: A Meditative Monologue," in *Robert Frost: Poetry and Prose*, ed. Edward Connery Lathen and Lawrence Thompson (New York: Holt, Rinehart, and Winston, 1972), 334.

44. Frost, 336.

45. Erin Manning, *The Minor Gesture* (Durham, NC: Duke University Press, 2016), 189.

46. Veta Goler, "*Love Poems to God*: The Contemplative Artistry of Dianne McIntyre," *Dance, Movement and Spiritualties* 1, no. 1 (2014): 79.

47. Cynthia Winton-Henry, *Dance—the Sacred Art: The Joy of Movement as Spiritual Practice* (Woodstock, VT: Skylight Paths, 2009), 13.

48. Koontz, "Rhetoric in the Service of the Real," 67.

49. Brown, *Retreat with Thea Bowman and Bede Abram*, 135; James H. Cone, *The Spirituals and the Blues: An Interpretation* (New York: Seabury, 1972), 7.

50. Joseph A. Brown, "This Little Light of Mine: The Possibility of Prophecy in the Black Catholic Church," in *Thea Bowman: Handing on Her Legacy*, ed. Christian Koontz (Kansas City, MO: Sheed & Ward, 1991), 74.

51. Brown, *Retreat with Thea Bowman and Bede Abram*, 49.

52. Brown, "This Little Light of Mine," 74.

53. Brown, "This Little Light of Mine," 75; James H. Cone, *Speaking the Truth: Ecumenism, Liberation, and Black Theology* (Grand Rapids: Eerdmans, 1986), 24.

54. Goler, "*Love Poems to God*," 73–74.

55. Goler, 74.

56. Sister Thea had sayings that she shared repeatedly. In addition to emphasizing the "true truth," being an "old folks' child" and being "fully functioning," she referred to African American "song and dance"—repeatedly treating song and dance as a proclamatory unit.

57. Henry H. Mitchell, *Celebration and Experience in Preaching* (Nashville: Abingdon, 1990), 39–40; Frank A. Thomas, *They Like to Never Quit Praisin' God: The Role of Celebration in Preaching* (Cleveland: United Church Press, 1997), 9.

58. Richard Lischer, *The Preacher King: Martin Luther King Jr. and the Word That Moved America* (New York: Oxford University Press, 1995), 49.

59. Gennifer Brooks, "Drama and Delivery in Preaching," paper presented at the Academy of Homiletics Annual Meeting, Chicago, 2012, 2.

60. Carla De Sola, ". . . And the Word Became Dance: A Theory and Practice of Liturgical Dance," in *Dance as Religious Studies*, ed. Doug Adams and Diane Apostolos-Cappadona (New York: Crossroad, 1990), 155–56, 158.

61. Brown, *Retreat with Thea Bowman and Bede Abram*, 129. The "true truth" also encompasses past and present, beginning with the slave trade and continuing to the present. Brown, "This Little Light of Mine," 75–76.

62. Joseph A. Brown, *To Stand on the Rock: Meditations on Black Catholic Identity* (Maryknoll, NY: Orbis, 1998), 164–65.

63. Winton-Henry, *Dance—the Sacred Art*, ix.

64. Teresa L. Fry Brown, "The Action Potential of Preaching" in *Purposes of Preaching*, ed. Jana Childers (St. Louis: Chalice Press, 2004), 50.
65. Brown, "This Little Light of Mine," 76–77.
66. Brown, 78.
67. John Miller Chernoff, *African Rhythm and African Sensibility: Aesthetics and Social Action in African Musical Idioms* (Chicago: University of Chicago Press, 1979), 144, 147, 154.
68. Farah Jasmine Griffin, *Harlem Nocturne: Women Artists and Progressive Politics during World War II* (New York: Basic Civitas, 2013), 24.
69. Aaron Mermelstein and Willard E. Shaw, *Sister Thea, Her Own Story: A Video Autobiography* (Bucksport, ME: Northeast Historic Film, 2013).
70. Phyllis Zagano, *Twentieth-Century Apostles: Contemporary Spirituality in Action* (Collegeville, MN: Liturgical Press, 1999), 150.
71. Joan Lybarger, "E Pluribus Unum," *La Crosse Tribune,* January 22, 1976, 6.
72. Pearl Primus, "African Dance," in *African Dance: An Artistic, Historical, and Philosophical Inquiry,* ed. Kariamu Welsh Asante (Trenton, NJ: Africa World Press, 1996), 3; Griffin, *Harlem Nocturne,* 24.
73. Langston Hughes, "On Leaping and Shouting," *Chicago Defender,* July 3, 1943; republished in Langston Hughes, *Langston Hughes and the Chicago Defender: Essays on Race, Politics, and Culture: 1942–1962,* ed. Christopher C. Santis (Champaign: University of Illinois Press, 1995), 199.
74. Brown, *To Stand on the Rock,* 26; Primus shares this view. Primus, "African Dance," 8.
75. Brown, "This Little Light of Mine," 86.
76. Evans Crawford with Thomas H. Troeger, *The Hum: Call and Response in African American Preaching* (Nashville: Abingdon, 1995), 38, 44.
77. Brown, *To Stand on the Rock,* 24.
78. Winton-Henry, *Dance—the Sacred Art,* 138–55.
79. Turner, *And We Shall Learn through the Dance,* 9.
80. Turner, 13.
81. Goler, "*Love Poems to God,*" 80. Dianne McIntyre's study of the ring shout is depicted in Jonathan Demme's film *Beloved,* which was based on Toni Morrison's novel.
82. Barbara Jean LaRochester, "She Walked by Faith and Not by Sight," in *Thea Bowman: Handing on Her Legacy,* ed. Christian Koontz (Kansas City, MO: Sheed & Ward, 1991), 49.
83. Mermelstein and Shaw, *Sister Thea, Her Own Story.*
84. Cleophus LaRue, *The Heart of Black Preaching* (Louisville: Westminster John Knox, 2000), 19.
85. Henry H. Mitchell, *Black Preaching: The Recovery of a Powerful Art* (Nashville: Abingdon, 1990), 104, 110, 122.
86. Frank Thomas, *They Like to Never Quit Praisin' God: The Role of Celebration in Preaching* (Cleveland: Pilgrim Press, 1997), 3.
87. Gennifer Benjamin Brooks, *Good News Preaching: Offering the Gospel in Every Sermon* (Cleveland: United Church Press, 2009), 2.
88. Brooks, 5, 23.
89. Richard Lischer, ed., *The Company of Preachers: Wisdom on Preaching, Augustine to the Present* (Grand Rapids: Eerdmans, 2002), 32.
90. Koontz, "Rhetoric in the Service of the Real," 69; Nutt, *Thea Bowman,* 97. Sister Thea sometimes demanded more from her audiences than they were

willing or accustomed to give. For example, during her presentation at the William Faulkner Conference at the University of Mississippi in 1989, she chided members of the audience (mostly academics) for their restrained responses. She accused them of wanting to discuss Faulkner on a literary and philosophical level while resisting the Black religion that shaped his thought. William Faulkner Conferences Collection, Archives and Special Collections, J. D. Williams Library, University of Mississippi.

91. Koontz, "Rhetoric in the Service of the Real," 68.
92. Thea Bowman, "Black History and Culture," *U.S. Catholic Historian* 7, no. 2/3 (1988): 309.
93. Bowman, *Sister Thea Bowman, Shooting Star*, 49–51.
94. Bowman, 46.
95. Brown, *Retreat with Thea Bowman and Bede Abram*, 60.
96. Bowman, *Sister Thea Bowman, Shooting Star*, 89–90.
97. Bowman, 78.
98. Bowman, "Black History and Culture," 307.
99. Bowman, 308.
100. Bowman, *Sister Thea Bowman, Shooting Star*, 89.
101. Chernoff, *African Rhythm and African Sensibility*, 150.
102. Chernoff, 150–51.
103. Schwartz and Schwartz, *Dance Claimed Me*, 39, 64.
104. Bowman, *Sister Thea Bowman, Shooting Star*, 98.
105. Bowman, 98.
106. Bowman, 121–22.
107. Quoted in Nutt, *Thea Bowman*, 86.
108. Brown, *Retreat with Thea Bowman and Bede Abram*, 130.
109. Marie Augusta Neal, "She Made the Bishops Dance," in *Thea Bowman: Handing on Her Legacy*, ed. Christian Koontz (Kansas City, MO: Sheed & Ward, 1991), 54.
110. Neal, 54.
111. Lindsey Stewart, *The Politics of Black Joy: Zora Neale Hurston and Neo-Abolitionism* (Evanston, IL: Northwestern University Press, 2021), 123.
112. Interviewed by Carol Jenkins, host, *Black America*, "Urban Bush Women with Jawole Willa Jo Zollar," November 4, 2017, https://www.youtube.com /watch?v=4FdBCbGf_GQ.

Chapter 4: The Intercessor

1. Howard Thurman, "Charting the Inward Sea," audio recording, January 25, 1952, Howard Thurman Collection, Boston University Libraries, Howard Gottlieb Archival Research Center. With a few emendations, this meditation was published in Howard Thurman, *Meditations of the Heart* (New York: Harper & Row, 1953; reprint, Richmond, IN: Friends United Press, 1976), 15. A portion of this material is also integrated in the body of a sermon on prayer and silence. Howard Thurman, *The Growing Edge* (New York: Harper, 1956; reprint, Richmond, IN: Friends United Press, 1980), 43.
2. Walter Earl Fluker and Catherine Tumber, eds., *A Strange Freedom: The Best of Howard Thurman on Religious Experience and Public Life* (Boston: Beacon Press, 1998), 1.
3. Howard Thurman, *Conversations with Howard Thurman* (San Francisco: Howard Thurman Educational Trust, 1987).
4. Howard Thurman, *With Head and Heart: The Autobiography of Howard Thurman* (San Diego: Harcourt Brace, 1979), 5.

5. Thurman, 6.

6. Thurman, 7–8.

7. Timothy Robinson, "He Talked to Trees! 'Thinking Differently' about Nature with Howard Thurman," *Spiritus: A Journal of Christian Spirituality* 21, no. 1 (2021): 1–19.

8. Thurman, *With Head and Heart*, 18.

9. Thurman, 18.

10. Thurman, 44–45.

11. Thurman, 71.

12. Thurman, 72.

13. Thurman, 72.

14. Thurman, 72.

15. "To What Loyalty Are You True?" is included in both Thurman, *Meditations of the Heart*, 74, and Howard Thurman, *The Mood of Christmas* (New York: Harper & Row, 1973; reprint, Richmond, IN: Friends United Press, 1985), 76.

16. Thurman, *With Head and Heart*, 73.

17. Thurman, 81.

18. Thurman, 84.

19. Thurman, 220.

20. Howard Thurman, *Jesus and the Disinherited* (Boston: Beacon Press, 1996), 15.

21. Fluker and Tumber, *Strange Freedom*, 5.

22. Thurman, *With Head and Heart*, 159.

23. Thurman, 160.

24. Thurman, 160.

25. Leslie Paul, *The Meaning of Human Existence* (Philadelphia: J. B. Lippincott, 1950), 175.

26. Thurman, *With Head and Heart*, 160.

27. Thurman, 161.

28. Miles Lowell Yates, *God in Us: The Theory and Practice of Christian Devotion*, ed. W. Norman Pittenger and William H. Ralston Jr. (Greenwich, CT: Seabury Press, 1959), 33, 38.

29. Fluker and Tumber, *Strange Freedom*, 6.

30. Thurman, *With Head and Heart*, 167.

31. Thurman, 172.

32. Thurman, 175, 179.

33. Luke A. Powery, *Becoming Human: The Holy Spirit and the Rhetoric of Race* (Louisville: Westminster John Knox, 2022), 107.

34. Thurman explains that the fruit of meditation is unsolicited. Patrick Clayborn, "Preaching as an Act of Spirit: The Homiletical Theory of Howard Thurman," *Homiletic* 35, no. 1 (2010): 14.

35. Miles Lowell Yates, *God in Us: The Theory and Practice of Christian Devotion*, ed. W. Norman Pittenger and William H. Ralston Jr. (Greenwich, CT: Seabury Press, 1959), 142.

36. "Holding someone in the Light" (of God) essentially means praying for the sustaining power of God in whatever the person faces.

37. Edward P. Wimberly, *Moving from Shame to Self-Worth: Preaching and Pastoral Care* (Nashville: Abingdon, 1999), 17–18. Wimberly draws on homiletical scholarship by Henry Mitchell and Frank Thomas, who discuss the elimination and replacement of negative tapes. Howard Thurman, *Deep River and the Negro Spiritual Speaks of Life and Death* (Richmond, IN: Friends United Press, 1975), 12.

38. Edward K. Kaplan, "Howard Thurman: Meditation, Mysticism, and Life's Contradictions," *Debate and Understanding* (1982): 22. An earlier draft of Kaplan's

article is included in box 17, folder 5, Howard Thurman Collection, Boston University Libraries, Howard Gotlieb Archival Research Center.

39. Along this line, Henry Mitchell cites Thurman's skill of tucking into the listener's "stream of consciousness" to facilitate divine encounter. Mitchell treats stream of consciousness as a literary vehicle alongside others, such as metaphor, monologue, dialogue, and character sketch and frames them as "Genres: Vehicles for Divine Encounter." Henry H. Mitchell, *Celebration and Experience in Preaching* (Nashville: Abingdon, 1990), 37, 46.

40. Kaplan, "Howard Thurman," 22.

41. Thurman, *Meditations of the Heart*, 48.

42. Thurman, 52.

43. Thurman, 61.

44. Thurman, 113.

45. Thurman, 86.

46. Thurman, 145.

47. Clayborn, "Preaching as an Act of Spirit," 11.

48. Clayborn, 9, 13–14. Drawing on James Earl Massey and Evans Crawford, Clayborn notes that Thurman's pauses could be "devotional," or "meditative." Pauses and silences also reveal his spiritual preparation for preaching. Evans Crawford explores the theological and practical aspects of sermonic pausing and timing in Evans E. Crawford and Thomas H. Troeger, *The Hum: Call and Response in African American Preaching* (Nashville: Abingdon, 1995), 25–32.

49. Kaplan, "Howard Thurman," 21–22.

50. Pamela Burnard, "Critical Openings in Performing Transdisciplinary Research as/in Rebellion," in *Doing Rebellious Research: In and beyond the Academy*, ed. Pamela Burnard, Elizabeth Mackinlay, David Rousell, and Tatjana Dragovic (Leiden: Brill, 2022), 25.

51. Paul, *Meaning of Human Existence*, 141.

52. Kaplan, "Howard Thurman," 20.

53. Thurman, *Meditations of the Heart*, 123.

54. Thurman, 82.

55. Thurman understands freedom to consist of a sense of alternative. He explains, "The essential word here is 'sense'; for it is the sense of alternative that guarantees the freedom." Howard Thurman, "Human Freedom and the Emancipation Proclamation," *Pulpit Digest* 43, no. 294 (December 1962): 15.

56. Powery, *Becoming Human*, 108.

57. Powery, 107, 109.

58. Kaplan, "Howard Thurman," 21.

59. Clayborn, "Preaching as an Act of Spirit," 6.

60. Clayborn, 13; Crawford and Troeger, *The Hum*, 26–27.

61. Clayborn, 5; Howard Thurman, "Worship and Word: A View of the Liberal Congregation and Its Sermons," box 7, folder 35, 4, Howard Thurman Collection, Boston University Libraries, Howard Gotlieb Archival Research Center.

62. Kaplan, "Howard Thurman," 22.

63. Annouchka Bayley, "The Heart of Research: Fictioning and Diffractive Writing as Critical Research Practice," in *Doing Rebellious Research: In and beyond the Academy*, ed. Pamela Burnard, Elizabeth Mackinlay, David Rousell, and Tatjana Dragovic (Leiden: Brill, 2022), 283.

64. Teresa L. Fry Brown explains, "The communication of the word of God is similar to that explosion of electrical activity across membrane of the nerve cell."

Teresa L. Fry Brown, "The Action Potential of Preaching," *Purposes of Preaching*, ed. Jana Childers (St. Louis: Chalice Press, 2004), 49–50.

65. Clayborn, "Preaching as an Act of Spirit," 5–6.
66. Howard Thurman, "Notes on Homiletics Course," box 16, folder 47, 5, Howard Thurman Collection, Boston University Libraries, Howard Gotlieb Archival Research Center.
67. Thurman, 2.
68. Thurman, 2.
69. Henry H. Mitchell, *Black Preaching: The Recovery of a Powerful Art* (Nashville: Abingdon, 1990), 104–5.
70. Thurman, "Notes on Homiletics Course," 7.
71. Proctor asserts that the "word comes as a major proposition, a one-sentence statement that embraces a salient truth for that audience at that time. When that proposition, that theme, that word, that declarative sentence comes, it brings with it a kind of self-evident authority. It will have a resonance, a ring, a vibration that assures the preacher that it has the warrant to be preached." Samuel D. Proctor, *The Certain Sound of the Trumpet: Crafting a Sermon of Authority* (Valley Forge, PA: Judson Press, 1994), 25–26. Thomas Long says, "A text's claim involves both a message *and* an intention bound up in the text's own manner of embodying that message, both what the text wishes to say *and* what the text wishes to do through its saying. . . . What the sermon aims to say can be called its 'focus,' and what the sermon aims to do can be called its 'function.'" Thomas G. Long, *The Witness of Preaching* (Louisville: Westminster John Knox, 1989), 85–86.
72. Thurman, "Notes on Homiletics Course," 4.
73. Thurman, 3.
74. Thurman, 9. Thurman attributes his training at Rochester Seminary for the idea of the sermon as an occasion to wrestle with a great idea. Clayborn, "Preaching as an Act of Spirit," 6.
75. Thurman, "Notes on Homiletics Course," 9.
76. Thurman, 4.
77. Thurman, 9.
78. Thurman, *Meditations of the Heart*, 67; Thurman, *Deep River and the Negro Spiritual Speaks of Life and Death*, 23, [32]–[34].
79. Thurman, "Notes on Homiletics Course," 6.
80. Thurman, 6.
81. Paul, *Meaning of Human Existence*, 53.
82. Paul, 53.
83. Paul, 123.
84. Thurman, *Deep River and the Negro Spiritual Speaks of Life and Death*, [50], 22–23; 80–81, 86.
85. Thurman, [32], [23].
86. Thurman, [5].
87. Thurman, [4].
88. Thurman, "Notes on Homiletics Course," 6.
89. Thurman, 6.
90. Abraham Joshua Heschel, *The Sabbath: Its Meaning for Modern Man* (New York: Farrar, Straus, and Giroux, 1951), 79.
91. Susannah Heschel, introduction to *The Sabbath: Its Meaning for Modern Man*, by Abraham Joshua Heschel (New York: Farrar, Straus, and Giroux, 1951), xiv.
92. Heschel, 96.

93. Heschel, 76.

94. Thurman, *Conversations with Howard Thurman*.

95. This insight on truth as encounter emerged in Ockert Meyer's research on Franz Rosenzweig's *Der Stern der Erlösung*. Ockert Meyer, "Preaching the Truth and the Truth of Preaching: Rosenzweig's Jewish Lessons for Christian Preaching" (paper, *Societas Homiletica*, Budapest, Hungary, August 16, 2022), 15. Lisa Thompson similarly emphasizes the role of preaching in facilitating divine encounter. Lisa L. Thompson, *Ingenuity: Preaching as an Outsider* (Nashville: Abingdon, 2018), 24, 63.

96. Ockert Meyer, "Preaching the Truth and the Truth of Preaching," 11.

97. Evelyn Underhill, *The Ways of the Spirit*, ed. Grace Adolphsen Brame (New York: Crossroads, 1994), 131.

98. Underhill, 52.

99. Underhill, 108.

100. Underhill, 170.

101. Thurman, "Notes on Homiletics Course," 5.

102. Thurman, 5.

103. Along this line, Henry H. Mitchell notes the value of at least initially slowing the pace for preaching. "The fundamental significance of the slow rate is impact on the whole person: on cognitive, intuitive, and emotive consciousness." Mitchell, *Black Preaching*, 97.

104. Yates, *God in Us*, 139–40.

105. Carolyn Denard, "The Long, High Gaze: The Mythical Consciousness of Toni Morrison and William Faulkner," in *Unflinching Gaze: Toni Morrison and William Faulkner Re-envisioned*, ed. Carol A. Kolmerten, Stephen M. Ross, and Judith Bryant Wittenberg (Jackson: University of Mississippi Press, 1997), 19–20.

106. Thurman, *Meditations of the Heart*, 136–37.

107. Thurman, 136–37.

108. Thurman, 137–38.

Chapter 5: The Parabler

1. William Muehl, "The Dark Reflection of God: A Sermon Preached in the University Chapel on Sunday, November 20, 1960," box 20, folder 9, Howard Thurman Collection, Boston University Libraries, Howard Gotlieb Archival Research Center.

2. Leo G. Perdue, "Sages, Scribes, and Seers in Israel and the Ancient Near East: An Introduction," in *Scribes, Sages, and Seers: The Sage in the Eastern Mediterranean World*, ed. Leo G. Perdue (Göttingen: Vandenhoeck & Ruprecht, 2008), 3.

3. Perdue, 16.

4. It is helpful to note that some figures, like Isaiah, hold the role of both prophet and sage and that Wisdom appears as a prophetess in Sirach. R. B. Y. Scott, *The Way of Wisdom: In the Old Testament* (New York: Macmillan, 1971), 130.

5. Scott, 114.

6. Scott, 117–19.

7. Scott, 118.

8. Toni Morrison, *The Nobel Laureate Lecture in Literature, 1993* (New York: Alfred A. Knopf, 1999), 13.

9. Cheryl Lester, "Meditations on a Bird in the Hand: Ethics and Aesthetics in a Parable by Toni Morrison," in *The Aesthetics of Toni Morrison: Speaking the Unspeakable*, ed. Marc C. Conner (Jackson: University Press of Mississippi, 2000), 129.

10. Toni Morrison, "An Interview with Toni Morrison," interview by Nellie McKay, *Contemporary Literature* 24, no. 4 (Winter 1983): 416.

11. Morrison, 416.

12. Toni Morrison, "'I Come from People Who Sang All the Time': A Conversation with Toni Morrison," interview by Sheldon Hackney in *Toni Morrison: Conversations*, ed. Carolyn C. Denard (Jackson: University Press of Mississippi, 2008), 131.

13. Morrison, 131.

14. Morrison, "Interview with Toni Morrison," 414.

15. Toni Morrison, "'I Regret Everything': Toni Morrison Looks Back on Her Personal Life," interview by Terry Gross, *Fresh Air*, NPR, August 20, 2015.

16. Nick Ripatrazone, *Longing for an Absent God: Faith and Doubt in Great American Fiction* (Minneapolis: Fortress, 2020), 118.

17. In an undrafted note to Carolyn Denard, Morrison explains that she never abandoned "Ardelia," her grandmother's name. Box 75, folder 5, Toni Morrison Papers, Manuscript Division, Department of Special Collections, Princeton University.

18. Morrison, "I Regret Everything."

19. Middleton A. Harris, *The Black Book*, with the assistance of Morris Levitt, Roger Furman, and Ernest Smith (New York: Random House, 1974).

20. Toni Morrison, "The Triumphant Song of Toni Morrison," interview by Paula Giddings in *Toni Morrison: Conversations*, ed. Carolyn C. Denard (Jackson: University Press of Mississippi, 2008), 13.

21. Box 90, folder 8, Toni Morrison Papers, Manuscript Division, Department of Special Collections, Princeton University.

22. Morrison, "I Regret Everything."

23. Toni Morrison, *The Source of Self-Regard: Selected Essays, Speeches, and Meditations* (New York: Alfred A. Knopf, 2019), 47–48.

24. Morrison, 53.

25. Toni Morrison, "The Language Must Not Sweat," interview by Thomas LeClair, in *Conversations with Toni Morrison*, ed. Danille Taylor-Guthrie (Jackson: University Press of Mississippi, 1994), 121.

26. Morrison, 121.

27. Morrison, "Interview with Toni Morrison," 428.

28. *Merriam-Webster*, s.v. "edify (v.)," accessed December 14, 2022, https://www.merriam-webster.com/dictionary/edify.

29. Flannery O'Connor, *Mystery and Manners: Occasional Prose*, selected and edited by Sally and Robert Fitzgerald (New York: Farrar, Straus, and Giroux, 1974), 145.

30. While I focus on *Beloved* and *Paradise*, one might similarly include *Song of Solomon*. Wahneema Lubiano, "The Postmodernist Rag: Political Identity and the Vernacular in *Song of Solomon*," in *New Essays on Song of Solomon*, ed. Valerie Smith (Cambridge: Cambridge University Press, 1995), 103.

31. Toni Morrison, *Beloved*, with a new foreword by the author (New York: Vintage, 2004), 5.

32. Cynthia Griffin Wolff, "'Margaret Garner': A Cincinnati Story," *Massachusetts Review* 32, no. 3 (Autumn 1991): 427–28. Wolff notes that the Garner family was part of a larger group of seventeen who escaped to Ohio.

33. Harris, *Black Book*, 10.

34. Morrison, *Beloved*, 101.

35. Morrison, 102.

36. Morrison, 102.

37. Morrison, 102–3.

38. Gerhard von Rad, *Wisdom in Israel* (Nashville: Abingdon, 1972), 158.

39. Morrison, *Beloved*, 103; Judylyn S. Ryan, "Spirituality and/as Ideology in Black Women's Literature: The Preaching of Maria W. Stewart and Baby Suggs, Holy," in *Women Preachers and Prophets: Through Two Millennia of Christianity*, ed. Beverly Mayne Kienzle and Pamela J. Walker (Berkeley: University of California Press, 1998), 280. Ryan also compares Baby Suggs, holy's battered body to that of Jesus.

40. Morrison, *Beloved*, 103–4.

41. Morrison, 104.

42. Henry Mitchell and Frank Thomas allude to this phenomenon in their discussions of Uncle Wash's funeral. Henry H. Mitchell, *Black Preaching: The Recovery of a Powerful Art* (Nashville: Abingdon, 1990), 34–36; Frank A. Thomas, *They Like to Never Quit Praisin' God* (Cleveland: United Church Press, 1997), 1–2. Morrison's attention to memory also involves what she calls "rememory," which according to Ashraf Rushdy is "mental recollection, both anamnesis and construction, that is never only personal but always interpersonal." Ashraf H. A. Rushdy, "'Rememory': Primal Scenes and Constructions in Toni Morrison's Novels," *Contemporary Literature* 31, no. 3 (1990): 304. Having cyclical, spiritual, and physical aspects, rememory points to the multidimensional effects of the past on individuals, communities, and spaces. It reflects a prismatic understanding of time.

43. Toni Morrison, *Paradise* (New York: Alfred A. Knopf, 1998), 141–42.

44. While I am making a point about the theological constitution of a sermon here, I also agree with Hortense Spillers when she suggests that the movement from the aural experience of listening to a sermon in its intended ritual setting differs greatly from the experience of reading a sermon manuscript, making that manuscript something of an "*anti*-sermon." Hortense J. Spillers, *Black, White, and in Color: Essays on American Literature and Culture* (Chicago: University of Chicago Press, 2003), 255.

45. Morrison, *Paradise*, 142.

46. Morrison, 147.

47. Fred Craddock offers an extended study of indirection in preaching in *Overhearing the Gospel* (St. Louis: Chalice Press, 2002).

48. David Z. Wehner, "To Live This Life Intensely and Well: The Rebirth of Milkman Dead in Toni Morrison's *Song of Solomon*," in *Toni Morrison and the Bible*, ed. Shirley A. Stave (New York: Peter Lang, 2006), 72.

49. Wehner, 75; Toni Morrison, "Talk with Toni Morrison," interview by Mel Watkins, in *Conversations with Toni Morrison*, ed. Danille Taylor-Guthrie (Jackson: University Press of Mississippi, 1994), 47.

50. Wehner, "To Live This Life Intensely and Well," 87.

51. Morrison, *Source of Self-Regard*, 328.

52. Wehner, "To Live This Life Intensely and Well," 72.

53. Zora Neale Hurston, *Their Eyes Were Watching God*, with a foreword by Mary Helen Washington and an afterword by Henry Louis Gates Jr. (New York: HarperCollins, 1998), 16.

54. Hurston, 192–93.

55. Quoted in David S. Reynolds, *Mightier Than the Sword: Uncle Tom's Cabin and the Battle for America* (New York: W. W. Norton, 2011), 13.

56. Richard Woods, preface to *Margaret Ebner: Major Works, ca. 1291–1351*, ed. and trans. Leonard P. Hindsley (New York: Paulist Press, 1993), 5.

57. Reynolds, *Mightier Than the Sword*, 33. Stowe also describes her preaching vocation in imagistic terms, thinking of herself as one called to paint a depiction of the
moral crisis that gripped the nation. Harriet Beecher Stowe, *The Oxford Harriet
Beecher Stowe Reader*, ed. Joan D. Hedrick (New York: Oxford University Press,
1999), 66.

58. Reynolds, *Mightier Than the Sword*, 37.

59. Reynolds, 43.

60. Charles L. Campbell, *Scandal of the Gospel: Preaching and the Grotesque* (Louisville:
Westminster John Knox, 2021), 26.

61. Campbell, 28. Alyce McKenzie explores how contemporary preachers might
draw on the strategies of novelists in sermons. Alyce M. McKenzie, *Novel Preaching: Tips from Top Writers on Crafting Creative Sermons* (Louisville: Westminster John
Knox, 2010).

62. Campbell, *Scandal of the Gospel*, 28.

63. Harriet Beecher Stowe, *Uncle Tom's Cabin, or Life among the Lowly* (New York: Penguin, 1981), 105. Stowe also preaches to her readers in *A Key to Uncle Tom's Cabin*,
published in 1853, and similarly uses the pattern of direct address to amplify her
message. Stowe, *Oxford Harriet Beecher Stowe Reader*, 406, 428.

64. Wolff, "Margaret Garner," 425–26.

65. Wolff, 418.

66. Nadra Nittle, *Toni Morrison's Spiritual Vision: Faith, Folktales, and Feminism in Her Life
and Literature* (Minneapolis: Fortress, 2021), 129–30.

67. Nittle, 136.

68. Kathleen Marks, *Toni Morrison's* Beloved *and the Apotropaic Imagination* (Columbia:
University of Missouri Press, 2002), 7, 29. There are apotropaic elements in communal prayers in some church settings in which the petitioner names evil to fend
it off. "We come against all manifestations of violence. We come against all works
of evil. . . ."

69. Marks, 126, 148–49.

70. Marks, 5.

71. Marks, 42.

72. Marks, 101.

73. Marks, 145.

74. Brennan Breed, "Reception of the Psalms: The Example of Psalm 91," in *The
Oxford Handbook of the Psalms*, ed. William P. Brown (Oxford: Oxford University
Press, 2014), 298–303.

75. Nittle, *Toni Morrison's Spiritual Vision*, 145; Zoë Heller, "Feathered Wombs," *London Review of Books* 20, no. 9 (May 1998), https://www.lrb.co.uk/the-paper/v20
/n09/zoe-heller/feathered-wombs.

76. Morrison, *Nobel Laureate Lecture*, 20.

77. Toni Morrison, *What Moves at the Margin: Selected Nonfiction* (Jackson: University
Press of Mississippi, 2008), 58–59.

78. Morrison, 59. She immediately goes on to make a musical comparison, stressing
that music is enriched by the audience's response.

79. Morrison, *Source of Self-Regard*, 329.

80. Morrison, "Interview with Toni Morrison," 426.

81. Stewarding is an "underutilized metaphor for preaching" according to Jared
Alcántara. "A steward is a person who has been entrusted with someone else's
most cherished possessions" and is called "to be a faithful guardian over that
which has been entrusted." I find this metaphor fitting for thinking about African

American preaching and ancestral wisdom. Jared E. Alcántara, *The Practices of Christian Preaching: Essentials for Effective Proclamation* (Grand Rapids: Baker Academic, 2019), 54.

82. Richard Lischer, *Reading the Parables*, Interpretation: Resources for the Use of Scripture in the Church (Louisville: Westminster John Knox, 2014), 14.

83. Morrison, *Nobel Laureate Lecture*, 10.

84. Morrison, 11.

85. Morrison, 26.

86. Morrison, 29.

87. Morrison, 30.

88. Lester, "Meditations on a Bird in the Hand," 129.

89. Box 297, folder 11, Toni Morrison, Toni Morrison Papers, Manuscript Division, Department of Special Collections, Princeton University.

90. Morrison, *What Moves at the Margin*, 36.

91. Russell Hamer, *Understanding Kierkegaard's Parables* (Jefferson, NC: McFarland, 2021), 43, 50–51; Donald D. Palmer, *Kierkegaard for Beginners* (Danbury, CT: For Beginners, 1996), 21, 24–25.

92. Daniel Berthold, "A Desire to Be Understood: Authorship and Authority in Kierkegaard's Work," in *Authorship and Authority in Kierkegaard's Writings*, ed. Joseph Westfall (London: Bloomberg Academic, 2019), 109.

93. Yvette Christiansë, *Toni Morrison: An Ethical Poetics* (New York: Fordham University Press, 2013), 26.

94. Box 91, folder 21, Toni Morrison Papers, Manuscript Division, Department of Special Collections, Princeton University.

95. Morrison, "Interview with Toni Morrison," 421.

96. Ockert Meyer, "Preaching the Truth and the Truth of Preaching: Rosenzweig's Jewish Lessons for Christian Preaching" (paper, *Societas Homiletica*, Budapest, Hungary, August 16, 2022), 10; Jonathan Sacks, *To Heal a Fractured World: The Ethics of Responsibility* (London: Continuum, 2005), 157.

97. Meyer, "Preaching the Truth and the Truth of Preaching," 11–12. Meyer refers to Søren Kierkegaard's famous quotation "The truth is a snare: you cannot have it, without being caught. You cannot have the truth in such a way that you catch it, but only in such a way that it catches you." Søren Kierkegaard, *The Last Years; Journals 1853–1855*, ed. and trans. Ronald Gregor Smith (London: Collins, 1965), 133.

98. C. H. Dodd, *Parables of the Kingdom*, rev. ed. (New York: Scribner, 1961), 5.

99. Lischer, *Reading the Parables*, 7.

100. Lischer, 3.

101. Lischer, 5.

102. Lischer, 11.

103. C. Clifton Black, *The Rhetoric of the Gospel: Theological Artistry in the Gospels and Acts*, 2nd ed. (Louisville: Westminster John Knox, 2013), 147.

104. David B. Gowler, *The Parables after Jesus: Their Imaginative Receptions across Two Millennia* (Grand Rapids: Baker Academic, 2017), 256.

105. Morrison, *What Moves at the Margin*, 60.

106. Morrison, *Source of Self-Regard*, 331; Morrison, "Interview with Toni Morrison," 429.

107. Morrison, *What Moves at the Margin*, 64.

108. L. Martina Young, "Beloved Bodies: Gestures toward Wholeness," in *Toni Morrison: Forty Years in the Clearing*, ed. Carmen Gillespie (Lewisburg, PA: Bucknell University Press; Lanham, MD: Rowman & Littlefield, 2012), 342.

109. Morrison, *What Moves at the Margin*, 62.
110. Christiansë, *Toni Morrison*, 22; Sharon Patricia Holland, *Raising the Dead: Readings of Death and (Black) Subjectivity* (Durham, NC: Duke University Press, 2000), 6.
111. Mitchell, *Black Preaching*, 57–58, 59.
112. Morrison, *What Moves at the Margin*, 62.
113. Morrison, *Source of Self-Regard*, 253.

Conclusion

1. Apparently the minister had some consciousness of guilt, because he downplayed his actions. John W. Blassingame, ed., *Slave Testimony: Two Centuries of Letters, Speeches, Interviews, and Autobiographies* (Baton Rouge: Louisiana State University Press, 1977), 717–18.
2. Blassingame, 420.
3. Hartmut Rosa, *Resonance: A Sociology of Our Relationship to the World*, trans. James C. Wagner (Cambridge: Polity Press, 2019), 122.
4. Rosa, 40–41.
5. Michelle Cliff, "'I Saw God in Myself and I Loved Her/I Loved Her Fiercely': More Thoughts on the Work of Black Women Artists," *Journal of Feminist Studies in Religion* 2, no. 1 (1986): 9.
6. Cliff, 9.
7. Hortense J. Spillers, *Black, White, and in Color: Essays on American Literature and Culture* (Chicago: University of Chicago Press, 2003), 259.
8. Michael Oppenheim, *What Does Revelation Mean to the Modern Jew? Rosenzweig, Buber, and Fackenheim* (Lewiston, NY: Edwin Mellen Press, 1985), 42.
9. Oppenheim, 97.
10. In keeping with Jared Alcántara, I would also say that their sermons had a "redemptive focus." Jared E. Alcántara, *The Practices of Christian Preaching: Essentials for Effective Proclamation* (Grand Rapids: Baker Academic, 2019), 37.
11. Robert H. Sitkoff and Jesse Dukeminier, *Wills, Trusts, and Estates*, 10th ed. (New York: Wolters Kluwer, 2017), 203.
12. Richard Lischer, ed., *The Company of Preachers: Wisdom on Preaching, Augustine to the Present* (Grand Rapids: Eerdmans, 2002), xvi.
13. I am drawing on my own perspective here, but Lis Valle-Ruiz and Andrew Wymer have edited a volume on homiletical whiteness that includes other viewpoints. Lis Valle-Ruiz and Andrew Wymer, eds., *Unmasking White Preaching: Racial Hegemony, Resistance, and Possibilities in Homiletics*, Postcolonial and Decolonial Studies in Religion and Theology (Lanham, MD: Lexington Books, 2022).
14. Dietrich Bonhoeffer, "The Proclaimed Word," in *The Company of Preachers: Wisdom on Preaching, Augustine to the Present*, ed. Richard Lischer (Grand Rapids: Eerdmans, 2002), 36.

Bibliography

Archival Sources

Alice Walker papers, Stuart A. Rose Manuscript, Archives, and Rare Book Library, Emory University, Atlanta

Boston Museum of Fine Arts

Carl Van Vechten Papers Relating to African American Arts and Letters, Beinecke Rare Book and Manuscript Library, Yale University, New Haven, CT

Howard Thurman Collection, Boston University Libraries, Howard Gotlieb Archival Research Center

Richard B. Russell Jr. Special Collections Libraries, University of Georgia, Athens

Rijksmuseum Research Library, Amsterdam, Netherlands

Toni Morrison Papers, Manuscript Division, Department of Special Collections, Princeton University, Princeton, NJ

William Faulkner Conferences Collection, Archives and Special Collections, J. D. Williams Library, University of Mississippi

Zora Neale Hurston Collection, Beinecke Rare Book and Manuscript Library, Yale University, New Haven, CT

Other Sources and Suggested Reading

Adams, Marie Jeanne. "The Harriet Powers Pictorial Quilts." *Black Art: An International Quarterly* 3, no. 4 (1979): 12–28.

Aelred of Rievaulx. *Treatises, Pastoral Prayer.* Introduction by David Knowles. Kalamazoo, MI: Cistercian Publications, 1995.

Alcántara, Jared E. *Learning from a Legend: What Gardner C. Taylor Can Teach Us about Preaching.* Eugene, OR: Cascade, 2016.

———. *The Practices of Christian Preaching: Essentials for Effective Proclamation.* Grand Rapids: Baker Academic, 2019.

Appelbaum, David. *Voice.* Albany: State University of New York Press, 1990.

Ballard, Horace D. "Rosie Lee Tompkins/Sacred Structures." In *Rosie Lee Tompkins: A Retrospective,* by Lawrence Rinder and Elaine Y. Yau, 39–49. Berkeley: University of California Berkeley Art Museum and Pacific Film Archive, 2020.

Bayley, Annouchka. "The Heart of Research: Fictioning and Diffractive Writing as Critical Research Practice." In *Doing Rebellious Research: In and beyond the Academy,* edited by Pamela Burnard, Elizabeth Mackinlay, David Rousell, and Tatjana Dragovic, 282–299. Leiden: Brill, 2022.

Berthold, Daniel. "A Desire to Be Understood: Authorship and Authority in Kierkegaard's Work." In *Authorship and Authority in Kierkegaard's Writings*, edited by Joseph Westfall, 107–20. London: Bloomberg Academic, 2019.

Bivins, Jason C. *Spirits Rejoice! Jazz and American Religion.* New York: Oxford University Press, 2015.

Black, C. Clifton. *The Rhetoric of the Gospel: Theological Artistry in the Gospels and Acts.* 2nd ed. Louisville: Westminster John Knox, 2013.

Blassingame, John W., ed. *Slave Testimony: Two Centuries of Letters, Speeches, Interviews, and Autobiographies.* Baton Rouge: Louisiana State University Press, 1977.

Blogg, Martin H. *Dance and the Christian Faith: A Form of Knowing.* London: Hodder and Stoughton, 1985.

Bonhoeffer, Dietrich. "The Proclaimed Word." In *The Company of Preachers: Wisdom on Preaching, Augustine to the Present,* edited by Richard Lischer, 31–37. Grand Rapids: Eerdmans, 2002.

Bowman, Thea. "The Gift of African American Sacred Song." In *Lead Me, Guide Me: The African American Catholic Hymnal.* Chicago: G.I.A., 1987.

———. "Black History and Culture." *U.S. Catholic Historian* 7, no. 2/3 (1988): 307–310.

———. *Sister Thea Bowman, Shooting Star: Selected Writings and Speeches.* Edited by Celestine Cepress, FSPA. Winona, MN: Saint Mary's Press, 1993.

Boyer, Horace. *The Golden Age of Gospel.* Urbana: University of Illinois, 2000.

Breed, Brennan. "Reception of the Psalms: The Example of Psalm 91." In *The Oxford Handbook of the Psalms,* edited by William P. Brown, 297–310. Oxford: Oxford University Press, 2014.

Brooks, Gennifer. "Drama and Delivery in Preaching." Paper presented at the Academy of Homiletics Annual Meeting, Chicago, 2012.

———. *Good News Preaching: Offering the Gospel in Every Sermon.* Cleveland: United Church Press, 2009.

Brown, Joseph A. *A Retreat with Thea Bowman and Bede Abram: Leaning on the Lord.* Cincinnati: St. Anthony Messenger Press, 1997.

———. "This Little Light of Mine: The Possibility of Prophecy in the Black Catholic Church." In *Thea Bowman: Handing on Her Legacy,* edited by Christian Koontz, 71–91. Kansas City, MO: Sheed & Ward, 1991.

———. *To Stand on the Rock: Meditations on Black Catholic Identity.* Maryknoll, NY: Orbis, 1998.

Brown, Teresa L. Fry. "The Action Potential of Preaching." In *Purposes of Preaching,* edited by Jana Childers, 49–65. St. Louis: Chalice Press, 2004.

———. *Delivering the Sermon: Voice, Body, and Animation in Proclamation.* Minneapolis: Fortress, 2008.

Buhring, Kurt. *Spirit(s) in Black Religion: Fire on the Inside.* Black Religion/Womanist Thought/Social Justice Series. Cham, Switzerland: Palgrave Macmillan, 2022.

Burford, Mark. *Mahalia Jackson and the Black Gospel Field.* New York: Oxford University Press, 2019.

———, ed. *The Mahalia Jackson Reader.* New York: Oxford University Press, 2020.

Burnard, Pamela. "Critical Openings in Performing Transdisciplinary Research as/in Rebellion." In *Doing Rebellious Research: In and beyond the Academy,* edited by Pamela Burnard, Elizabeth Mackinlay, David Rousell, and Tatjana Dragovic, 15–33. Leiden: Brill, 2022.

Butler, Judith. *Precarious Life: The Powers of Mourning and Violence.* London: Verso, 2004.

Buttrick, David. *Homiletic: Moves and Structures.* Philadelphia: Fortress, 1987.

Campbell, Charles L. *The Scandal of the Gospel: Preaching and the Grotesque.* Louisville: Westminster John Knox, 2021.

Case, Nancy Humphrey. "Quilts with Divine Inspiration." *Christian Science Monitor,* May 24, 2007. http://www.csmonitor.com/2007/0524/p19s01-hfes.html.

Chappell, Patricia. "Sister Thea Bowman: Faithful Life, Powerful Legacy, Continuing Lessons." Dahlgren Dialogue at the Georgetown University Initiative on Catholic Social Thought and Public Life, Washington, DC, May 3, 2022. https://catholicsocialthought.georgetown.edu/events/sister-thea-bowman.

Chernoff, John Miller. *African Rhythm and African Sensibility: Aesthetics and Social Action in African Musical Idioms.* Chicago: University of Chicago Press, 1979.

Christiansë, Yvette. *Toni Morrison: An Ethical Poetics.* New York: Fordham University Press, 2013.

Clayborn, Patrick. "Preaching as an Act of Spirit: The Homiletical Theory of Howard Thurman," *Homiletic* 35, no. 1 (2010): 3–16.

Cliff, Michelle. "'I Saw God in Myself and I Loved Her/I Loved Her Fiercely': More Thoughts on the Work of Black Women Artists." *Journal of Feminist Studies in Religion* 2, no. 1 (1986): 7–39.

Cone, James H. *God of the Oppressed.* New York: Seabury, 1975.

———. *Speaking the Truth: Ecumenism, Liberation, and Black Theology.* Grand Rapids: Eerdmans, 1986.

———. *The Spirituals and the Blues: An Interpretation.* New York: Seabury, 1972.

Craddock, Fred. *Overhearing the Gospel.* St. Louis: Chalice Press, 2002.

Crawford, Evans, and Thomas H. Troeger. *The Hum: Call and Response in African American Preaching.* Nashville: Abingdon, 1995.

Davis, Gerald L. *I Got the Word in Me and I Can Sing It, You Know: A Study of the Performed African-American Sermon.* Philadelphia: University of Pennsylvania Press, 1985.

Davis, Joseph M. "Gone—for Glory!" In *Thea Bowman: Handing on Her Legacy,* edited by Christian Koontz, 18–20. Kansas City, MO: Sheed & Ward, 1991.

Denard, Carolyn. "The Long, High Gaze: The Mythical Consciousness of Toni Morrison and William Faulkner." In *Unflinching Gaze: Morrison and Faulkner Re-envisioned,* edited by Carol A. Kolmerten, Stephen M. Ross, and Judith Bryant Wittenberg, 17–30. Jackson: University of Mississippi Press, 1997.

Derrida, Jacques. "The Law of Genre." Translated by Avital Ronell. In *Acts of Literature,* edited by Derek Attridge, 221–52. New York: Routledge, 1992.

De Sola, Carla. ". . . And the Word Became Dance: A Theory and Practice of Liturgical Dance." In *Dance as Religious Studies,* edited by Doug Adams and Diane Apostolos-Cappadona, 153–166. New York: Crossroad, 1990.

Dodd, C. H. *Parables of the Kingdom.* Rev. ed. New York: Scribner, 1961.

Driskell, David C. "Some Observations on Aaron Douglas as Tastemaker in the Renaissance Movement." In *Aaron Douglas: African American Modernist,* edited by Susan Earle, 87–93. New Haven, CT: Yale University Press; Lawrence, KS: Spencer Museum of Art, University of Kansas, 2007.

Earle, Susan, ed., *Aaron Douglas: African American Modernist.* New Haven, CT: Yale University Press; Lawrence, KS: Spencer Museum of Art, University of Kansas, 2007.

———. "Harlem, Modernism, and Beyond: Aaron Douglas and His Role in Art/ History." In *Aaron Douglas: African American Modernist*, edited by Susan Earle, 5–51. New Haven, CT: Yale University Press; Lawrence, KS: Spencer Museum of Art, University of Kansas, 2007.

Eubanks, W. Ralph. "I Will Move On Up a Little Higher: Mahalia Jackson's Power to Witness through Music." In *Can I Get a Witness? Thirteen Peacemakers, Community Builders, and Agitators for Faith and Justice*, edited by Charles Marsh, Shea Tuttle, and Daniel Rhodes, 197–225. Grand Rapids: Eerdmans, 2019.

Finch, Lucine. "A Sermon in Patchwork." *Outlook Magazine*. October 28, 1914.

Fluker, Walter Earl, and Catherine Tumber, eds. *A Strange Freedom: The Best of Howard Thurman on Religious Experience and Public Life*. Boston: Beacon Press, 1998.

Fraleigh, Sondra Horton. *Dance and the Lived Body: A Descriptive Aesthetics*. Pittsburgh: University of Pittsburgh Press, 1987.

Frost, Robert. "Education by Poetry: A Meditative Monologue." In *Robert Frost: Poetry and Prose*, edited by Edward Connery Lathen and Lawrence Thompson, 329–340. New York: Holt, Rinehart, and Winston, 1972.

Frow, John. *Genre*. 2nd ed. London: Routledge, 2015.

Fry, Gladys-Marie. "Harriet Powers: Portrait of a Black Quilter." In *Missing Pieces: Georgia Folk Art, 1770-1976* (catalog of an exhibition organized by Anna Wadsworth), 16–23. Atlanta: Georgia Council for the Humanities and Whittet & Shepperson, 1976.

———. "'A Sermon in Patchwork': New Light on Harriet Powers." In *Singular Women: Writing the Artist*, edited by Kristen Frederickson and Sarah E. Webb, 81–94. Berkeley: University of California Press, 2003.

———. *Stitched from the Soul: Slave Quilts from the Antebellum South*. Chapel Hill: University of North Carolina Press, 2002.

George-Graves, Nadine. *Urban Bush Women: Twenty Years of African American Dance Theater, Community Engagement, and Working It Out*. Madison: University of Wisconsin Press, 2010.

Gilbert, Kenyatta R. *The Journey and Promise of African American Preaching*. Minneapolis: Fortress, 2011.

Gilkes, Cheryl Townsend. "Shirley Caesar and the Souls of Black Folk: Gospel Music as Cultural Narrative and Critique." *African American Pulpit*, Spring (2003): 12–16.

Gill, Miriam. "Preaching and Image: Sermons and Wall Paintings in Later Medieval England." In *Preacher, Sermon, and Audience in the Middle Ages*, edited by Carolyn Muessig, 155–80. Leiden: Brill, 2002.

Goldman, Danielle. *I Want to Be Ready: Improvised Dance as a Practice of Freedom*. Ann Arbor: University of Michigan, 2010.

Goler, Veta. "*Love Poems to God*: The Contemplative Artistry of Dianne McIntyre." *Dance, Movement, and Spiritualties* 1, no. 1 (2014): 73–86.

Gowler, David B. *The Parables after Jesus: Their Imaginative Receptions across Two Millennia*. Grand Rapids: Baker Academic, 2017.

Gowran, Clay. "Gospel Singing Queen Lonely, Sad as a Child: Croons to Doll to Start Life." *Chicago Tribune*, July 31, 1955.

———. "Language No Bar as Mahalia Sings." *Chicago Tribune*, August 14, 1955.

Griffin, Farah Jasmine. *Harlem Nocturne: Women Artists and Progressive Politics during World War II*. New York: Basic Civitas, 2013.

Hale, Thomas A. *Griots and Griottes: Masters of Words and Music.* Bloomington: Indiana University Press, 1998.

Hamer, Russell. *Understanding Kierkegaard's Parables.* Jefferson, NC: McFarland, 2021.

Hardy, Clarence E., III. "Fauset's (Missing) Pentecostals: Church Mothers, Remaking Respectability, and Religious Modernism." In *The New Black Gods: Arthur Huff Fauset and the Study of African American Religions*, edited by Edward E. Curtis IV and Danielle Brune Sigler, 15–30. Bloomington: Indiana University Press, 2009.

Harris, Middleton A. *The Black Book.* With the assistance of Morris Levitt, Roger Furman, and Ernest Smith. New York: Random House, 1974.

Heller, Zoë. "Feathered Wombs." *London Review of Books* 20, no. 9 (May 1998). https://www.lrb.co.uk/the-paper/v20/n09/zoe-heller/feathered-wombs.

Heschel, Abraham Joshua. *The Sabbath: Its Meaning for Modern Man.* New York: Farrar, Straus, and Giroux, 1951.

Heschel, Susannah. Introduction to *The Sabbath: Its Meaning for Modern Man,* by Abraham Joshua Heschel, vii–xvi. New York: Farrar, Straus, and Giroux, 1951.

Hicks, Kyra E. *This I Accomplish: Harriet Powers' Bible Quilt and Other Pieces.* N.p.: Black Thread Press, 2009.

Holland, Sharon Patricia. *Raising the Dead: Readings of Death and (Black) Subjectivity.* Durham, NC: Duke University Press, 2000.

Holmes, Barbara A. "Christ, Coltrane, and the Jazz Sermon: Preaching a Love Supreme." *African American Pulpit* 6, (Fall 2003): 10–14.

Hooke, Ruthanna B. *Transforming Preaching.* New York: Church Publishing, 2010.

Hughes, Langston. *Langston Hughes and the Chicago Defender: Essays on Race, Politics, and Culture: 1942–1962.* Edited by Christopher C. Santis. Champaign: University of Illinois Press, 1995.

Hurston, Zora Neale. *Their Eyes Were Watching God.* Foreword by Mary Helen Washington. Afterword by Henry Louis Gates Jr. New York: HarperCollins, 1998.

Jabir, Johari. "On Conjuring Mahalia: Mahalia Jackson, New Orleans, and the Sanctified Swing." *American Quarterly* 61, no. 3 (2009): 649–69.

Jackson, Mahalia. Interview by Studs Terkel. WFMT, Studs Terkel Radio Archive, 1956.

———. *I Sing Because I'm Happy.* With songs recorded, annotated, and compiled by Jules Schwerin. Washington, DC: Smithsonian Folkways Records, 1992.

———. "Mahalia Jackson: Childhood Memories." In *The Mahalia Jackson Reader*, edited by Mark Burford, 23–31. New York: Oxford University Press, 2020.

Jackson, Mahalia, and Evan McLeod Wylie. *Movin' On Up.* New York: Avon, 1966.

Jacobson, Diane. "Wisdom Language in the Psalms." In *The Oxford Handbook of the Psalms*, edited by William P. Brown, 147–57. New York: Oxford University Press, 2014.

Jenkins, Carol, host. *Black America.* "Urban Bush Women with Jawole Willa Jo Zollar." November 4, 2017. http://www.youtube.com/watch?v=4FdBCbGf_GQ.

Jennings, Willie. "When Mahalia Sings: The Black Singer of Sacred Song as an Icon." In *The Mahalia Jackson Reader*, edited by Mark Burford, 195–200. New York: Oxford University Press, 2020.

Jones, Kirk Byron. *The Jazz of Preaching: How to Preach with Great Freedom and Joy.* Nashville: Abingdon, 2004.

Kaminska, Barbara A. *Pieter Bruegel the Elder: Religious Art for the Urban Community.* Leiden: Brill, 2019.

Kaplan, Edward K. "Howard Thurman: Meditation, Mysticism, and Life's Contradictions." *Debate and Understanding* (1982): 19–26.

Kienzle, Beverly Mayne. "Typology of the Medieval Sermon and Its Development in the Middle Ages: Report on a Work in Progress." In *De l'homélie au sermon: Histoire de la prédication médiévale, actes du colloque international de Louvain-la-Neuve,* edited by Jacqueline Hamesse and Zavier Hermand, 83–101. Louvain-la-Neuve: Institut d'études médiévales de l'université catholique de Louvain, 1993.

Kierkegaard, Søren. *The Last Years; Journals 1853–1855.* Edited and translated by Ronald Gregor Smith. London: Collins, 1965.

Kline, Peter. *Passion for Nothing: Kierkegaard's Apophatic Theology.* Minneapolis: Augsburg Fortress, 2017.

Koontz, Christian. "Rhetoric in the Service of the Real." In *Thea Bowman: Handing on Her Legacy,* edited by Christian Koontz, 58–70. Kansas City, MO: Sheed & Ward, 1991.

LaRochester, Barbara Jean. "She Walked by Faith and Not by Sight." In *Thea Bowman: Handing on Her Legacy,* edited by Christian Koontz, 45–50. Kansas City, MO: Sheed & Ward, 1991.

LaRue, Cleophus J. *The Heart of Black Preaching.* Louisville: Westminster John Knox, 2000.

Leon, Eli. *Accidentally on Purpose: The Aesthetic Management of Irregularities in African Textiles and African-American Quilts.* Davenport, IA: Figge Art Museum, 2006.

———. *Something Pertaining to God: The Patchwork Art of Rosie Lee Tompkins.* Shelburne, VT: Shelburne Museum, 2007.

Lester, Cheryl. "Meditations on a Bird in the Hand: Ethics and Aesthetics in a Parable by Toni Morrison." In *The Aesthetics of Toni Morrison: Speaking the Unspeakable,* edited by Marc C. Conner, 125–38. Jackson: University Press of Mississippi, 2000.

Lischer, Richard, ed. *The Company of Preachers: Wisdom on Preaching, Augustine to the Present.* Grand Rapids: Eerdmans, 2002.

———. *The Preacher King: Martin Luther King Jr. and the Word That Moved America.* New York: Oxford University Press, 1995.

———. *Reading the Parables.* Interpretation: Resources for the Use of Scripture in the Church. Louisville: Westminster John Knox, 2014.

———. "Why I Am Not Persuasive." *Homiletic* 24, no. 2 (1999): 13–16.

Llosa, Mario Vargas. *The Storyteller.* Translated by Helen Lane. New York: Farrar, Straus, and Giroux, 1989.

Long, Thomas G. *The Witness of Preaching.* Louisville: Westminster John Knox, 1989.

Lorensen, Marlene Ringgaard. *Dialogical Preaching: Bakhtin, Otherness, and Homiletics.* Göttingen: Vandenhoeck & Ruprecht, 2014.

Lubiano, Wahneema. "The Postmodernist Rag: Political Identity and the Vernacular in *Song of Solomon.*" In *New Essays on Song of Solomon,* edited by Valerie Smith, 93–113. Cambridge: Cambridge University Press, 1995.

Lybarger, Joan. "E Pluribus Unum." *La Crosse Tribune,* January 22, 1976.

"Mahalia Jackson Gospel Song Diva." *New York Amsterdam News,* October 7, 1950. In *The Mahalia Jackson Reader,* edited by Mark Burford, 247–48. New York: Oxford University Press, 2020.

Manning, Erin. *The Minor Gesture.* Durham, NC: Duke University Press, 2016.

Marks, Kathleen. *Toni Morrison's Beloved and the Apotropaic Imagination*. Columbia: University of Missouri Press, 2002.

Marks, Laura U. *The Skin of the Film: Intercultural Cinema, Embodiment, and the Senses*. Durham, NC: Duke University Press, 2000.

Mazloomi, Carolyn. *Spirits of the Cloth: Contemporary African American Quilts*. New York: Clarkson Potter/Publishers, 1998.

McClure, John S. *The Four Codes of Preaching: Rhetorical Strategies*. Minneapolis: Fortress, 1991.

McCray, Donyelle. *The Censored Pulpit: Julian of Norwich as Preacher*. Lanham, MD: Lexington/Fortress Academic, 2019.

———. "Quilting the Sermon: Homiletical Insights from Harriet Powers." *Religions* 9, no. 2, (2018): 46.

McKenzie, Alyce M. *Novel Preaching: Tips from Top Writers on Crafting Creative Sermons*. Louisville: Westminster John Knox, 2010.

———. *Preaching Biblical Wisdom in a Self-Help Society*. Nashville: Abingdon, 2002.

Mermelstein, Aaron, and Willard E. Shaw. *Sister Thea, Her Own Story: A Video Autobiography*. Bucksport, ME: Northeast Historic Film, 2013.

Meyer, Ockert. "Preaching the Truth and the Truth of Preaching: Rosenzweig's Jewish Lessons for Christian Preaching." Paper presented at *Societas Homiletica*, Budapest, Hungary, August 16, 2022.

Mitchell, Henry H. *Black Preaching: The Recovery of a Powerful Art*. Nashville: Abingdon, 1990.

———. *Celebration and Experience in Preaching*. Nashville: Abingdon, 1990.

Moore, Pat. "Liturgical Dance Reviews Mixed." *La Crosse Tribune*, February 14, 1975.

Morrison, Toni. *Beloved*. With a new foreword by the author. New York: Vintage, 2004.

———. "'I Come from People Who Sang All the Time': A Conversation with Toni Morrison." Interview by Sheldon Hackney. In *Toni Morrison: Conversations*, edited by Carolyn C. Denard, 126–38. Jackson: University Press of Mississippi, 2008.

———. "'I Regret Everything': Toni Morrison Looks Back on Her Personal Life." Interview by Terry Gross. *Fresh Air*, NPR, 20 August 2015.

———. "An Interview with Toni Morrison." Interview by Nellie McKay. *Contemporary Literature* 24, no. 4 (Winter 1983): 413–29.

———. "The Language Must Not Sweat." Interview by Thomas LeClair. In *Conversations with Toni Morrison*, edited by Danille Taylor-Guthrie, 119–28. Jackson: University Press of Mississippi, 1994.

———. *The Nobel Laureate Lecture in Literature, 1993*. New York: Alfred A. Knopf, 1999.

———. *Paradise*. New York: Alfred A. Knopf, 1998.

———. *The Source of Self-Regard: Selected Essays, Speeches, and Meditations*. New York: Alfred A. Knopf, 2019.

———. "Talk with Toni Morrison." Interview by Mel Watkins. In *Conversations with Toni Morrison*, edited by Danille Taylor-Guthrie, 43–47. Jackson: University Press of Mississippi, 1994.

———. "The Triumphant Song of Toni Morrison." Interview by Paula Giddings. In *Toni Morrison: Conversations*, edited by Carolyn C. Denard, 10–16. Jackson: University Press of Mississippi, 2008.

———. *What Moves at the Margin: Selected Nonfiction.* Jackson: University Press of Mississippi, 2008.

Moss, Otis, III. *Blue Note Preaching in a Post-Soul World: Finding Hope in an Age of Despair.* Louisville: Westminster John Knox, 2015.

Moten, Fred. *In the Break: The Aesthetics of the Black Radical Tradition.* Minneapolis: University of Minnesota Press, 2003.

Muehl, William. "The Dark Reflection of God: A Sermon Preached in the University Chapel on Sunday, November 20, 1960," Howard Thurman Collection, Boston University Libraries, Howard Gotlieb Archival Research Center, box 20, folder 9.

Murray, Pauli. *Dark Testament and Other Poems.* Norwalk, CT: Silvermine, 1970.

———. *Pauli Murray: Selected Sermons and Writings.* Edited by Anthony B. Pinn. Maryknoll, NY: Orbis, 2006.

Neal, Marie Augusta. "She Made the Bishops Dance." In *Thea Bowman: Handing on Her Legacy*, edited by Christian Koontz, 54–57. Kansas City, MO: Sheed & Ward, 1991.

Nel, Malan. "Preaching, Truth-Sharing, and 'Eager to Prophesy.'" Paper presented at *Societas Homiletica*, Budapest, Hungary, August 14, 2022.

Nittle, Nadra. *Toni Morrison's Spiritual Vision: Faith, Folktales, and Feminism in Her Life and Literature.* Minneapolis: Fortress, 2021.

Noel, James A. "African American Art and Biblical Interpretation." In *True to Our Native Land: An African American New Testament Commentary*, edited by Brian K. Blount, 73–81. Minneapolis: Fortress Press, 2007.

Nutt, Maurice J. *Thea Bowman: Faithful and Free.* Collegeville, MN: Liturgical Press, 2019.

O'Connor, Flannery. *Mystery and Manners: Occasional Prose.* Selected and edited by Sally and Robert Fitzgerald. New York: Farrar, Straus, and Giroux, 1974.

Oppenheim, Michael. *What Does Revelation Mean to the Modern Jew? Rosenzweig, Buber, and Fackenheim.* Lewiston, NY: Edwin Mellen Press, 1985.

Painter, Nell Irvin. *Sojourner Truth: A Life, a Symbol.* New York: W. W. Norton, 1996.

Palmer, Donald D. *Kierkegaard for Beginners.* Danbury, CT: For Beginners, 1996.

Parmal, Pamela A., and Jennifer M. Swope. *Quilts and Color: The Pilgrim/Roy Collection.* Boston: MFA Publications, 2014.

Parmal, Pamela A., Jennifer M. Swope, and Lauren D. Whitley. *Fabric of a Nation: American Quilt Stories.* With a preface by Laurel Thatcher Ulrich. Boston: MFA Publications, 2021.

Paul, Leslie. *The Meaning of Human Existence.* Philadelphia: J. B. Lippincott, 1950.

Perdue, Leo G. "Sages, Scribes, and Seers in Israel and the Ancient Near East: An Introduction." In *Scribes, Sages, and Seers: The Sage in the Eastern Mediterranean World*, edited by Leo G. Perdue, 1–34. Göttingen: Vandenhoeck & Ruprecht, 2008.

Perry, Regenia A. *Harriet Powers's Bible Quilts.* New York: Rizzoli International and St. Martin's Press, 1994.

Powell, Richard J. "The Aaron Douglas Effect." In *Aaron Douglas: African American Modernist*, edited by Susan Earle, 53–73. New Haven, CT: Yale University Press; Lawrence, KS: Spencer Museum of Art, University of Kansas, 2007.

Powers, Harriet. *Bible Quilt.* 1885–1886. Hand- and machine-stitched cotton. National Museum of American History, Washington, DC.

————, *Pictorial Quilt*. 1895–1898. Cotton plain weave, pieced, appliqued, embroidered, and quilted. Museum of Fine Arts, Boston.

Powery, Luke A. *Becoming Human: The Holy Spirit and the Rhetoric of Race*. Louisville: Westminster John Knox, 2022.

————. *Dem Dry Bones: Preaching, Death, and Hope*. Minneapolis: Fortress, 2012.

Primus, Pearl. "African Dance." In *African Dance: An Artistic, Historical, and Philosophical Inquiry*, edited by Kariamu Welsh Asante, 3–11. Trenton, NJ: Africa World Press, 1996.

Proctor, Samuel D. *The Certain Sound of the Trumpet: Crafting a Sermon of Authority*. Valley Forge, PA: Judson Press, 1994.

Reynolds, David S. *Mightier than the Sword:* Uncle Tom's Cabin *and the Battle for America*. New York: W. W. Norton, 2011.

Rinder, Lawrence, and Elaine Y. Yau. *Rosie Lee Tompkins: A Retrospective*. With a contribution by Horace D. Ballard. Berkeley: University of California Berkeley Art Museum and Pacific Film Archive, 2020.

Ripatrazone, Nick. *Longing for an Absent God: Faith and Doubt in Great American Fiction*. Minneapolis: Fortress, 2020.

Robinson, Timothy. "He Talked to Trees! 'Thinking Differently' about Nature with Howard Thurman." *Spiritus: A Journal of Christian Spirituality* 21, no. 1 (2021): 1–19.

Rock, Judith, and Norman Mealy. *Performer as Priest and Prophet: Restoring the Intuitive in Worship through Music and Dance*. San Francisco: Harper & Row, 1988.

Rosa, Hartmut. *Resonance: A Sociology of Our Relationship to the World*. Translated by James C. Wagner. Cambridge: Polity Press, 2019.

Rushdy, Ashraf H. A. "'Rememory': Primal Scenes and Constructions in Toni Morrison's Novels." *Contemporary Literature* 31, no. 3 (1990): 300–323.

Russell, Letty. *Church in the Round: Feminist Interpretation of the Church*. Louisville: Westminster John Knox, 1993.

Ryan, Judylyn S. "Spirituality and/as Ideology in Black Women's Literature: The Preaching of Maria W. Stewart and Baby Suggs, Holy." In *Women Preachers and Prophets: Through Two Millennia of Christianity*, edited by Beverly Mayne Kienzle and Pamela J. Walker, 267–87. Berkeley: University of California Press, 1998.

Sacks, Jonathan. *To Heal a Fractured World: The Ethics of Responsibility*. London: Continuum, 2005.

Schwartz, Peggy, and Murray Schwartz. *The Dance Claimed Me: A Biography of Pearl Primus*. New Haven, CT: Yale University Press, 2011.

Schwerin, Jules. *Got to Tell It: Mahalia Jackson, Queen of Gospel*. New York: Oxford University Press, 1992.

Scott, R. B. Y. *The Way of Wisdom: In the Old Testament*. New York: Macmillan, 1971.

Shange, Ntozake. *For Colored Girls Who Have Considered Suicide When the Rainbow Is Enuf: A Choreopoem*. New York: Scribner, 1997.

Shelley, Braxton. *Healing for the Soul: Richard Smallwood, the Vamp, and the Gospel Imagination*. New York: Oxford University Press, 2021.

Simmons, Martha. "Whooping: The Musicality of African American Preaching Past and Present." In *Preaching with Sacred Fire: An Anthology of African American Sermons, 1750 to the Present*, edited by Martha Simmons and Frank A. Thomas, 864–84. New York: W. W. Norton, 2010.

Sitkoff, Robert H., and Jesse Dukeminier. *Wills, Trusts, and Estates*. 10th ed. New York: Wolters Kluwer, 2017.

Sittler, Joseph. "Imagining a Sermon." In *The Company of Preachers: Wisdom on Preaching, Augustine to the Present*, edited by Richard Lischer, 331–36. Grand Rapids: Eerdmans, 2002.

Smith, Charlene, and John Feister. *Thea's Song: The Life of Thea Bowman*. Maryknoll, NY: Orbis, 2009.

Smith, Christine M. *Weaving the Sermon: Preaching in a Feminist Perspective*. Louisville: Westminster John Knox, 1989.

Smith, Roberta. "The Radical Quilting of Rosie Lee Tompkins." *New York Times*, June 29, 2020. http://www.nytimes.com/interactive/2020/06/26/arts/design/rosie-lee-tompkins-quilts.html.

Smith, Ted A. *Weird John Brown: Divine Violence and the Limits of Ethics*. Stanford, CA: Stanford University Press, 2015.

Spencer, Jon Michael. *Sacred Symphony: The Chanted Sermon of the Black Preacher*. Westport, CT: Greenwood Press, 1987.

Spillers, Hortense J. *Black, White, and in Color: Essays on American Literature and Culture*. Chicago: University of Chicago Press, 2003.

Stewart, Lindsey. *The Politics of Black Joy: Zora Neale Hurston and Neo-Abolitionism*. Evanston, IL: Northwestern University Press, 2021.

Stowe, Harriet Beecher. *The Oxford Harriet Beecher Stowe Reader*. Edited by Joan D. Hedrick. New York: Oxford University Press, 1999.

———. *Uncle Tom's Cabin, or Life among the Lowly*. New York: Penguin, 1981.

Taylor, Gardner C. *The Words of Gardner Taylor: Special Occasion and Expository Sermons*. Vol. 4. Edited by Edward L. Taylor. Valley Forge, PA: Judson Press, 2004.

Taylor, Margaret Fisk. *A Time to Dance: Symbolic Movement in Worship*. Edited by Doug Adams. Austin: Sharing Co., 1980.

Thomas, Frank A. *They Like to Never Quit Praisin' God: The Role of Celebration in Preaching*. Cleveland: United Church Press, 1997.

Thompson, Lisa L. *Ingenuity: Preaching as an Outsider*. Nashville: Abingdon, 2018.

Thurman, Howard. *Conversations with Howard Thurman*. San Francisco: Howard Thurman Educational Trust, 1987.

———. *Deep River and the Negro Spiritual Speaks of Life and Death*. Richmond, IN: Friends United Press, 1975.

———. *The Growing Edge*. New York: Harper, 1956; reprint, Richmond, IN: Friends United Press, 1980.

———. "Human Freedom and the Emancipation Proclamation." *Pulpit Digest* 43, no. 294 (December 1962): 13–16.

———. *Jesus and the Disinherited*. Boston: Beacon Press, 1996.

———. *Meditations of the Heart*. New York: Harper & Row, 1953; reprint, Richmond, IN: Friends United Press, 1976.

———. *The Mood of Christmas*. New York: Harper & Row, 1973; reprint, Richmond, IN: Friends United Press, 1985.

———. "Notes on Homiletics Course," Howard Thurman Collection, Boston University Libraries, Howard Gotlieb Archival Research Center.

———. *With Head and Heart: The Autobiography of Howard Thurman*. San Diego: Harcourt Brace, 1979.

———. "Worship and Word: A View of the Liberal Congregation and Its Sermons," Howard Thurman Collection, Boston University Libraries, Howard Gotlieb Archival Research Center.

Tompkins, Rosie Lee. *String*, 1985. Quilted and reconstructed by Willia Ette Graham, 1985. Photographed by Sharon Risedorph. In *Rosie Lee Tompkins: A Retrospective*, edited by Lawrence Rinder and Elaine Y. Yau, plate 16, page 69. Berkeley: University of California Berkeley Art Museum and Pacific Film Archive, 2020.

———. *Untitled*, 1970s with embroidered Scripture added mid-1980s. Quilted by Irene Bankhead, 1997. Photographed by Ben Blackwell. In *Rosie Lee Tompkins: A Retrospective*, edited by Lawrence Rinder and Elaine Y. Yau, plate 7, page 38. Berkeley: University of California Berkeley Art Museum and Pacific Film Archive, 2020.

———. *Untitled*, c. 1996. Photographed by Ben Blackwell. In *Rosie Lee Tompkins: A Retrospective*, edited by Lawrence Rinder and Elaine Y. Yau, plate 44, pages 124–25. Berkeley: University of California Berkeley Art Museum and Pacific Film Archive, 2020.

———. *Untitled*, c. 2002. Photographed by Ben Blackwell. In *Rosie Lee Tompkins: A Retrospective*, edited by Lawrence Rinder and Elaine Y. Yau, plate 51, pages 138–39. Berkeley: University of California Berkeley Art Museum and Pacific Film Archive, 2020.

———. *Untitled*, c. 2002. Photographed by Ben Blackwell. In *Rosie Lee Tompkins: A Retrospective*, edited by Lawrence Rinder and Elaine Y. Yau, plate 52, pages 140–41. Berkeley: University of California Berkeley Art Museum and Pacific Film Archive, 2020.

———. *Untitled*, c. 2005. Quilted by Irene Bankhead, 2008. Photographed by Ben Blackwell. In *Rosie Lee Tompkins: A Retrospective*, edited by Lawrence Rinder and Elaine Y. Yau, plate 63, pages 158–59. Berkeley: University of California Berkeley Art Museum and Pacific Film Archive, 2020.

Tucker, JoAnne, and Susan Freeman. *Torah in Motion: Creating Dance Midrash*. N.p.: Open Road Media, 2014.

Turner, Kathleen S. *And We Shall Learn through the Dance: Liturgical Dance as Religious Education*. Eugene, OR: Pickwick Publications, 2021.

Turner, Patricia A. *Crafted Lives: Stories and Studies of African American Quilters*. Foreword by Kyra E. Hicks. Jackson: University Press of Mississippi, 2009.

Turner, William Clair, Jr. "The Musicality of Black Preaching: Performing the Word." In *Performance in Preaching: Bringing the Sermon to Life*, edited by Jana Childers and Clayton Schmit, 191–209. Grand Rapids: Baker Academic, 2008.

Ulrich, Laurel Thatcher. "'A Quilt unlike Any Other:' Rediscovering the Work of Harriet Powers." In *Writing Women's History: A Tribute to Anne Firor Scott*, edited by Elizabeth Anne Payne, 82–116. Jackson: University of Mississippi Press, 2011.

Underhill, Evelyn. *The Ways of the Spirit*. Edited by Grace Adolphsen Brame. New York: Crossroads, 1994.

Valle-Ruiz, Lis, and Andrew Wymer, eds. *Unmasking White Preaching: Racial Hegemony, Resistance, and Possibilities in Homiletics*. Postcolonial and Decolonial Studies in Religion and Theology. Lanham, MD: Lexington Books, 2022.

von Rad, Gerhard. *Wisdom in Israel*. Nashville: Abingdon, 1972.

Wahlman, Maude Southwell. *Signs and Symbols: African Images in African-American Quilts*. Atlanta: Tinwood Books, 2001.

Washington, Booker T. "Atlanta Exposition Speech." Transcript of speech delivered in Atlanta on September 18, 1895. Library of Congress. https://blogs.loc.gov/teachers/2011/07/booker-t-washington-and-the-atlanta-compromise.

Wehner, David Z. "To Live This Life Intensely and Well: The Rebirth of Milkman Dead in Toni Morrison's *Song of Solomon.*" In *Toni Morrison and the Bible*, edited by Shirley A. Stave, 71–93. New York: Peter Lang, 2006.

White, Major C. "Missionary Work of the Highest Order." *Pacific Union Recorder* 74, no. 48 (1975): 1.

Wilder, Amos N. *Early Christian Rhetoric: The Language of the Gospel.* Cambridge, MA: Harvard University Press, 1971.

Wimberly, Edward P. *Moving from Shame to Self-Worth: Preaching and Pastoral Care.* Nashville: Abingdon, 1999.

Winton-Henry, Cynthia. *Dance—the Sacred Art: The Joy of Movement as Spiritual Practice.* Woodstock, VT: Skylight Paths, 2009.

Wolff, Cynthia Griffin. "'Margaret Garner': A Cincinnati Story." *Massachusetts Review* 32, no. 3 (Autumn 1991): 417–40.

Woods, Richard. Preface to *Margaret Ebner: Major Works, ca. 1291–1351.* Edited and translated by Leonard P. Hindsley. New York: Paulist Press, 1993.

Woolf, Rosemary. *Art and Doctrine: Essays on Medieval Literature.* Edited by Heather O'Donoghue. London: Hambledon Press, 1986.

Yang, Sunggu A. *Arts and Preaching: An Aesthetic Homiletic for the Twenty-First Century.* Eugene, OR: Cascade, 2021.

Yates, Miles Lowell. *God in Us: The Theory and Practice of Christian Devotion.* Edited by W. Norman Pittenger and William H. Ralston Jr. Greenwich, CT: Seabury Press, 1959.

Yau, Elaine Y. "The Craft and Art of Rosie Lee Tompkins." In *Rosie Lee Tompkins: A Retrospective,* edited by Lawrence Rinder and Elaine Y. Yau, 13–25. Berkeley: University of California Berkeley Art Museum and Pacific Film Archive, 2020.

Young, L. Martina. "Beloved Bodies: Gestures toward Wholeness." In *Toni Morrison: Forty Years in the Clearing,* edited by Carmen Gillespie, 329–53. Lewisburg, PA: Bucknell University Press; Lanham, MD: Rowman & Littlefield, 2012.

Zagano, Phyllis. *Twentieth-Century Apostles: Contemporary Spirituality in Action.* Collegeville, MN: Liturgical Press, 1999.

Zakkai, Jennifer Donohue. *Dance as a Way of Knowing.* Los Angeles: Stenhouse, 1997.

Index

Italicized page numbers followed by an *i* indicates an image on that page.

Printed in the USA
CPSIA information can be obtained
at www.ICGtesting.com
CBHW020545160924
14223CB00001B/1